Miguel Maria Arribas, O. Carm.

The Price of Truth
Titus Brandsma
Carmelite

Carmelite Media

Edited by William J. Harry, O. Carm.
Layout and Cover design by William J. Harry, O. Carm.

© 2022 by Carmelite Media (Second Edition)
Printed in the United States of America
All rights reserved

No part of this book may be reproduced, stored in a retrieval system, or transmitted in any form, or by any means, electronic, mechanical, photocopying, or otherwise, without the prior written permission of the publisher, except by a reviewer, who may quote brief passages in a review.

Jointly Published:
Carmelite Media
8501 Bailey Road
Darien, Illinois 60561

Phone: 1-630-971-0724
Email: publications@carmelnet.org
Website: carmelites.info/publications

Office of the Postulator General of the Carmelite Order
Carmelite Curia
Via Giovanni Lanza, 138
00184 Rome, Italy

This is a translation with additions of the work *El precio de la verdad: Tito Brandsma, Carmelite*, by Miguel Maria Arribas, O. Carm. 1998. ISBN: 88-87275-00-9

Current Printed Edition ISBN: 978-1-936742-26-4
E-Book ISBN: 978-1-936742-27-1

Table of Contents

Preface i
Editor's Introduction v
Abbreviations vii

I. A Shoot from Good Stock 1

II. Formation 17

III. Plans and Hopes 35

IV. At the University 45

V. *Rector Magnificus* of the University 59

VI. Seeking God 75

VII. "That Dangerous Little Friar" 103

VIII. Apologia from Prison 133

IX. An Exceptional Prisoner 163

X. His Final Sentence 179

XI. A Break Along the Way 185

XII. Dachau Concentration Camp 197

XIII. Holocaust 221

XIV. Saint and Hero 235

> Appendix I: North American Lecture Tour 253
> Appendix II: Trips to Ireland in 1935 257
> Appendix III: Brother Raphael Tijhuis, O. Carm. 259
> Appendix IV: Blessed Titus' Rosaries 261
> Appendix V: "Before a Picture of Jesus in My Cell" 265
> Appendix VI: The "Carmelite Priory" in Dachau 267
> Appendix VII: The 1985 Beatification 271
> Appendix VIII: Homilies on Titus Brandsma 279
> Appendix IX: Chronology of Titus Brandsma's Life 297
>
> List of Illustrations 303
> Bibliography 305
> Recommended Carmelite Websites 321

Preface

It was around six o'clock Monday evening, January 19, 1942, when two burly young men rang the doorbell of the Carmelite priory in Nijmegen in the Netherlands. The brother porter hastened to respond, greeted the visitors and inquired, "How may I help you, gentlemen?" The younger of the two responded in perfect Dutch, "We would like to speak with Professor Brandsma. I am the student who has been trying to reach him by telephone, but without success. We are in a hurry. Please let him know." The other said not a word, not even giving his name.

The brother ushered them into a parlor and called Father Titus Brandsma. As was his custom, Titus came down at once and greeted his guests cordially. It was at this point that the previously silent visitor announced in German: "My name is Steffen; I am an agent of the State Security Police. By order of the Security Service (*Sicherheitsdienst*) you are under arrest. You are to come with me on the 7:35 train to Arnhem. First, however, I must search your personal quarters. Please conduct me to them." "What is the charge?" the Carmelite priest asked calmly. "I have ordered you to show me to your rooms, Professor. Now!" The Gestapo agent responded in clipped tones as he prepared officiously to enter the monastery.

The search was meticulous. The agents gathered whatever they thought might be useful for their purpose. Then they sealed the rooms and escorted the prisoner down the stairs toward the street. Meanwhile, aware that this was to be a farewell, the community had gathered near the front door.

Father Titus took each one warmly by the hand, and then, as was the custom before leaving the house, knelt to ask the prior's blessing. At the threshold he turned and with a little smile whispered a "*Memento mei*"– pray for me– and then departed with the police.

The night was very cold. "What was the charge?" we too wonder. As soon as Hitler's forces invaded the Netherlands, May 10, 1940, the Nazis took steps to seize control of both education and the press. This they considered essential for changing the outlook of the Dutch people and so mastering them.

For Dutch Catholics, the Nazi plan triggered a brutal confrontation with two of the Church's most cherished public expressions. Fr. Titus Brandsma was both Ecclesiastical Advisor to the Union of Dutch Catholic Journalists (UCIP) and President of the Union of Directors of Catholic Schools. As such he had raised his voice courageously to denounce in public what many others– for fear of being incriminated by an informer in the pay of the Gestapo– had condemned only in the privacy of their homes or in the unspoken conviction of their own consciences. Well aware that his actions might lead to his detention, Doctor Titus Brandsma had refused to be silent.

Titus was not, of course, the official head of the Catholic Church in rhe Netherlands, but in these matters– journalism and education– he was her official spokesperson. Several friends advised him to leave the entire matter in the hands of the Dutch Bishops and to take refuge in some out-of-the-way Carmelite house. "No," he replied. "That I cannot do. I have certain responsibilities. Moreover, it would cause irreparable damage to the Church were the Archbishop made to appear as the only defender of truth. Every conscientious Catholic must be ready to stand alongside him."

The Security Police, who had been keeping Titus under close surveillance for some time, would not long tolerate this diminutive Dutch Carmelite who dared raise his voice against the all-powerful Deutsches Reich. They acknowledged: "*Er is sehr gefährlich*! ... He is very dangerous! He is sabotaging all our plans in the press. He must be sent away immediately to a concentration camp."

Within a short time, he was arrested. Titus Brandsma was to pass through five prisons and camps before ending up in the concentration and extermination camp at Dachau. Dachau was a nightmarish world where the Nazis went beyond every conceivable definition of degradation and brutality. There he was to undergo unspeakable physical and moral torture: he was used for infamous biochemical experiments until finally, July 26, 1942, he was killed with an "injection of mercy"– carbolic acid.

On Sunday, November 3, 1985, in St. Peter's Basilica, Rome, Pope John Paul II raised the Carmelite Titus Brandsma to the honors of the altar in the presence of thousands of the faithful from all parts of the world. It was the final act in the process of beatification that had begun in 1955 in the Dutch Diocese of s'-Hertogenbosch.

In his homilies during the celebrations of beatification, the Holy Father deftly recapped Titus' life: "No barrier was able to stop the impulse of charity which animated this great Carmelite." He was "absolutely faithful to his vocation and to religious observance, obedient to the successors of the apostles, and to the task they imposed on him which led him to martyrdom; full of love for everyone, even his enemies, unimpeachable in his scientific work, totally convinced of the need for truly Catholic education and a really Catholic press, unyielding in his opposition to an ideology that threatened the foundations of faith and morals."[1]

Heroism does not just happen. Titus spent his whole life bringing it to maturity. As the Holy Father noted, it was not the martyrdom which ended his life that made him a saint; his sanctity was the fruit of his entire life. Titus Brandsma was a religious priest— a status totally infused with his faith. To this vocation he brought a long familiarity with the field of higher education, the vast erudition of a truly enlightened man, and especially his own intense experience in the ways of the spirit, ways along which— if we are to believe his contemporaries— he personally journeyed to the heights of Christian mysticism.

In the case of Father Titus, the process of beatification was twofold: he was both a confessor and a martyr. Titus Brandsma was also a journalist. Death was the price he paid for his professional integrity as well as for his commitment to his faith in Christ. For him these two were but different facets of a single reality.

The Nazis condemned him as a "political saboteur;" nevertheless, those who knew him most intimately are convinced that nothing was farther from his concerns than politics. The record of his trials— almost miraculously preserved by the very people who had intended to destroy all trustworthy evidence of their atrocities— makes this absolutely clear. The same can be said of the long canonical process that identifies him as "a martyr for the freedom of expression," possibly the first journalist martyr in the two-thousand-year history of the Church.

In this instance the ecclesiastical process goes beyond the traditional model of martyrdom and examines it in light of the conflicts of our era: death for the faith directly coupled to the socio-politico-military action known as war. These two realities have become so intermingled that they can be separated only with great difficulty for the purpose of analysis. This is no accident. The National Socialists knew all too well the importance of camouflaging their true intentions: by causing confusion they hoped to escape the condemnation of history.

But their designs were revealed in the pure light of truth. Put very simply, the Nazis condemned Titus Brandsma because he defended Christian ideals in the face of the neo-paganism they sought to impose. He is the first victim of Nazism beatified as a martyr. Even before the war Fr. Titus Brandsma was so well-known in the Netherlands that a letter addressed to him with nothing but his name on the envelope would have been delivered promptly. Today his name and his message have been placed on a lamp stand as "a luminous and timely example for the Church and the faithful in these times."[2]

This too is goal of this biography: that the person and message of St. Titus Brandsma reach beyond the boundaries of the Netherlands and of the Carmelite Order and bring light to a world that remains tragically divided and in darkness. These pages will put before your eyes his life as a Carmelite religious, as a priest of many apostolates, as a mystic; as a keen journalist, as a professor, as the *Rector magnificus* of a university; as a long-suffering prisoner, and, finally, as a heroic martyr for Christ.[3]

Miguel Maria Arribas, O. Carm.

ENDNOTES

1. Cf. *L'Osservatore Romano*, November 4-5, 1986. See too *The Beatification of Father Titus Brandsma, Carmelite (1881-1942): Martyr in Dachau*, edited by Redemptus Maria Valabek, O. Carm. (Rome: Institutum Carmelitanum: 1986), pp. 50, 69.

2. Pope John Paul II, in *The Beatification of Father Titus Brandsma, Carmelite*, p. 69.

3. I want to thank Fr. Adrian Staring, O. Carm., Vice-Postulator of the Cause for Beatification, for having read and approved this entire text. –Author's note.

Editor's Introduction

Carmel is a name to conjure with. For the average person the word opens vistas of enclosed gardens, of silent religious women clothed in brown and wearing sandals, perhaps with an off-white mantle, possibly gazing at a crucifix. There would be a certain foundation for their musings. For many Carmel has come to be identified with some of the most popular saints of our times: Thérèse of Lisieux being but the first of many heroic women who come to mind, along with Teresa of Avila, and the more recently canonized young nun of Chile, Teresa of Los Andes.

Yet there are many Carmelites, men and women, whose living out of Carmel's charism involved a lifestyle considerably removed from that of cloistered women, men and women who– even as they made the arduous ascent to the summit of Mount Carmel– were following in the footsteps of the Lord by proclaiming the Good News in both word and deed. Today they may not be as well-known as they deserve, but they lived out their vocation to Carmel by bringing the healing ministry of Jesus to both individuals and society.

Carmel is a place, indeed a mountain– more accurately a mountain ridge– in the northwestern part of the Holy Land, rising sharply from the Mediterranean. In the Old Testament it was known for its natural beauty and as a place of encounter with God. In his 1935 North American lecture tour,[1] St Titus Brandsma remarked that from Carmel's summit one may look over the plain of Esdraelon and contemplate "the mystery of Nazareth;" he went on to describe Carmel as "the natural retreat of the contemplative."

But Carmel has other, less peaceful, associations as well: it was on Carmel that Elijah reproached Israel for its infidelity to God and challenged them: "How long will you straddle the issue? If the Lord is God, follow him; if Baal, follow him" (1 Kgs 18:21). In the New Testament Carmel is not mentioned explicitly, but it is neither out of sight nor out of mind: the Old Testament characters most intimately connected with Carmel have important roles in the four gospels, in the letters of Paul and James, and even in Revelations.

The Church Fathers, both eastern and western, frequently comment on the Biblical texts that mention Elijah the Prophet of Carmel; they recognize him as type and symbol of the Christian mission to proclaim the Good News, of the efficacy of prayer, of the importance of the desert; describing him as "a man like us," they praise his zeal for the things of God in the face of persecution, his constancy in prayer, his living in the presence of God.

Historical and archaelogical evidence place Christian hermits on Mount Carmel as early as the fifth century. The ascent of the mountain is not easy, but at its summit one enjoys intimate fellowship with the living God.

ENDNOTES

1. Titus Brandsma, O. Carm. *Carmelite Mysticism: Historical Sketches* (50th Anniversary Edition. Darien, Illinois: The Carmelite Press, 1986), p. 1.

Abbreviations

INF 68: *Informatio super dubio beatificationis seu declarationis martyrii servi Dei Titi Brandsma, Sacerdotis profesi Ordinis beatissimae Virginis Mariae de Monte Carmelo* (Romae, 1968), p. 17.

Summarium super dubio beatificationis seu declarationis martyrii servi Dei TITI BRANDSMA, sacerdotis professi Ordinis beatissijmae Virginis Mariae de Monte Carmelo. (Romae, 1965), p. 23. (Hereafter SU65)

Chapter 1

A Shoot from Good Stock

The Netherlands

It is said that the Netherlands is a "diminutive world giant."

Certainly, the country's small size has little to do with its influence on world history. When a Dutchman holds up the map of his country, he has a right to be proud. As the saying goes, "God made the earth, but the Dutch made the Netherlands." Hyperbole, but with a grain of truth.

The Netherlands is a typical coastal plain, the product of two underlying forces: one, the silt deposited by the Rhine, Meuse, and Schelde rivers which form a single delta; the other the continual struggle of the Dutch themselves who for centuries have been waging a relentless war of titanic proportions to salvage additional land from the sea.

Known officially as the Netherlands or Low Countries but often incorrectly called Holland, the country is located in a geographical depression, with over a third (38%) lying between 23 and 100 feet below sea level. This area is protected by a chain of coastal dunes that provide a natural barrier to the sea, and, where dunes are lacking, the Dutch have constructed huge dykes or sea walls.

The actual surface area of the country is approximately 16,000 square miles, of which 13,000 are dry land and the rest (a little more than one fifth of the country), water. In the course of their history the Dutch have extended their dominion over the land with incredible feats of engineering: inch by inch they have drained swamps and lakes, diverted river channels, solidified fluvial sediment, and built canals.

Still not content, they have taken their battle to the sea itself: with unconquerable spirit, they have managed to wrest nearly 1,200 square miles, i.e., nearly 10% of their national territory from the sea. In this constant battle between the sea and the Dutch– the former striving to submerge, the latter to rescue the land— on hundreds of occasions the fury of the elements has conquered, nullifying in moments the work of centuries, flooding enormous areas of hard-earned farmland, and exacting a tribute in human lives as well.

But just as often the Dutch have tenaciously returned to reclaim the land from the sea, rebuilding their dykes, their homes, their fields. Today land reclaimed from the sea— called *polders*— forms the country's twelfth province: Flevoland, famous for its broad, meadowed plains and magnificent fields of tulips.

During a trip I made one August some years ago I visited just about the entire country. It felt as though I were traveling across the bottom of a vast dry lake, where everything was green; it was as though I were part of an incredibly domesticated environment, almost like moving through an artificial landscape.

Frequently I asked myself where those 950 Dutchmen per square mile—one of the earth's most dense populations—were hiding. Except for the teeming city-centers the country seemed half empty. The silence, the quiet, were palpable.

The inhabitants, a restrained and gentle people, appeared to reflect the unrestricted plains of their country. It seemed that no one wanted to stand out, although they were certainly not without pride in their history and in their heroes.

It is a country that is well organized and frugal, where every person and everything has its proper place, but at the same time a country that puts great value on its independence. Dutch socio-politico-religious development is frequently admired but somewhat disconcerting for an observer from the south of Europe.

The Netherlands, finally, is a country that its nearly 16,000,000 energetic inhabitants have transformed into one of the most beautiful of the old continent, and second to none in its standard of living. Following the rupture in the Church caused by the Protestant Reformation, which held sway in most of the Netherlands, Dutch Catholicism was forced underground. During a considerable part of the 17th and 18th centuries, especially after 1648 when the country gained its independence, many Dutch citizens were deprived of even the most basic human rights simply for declaring themselves Catholic.

Although by 1796 the rights of Catholics were recognized, the Orange Monarchy restricted the activity of the Catholic Church through a combination of minimal freedom and a series of constraints and restrictions. It was during this period when Catholics began what came to be known as the "process of emancipation." Dutch Catholics made up a third of the population: 95% in the south, 30% in the center, 5% in the north. Nevertheless, the Church in the Netherlands did not yet have its own hierarchy; the country was considered mission territory, under the jurisdiction of a papal nuncio who lived in Brussels.

It was not until 1848 that religious orders were permitted to return to the country. In 1855 a national hierarchy was created, with five dioceses subject to the Sacred Congregation for the Propagation of the Faith. It was 1909 before the Netherlands enjoyed its own independent hierarchy. By 1998, Catholics constituted the largest religious denomination in the Netherlands, numbering some five million members– 31% of the population– although less than half are practicing. About 40% claimed no religious affiliation. In 2015 there were an estimated 3.88 million Catholics registered or 22% of the population.

The Dutch Catholic Church, immersed in an intensely secularized environment, practices a Catholicism that in many ways is bold. Following Vatican II many Dutch Catholics–directed, even instigated by the clergy itself–arrived at positions no one could have foreseen from a people traditionally restrained and tolerant. Its theologians have been on the cutting edge in many areas of dogmatic and pastoral theology, a development that has produced not a few hazards and tensions.

Friesland

Departing from Amsterdam I trod for the first time on the earth of Friesland. The motorbus had taken me 20 miles along the impressive *afsluitdijk*, the dyke that since its completion in 1932 has separated the tempestuous waters of the North Sea from the brackish waters of Lake Ijsselmeer. Now in Frisian country, I began to experience that special seduction that always awaits me in lands charged with history.

Friesland is the northernmost province of the Netherlands and, without a doubt, it is among the most picturesque. After passing through the monotonous territory of Flevoland, which until recently had been submerged in the depths of the sea, Friesland seemed teeming with personality. It is a region of great plains, a tangle of rivers and canals that cut across the land in all directions; it is sprinkled with poplar trees, gothic towers, and the sails of windmills, that from a distance give the impression of ships sailing among planted fields and cattle. The soil, composed largely of clay mixed with peat, is well suited as pasture for the Frisian cattle, whose products are one source for the wealth of the area. The climate is humid; heavy mist absorbs the brightness of the sun but gives vitality to the scenery.

As a people, Frisians are proud of their Scandinavian, not Saxon, heritage. They preserve their own customs, their own language. They are known for their serious-mindedness and their love of freedom. Due to the climate they tend to be homebodies. Their houses are comfortable, with large windows to take maximum advantage of the light and warmth of whatever sun breaks through.

Bolsward

This small Frisian city–about 10,000 inhabitants–was the goal of my trip. From the distance, I glimpsed the silhouette of the ancient rectangular tower of the Martinkerk (the Church of St. Martin), a gothic structure with some aspects of a cathedral, once Catholic but now Protestant. Just beyond this historic municipality is the farmstead of Oegeklooster, the destination of my pilgrimage: the family home of the Brandsmas.

As soon as I had left the bus, I headed toward the sharp steeple of another more modern church that might be Catholic. My suspicion was confirmed when I saw the figure of St. Francis of Assisi on the façade. I rang the bell of the parish house; a housekeeper responded. "Is Fr. Stolk at home?" I asked.

The women responded in Dutch that he was not. With difficulty I was given to understand that he would not get back until four o'clock that afternoon.

Since it was then only two, I passed the time visiting the picturesque town: St. Martin's Church, the carefully maintained streets, the canals, the town hall. At four I returned to the rectory. The Franciscan was waiting for me. When I told him I wanted to visit the farmhouse where Fr. Titus Brandsma had been born; he immediately invited me into a parlor whose focal point was a photograph of Fr. Titus. He apologized that, since it was Saturday and he had services and meetings, he could not accompany me. Instead he drew a map so that I could find the place myself. "Even though it is not part of the village," he told me, "the house is not very far. You will find it easily. I will call the people who live there, the Terwisscha van Sheltinga family, to expect you."

Thanking him for his help, I set out. In my excitement I covered the ground rapidly. I crossed a street with a canal down its center, and another with modern chalets on either side, each similar to the others in form and color. Finally, I came to an open area of broad meadows with poplars and a few houses scattered here and there.

The pastor's map was perfect. In a few hundred yards I found the Oegeklooster farmstead. I picked it out immediately from a dozen others. Its outline was familiar because of the photographs I had seen so often.

Without taking my eyes off the house, I continued along the road made at first of paving stones–the original–and then of packed earth, the same road often used by the Brandsma family. The farm is in an open, somewhat melancholy area: tall poplars, drainage ditches, blocks of flowers, and extensive pastures with a large number of livestock.

The house itself is built in the pure Frisian style, called *stelp*. A rectangular building, it includes the living quarters in the front, stables in the rear. Its enormous pyramidal roof is three-fourths of the height of the structure; dark red shingles cover the entire building like some kind of giant hat, descending on the sides almost to the ground in order to protect it from the heavy rain and snow.

The name *Oegeklooster* (Hugh's Convent) recalls the rest home that the Cistercian Monastery of Hartwerd once owned there; the name embraces three neighboring farms that, at the beginning of the century, had worked some two hundred and fifty acres of land. The houses were at some distance one from the other. The Brandsma house had been purchased by Titus' grandfather, Hendrik Mevis Brandsma, in 1820 from the Terwisscha van Sheltinga family, to whom it had now returned.

A couple, clearly of nordic descent and about forty years of age, was waiting for me at the door; they greeted me hospitably and showed me every part of the house. Apart from the inevitable small changes that come with the passage of time, I felt it was the same exact home of the Brandsma family, both inside and out.

A large photograph of Fr. Titus in his Carmelite habit occupied the place of honor in the entrance. I took pictures of the various rooms and of all their details, and I did the same of the outside of the house and of the surrounding countryside. My hosts showed me an album about Fr. Titus that I paged through while enjoying a cup of coffee. Showing me a drawing of her family tree, my hostess pointed out that she was a relative of the Brandsma family: the paternal grandmother of Fr. Titus was Apolonia Theodora Terwisscha van Scheltinga, a member of one of the oldest Catholic families of Friesland.

As I took my leave, I encouraged them to preserve the house of their dear and saintly relative as a venerable relic.

Family

The fire never died out in Oegeklooster on the frigid night between February 21-22, 1881. The Brandsmas were impatiently awaiting the birth of a new shoot. It would be their fifth. The newcomer was born in the early hours of February 23, and his arrival filled the entire family of hardworking farmers with joy. It was a boy, another pair of hands to work their enormous farm.

Overcome with gratitude the father fell to his knees, thanking God because at last his four daughters had been joined by the hoped-for male heir. Following this newborn son, there was to be another brother.

Everyone who saw the infant praised his delicate complexion and agreed that he looked like his mother.

In accord with the old ways, that same afternoon the entire family hurried to the parish church to baptize the newcomer. He was given typically Frisian names: Anno Sjoerd. St. Anno had been a famous Bishop of Cologne who had founded monasteries in the northern part of Europe around 1056.

Three generations of Brandsmas had lived in the family home at Oegeklooster. Theirs was a complete and noble family of farmers, accustomed to living in a patriarchal society and to practicing their Catholic faith zealously in order, in their turn, to pass it on to their descendants. The Brandsma family had given some important members to the Church, among them a cousin, Gorgonius, who, after having worked the farm at Oegeklooster, entered the Mill Hill Society and became Bishop of Kisoemoe in Africa. Years later, with a twinkle in his eye, Anno was to say of this prelate: "We two were brought up near the tail of the same cow." Another relative was Constans Kramer, who became Bishop of Loeanfoe in China.[1]

The Lord gave Anno exemplary parents, religious people who diligently and zealously watched over his education from the very beginning.

His mother, Tjitje Postma, was a woman of extraordinary Christian faith. It was in her parish church that she found the spiritual hearth where her outstanding domestic virtues were kneaded and rose and became both the foundation for the education of her children and the inheritance, she left them. It was frequent communion–unusual in those days–that strengthened her spirit in spite of her weak constitution.

Her husband, Titus Hendriks Brandsma, was always at her side. He was a man who appeared stern and severe to outsiders, but within the family circle he was known to be optimistic and cheerful. No matter where he had been on a given day, every evening he prayed the rosary with his family and read aloud some passage from the Bible, the *Imitation of Christ,* or the *Lives of the Saints.* As a member of the local council, he fought for improved education and for the Catholic press. The acorn did not fall far from the tree, we might say of his son.

The elder Brandsma loved music, played the piano and sang in the parish choir throughout his life–one area where his son did not follow in his father's footsteps, although not for lack of desire.

Years later, with a twinkle in his eyes, Anno reported that the first thing his father did on rising was to offer the Lord the incense of his beloved pipe.

The Parents of Titus Brandsma, O. Carm. — Titus and Tjitje Annes (née Postma) Brandsma. They were farmers with a profound Catholic faith. Five of their six children embraced religious life. The senior Titus died in 1920. Tjitje died in 1933. *(Photos courtesy of the Nederlands Carmelitaans Instituut)*

It is not surprising that such a tree would have branches with above average human and religious sensibilities. It is a witness to the practical faith of this home that five of its six children embraced vocations to the priesthood and religious life.[2]

Fun Loving Yet Pious

Anno passed his childhood in this peaceful and quiet rural environment.

He was a small lad but fun-loving. Although he was not as healthy or strong as his siblings, he surpassed them in intelligence, kindheartedness, and native piety. It is generally admitted that physically he took after his mother: short and thin, brown hair and blue eyes, broad forehead, prominent nose, wide cheek bones, and a pointed chin.

He was unusually precocious. When told about the life of his patron saint, the holy bishop Anno, he announced enthusiastically: "I want to be a bishop too."

He possessed a prodigious memory and was gifted with almost total recall. Most evenings, due to his delicate health, he was sent early to bed; nevertheless, he could follow the family's reading of the Bible. It was not unusual that when no one else could recall the passage from the previous evening, a small voice would come through the door of his bedroom and give precise details that would bring it to mind.

On the evening following his First Holy Communion, his sister Gatske remarked: "Anno, you were very devout in church today; our parents were overcome with emotion when they saw you with your hands folded and your eyes closed." "When you are alone with God," the lad–then eleven years old–responded, "you don't have time for other things."

At the close of the ceremony, all the First Communicants were to recite the long, complex Tridentine profession of faith. Anno had no need to read the formula; he knew it by heart. No small feat!

The Brandsma children attended the Catholic school. Anno was a good, quick-witted student who made continual progress in his studies.

At times he could be independent, even imprudent and stubborn. When daily classes were over, he and some of his companions also attended classes in French. It was customary for the students to take turns bringing treats to share with the others. When it was Anno's turn, he let it be known that he thought the practice foolish and he did not intend to take part in it. Naturally the others did not take kindly to his rebellion and drenched him with a hose. He arrived home soaked and shivering, but satisfied that he had made his point.

On other occasions his kindlier nature asserted itself. From time to time the local area was plagued by a petty thief who stole honey. Anno's father tried to catch him; on one such occasion he returned to the house with little more than a bad temper and blustered: "Just let me get my hands on him!"

Anno replied, "No, Papá; it's better that you didn't catch him, so you won't even know who it is." "You're right, son," the father responded. "This way I can keep the peace, and I can clap him on the shoulder."

Each day, before leaving for school, the Brandsma children walked to the parish church for Mass. Anno and Hendrik served, and frequently received Holy Communion. Otherwise, although it was customary in their region for men and women to be separated, the Brandsma children stayed together.

In thanksgiving for a gift of healing, the two brothers made a promise—and fulfilled it—to the Virgin Mary to pray the *Little Office of the Blessed Virgin* daily for several months.

In general, the Brandsmas were not particularly popular among the other children of Bolsward. They were considered too enclosed within their own family circle on the farm. The only friends who went to the farm to play were their cousins.

Due largely to her own precarious health, Mother Brandsma did not encourage visitors. Years later Hendrik, the younger son, wrote: "Mamá was overly cautious about any contact with children of non-Catholic families, and that was one reason for our isolation."[3] At that time it was not uncommon for there to be a very strict separation between Catholics and Protestants.

His mother's protectiveness does not appear to have affected Anno's development, however; throughout his life he maintained

The Complete Brandsma Family (1891): (From left to right) Anno (Fr. Titus), Gatsche, Siebrigje, Titus Brandsma, Tjitje Brandsma, Hendrik, Apollonia (Plône), and Baukje. *(Photo courtesy of the Nederlands Carmelitaans Instituut)*

positive, even compassionate relationships with people of all faiths.

In any case, life on the Brandsma farm was anything but boring, and the family's work brought increasing prosperity. The children not only helped with churning butter and making cheese, they apparently turned these chores into useful games. Titus had a fertile imagination that cooked up all kinds of projects. His siblings, even the older ones, participated wholeheartedly. To Anno's disappointment his health would not allow him to take part in all the chores on the farm. One year during the hay harvest, for example, he was told that he would do better to work at less strenuous tasks. His dissatisfaction was apparent: he would have preferred being with the others rather than being relegated to taking the cows to pasture, cleaning harness and tools, or helping his mother with domestic chores. Like it or not, he was unable to imitate his father's physical strength; he would try to make up for it by being like him in spirit and resolve. On the other hand, the lad showed a marked inclination toward books. Often, he was found in his father's small library absorbed in a book on farming or botany or religion.

Life on the Brandsma farm was not terribly difficult since their economic situation was improving. Still his parents must have wondered what profession he would follow. He had aptitude for just about anything, except for farming.

Religious Vocation

When Anno was ten, he announced that he wanted to be a priest. This surprised no one; indeed any other choice would have seemed strange.[4] His parents, with their deep religious faith, were happy; nevertheless the news affected the family deeply since not long before his younger brother Hendrik had expressed a similar decision.

Their father, however, was worried. How could he, all alone, carry on with all the work of the farm? And how was he to find the resources to underwrite the expenses of both his sons' studies? Nevertheless, trusting as ever in divine providence, he generously gave both his blessing and humbly thanked God for showing His special love by calling his sons into His service.

Following the advice of the Franciscans of his parish, Anno entered the preparatory school operated by their order in Megen, an almost totally Catholic city in the province of Brabant in the south of the Netherlands. There he would complete the first stage of his studies. Later, if he persevered in this first step, there would be time to determine how best to proceed. One misty morning in September 1892, Anno left his native Friesland for Megen. At the Bolsward station he joined a group of ten other boys who were setting out for the same school, among them his cousin Gorgonius, the future bishop in Africa.

There were some 115 students at the school, divided into groups of eight or ten. They lived in private homes that had been approved by the religious and were under their supervision. They went to the school only for classes and spiritual formation.

How accurate his pastor had been when he had written the recommendation required for admission: "He is a complete little man, but he has a weak constitution that will require special attention; otherwise he is an intelligent young man with good judgment, one

Anno (Fr. Titus) at the age of 17 years shortly before he entered the novitiate of 1898 at the Carmelite monastery in Boxmeer, Netherlands. *(Photo courtesy of the Nederlands Carmelitaans Instituut)*

who loves his studies and is a generous friend of Our Lord. There is nothing to worry about as far as his vocation. He has excellent gifts for studies, his physical strength will come with time."[5] Short and thin, he was almost immediately given the nickname *punt* ("Runt"). Within a few months he was at the head of his class in academics, in discipline, and in piety, positions he maintained during his entire six-year stay. Soon he demonstrated a special liking for history and literature, but he held the last place when it came to public speaking: his delivery was monotonous.[6]

It was not long before the cross he was to bear throughout his life appeared.

His instructors admired his lively spirit, his ability to assimilate, his willingness to help others, his courtesy, his noble heart, his deep piety. But they were concerned for his health and required him to get extra rest and to drink lots of milk.

The Father Prefect was disturbed when he observed the extreme delicacy of this student, and one day he asked, "What's wrong, Anno? Don't you feel well? Are you tired? Are you sick?"

"No, it's nothing, Father," he replied. "I have never been strong. I am not sick, but sometimes at night I have a pain in my stomach; but don't let it worry you because they say it has to do with growth. One of these days I do have to grow, don't I? My Father always said his little man would develop once he was fourteen."

All to no avail. His father suggested that he return to the farm until, in that healthy, pleasant environment, he recovered his strength. However, as the term was almost over, Anno pleaded to stay at the school, and promised to take better care of himself and to follow the medical advice he had received. This enabled him to complete his six years of humanistic studies brilliantly.

The time had come for him to make a definitive choice about his future. His brother, Hendrik, had decided to become a Franciscan. His parents encouraged Anno to enter the same order, one well known to the entire family. One of his professors, however, noting his interest in studies, said to him in jest: "You are too bright to become a Franciscan; you should be a Jesuit!"

He discussed his vocation with his two best friends at the school. Together, they decided to read everything they could find about the various orders and religious congregations. One of their classmates later recalled that during that period the three were found on their knees in the chapel more often than before.

Not long before, Anno's older sister, Baukje, had entered the Poor Clare monastery in Megen. Possibly influenced by this, he recognized his own attraction to the contemplative ideal. He considered the Carthusians and the Trappists, but feared his health would not hold up.

Moreover, he also felt the need to have direct contact with souls through an active apostolate. What to do?

ENDNOTES

1. Joseph Rees, Titus Brandsma, *A Modern Martyr* (London: Sidgwick & Jackson, 1971). p. 18. (Hereafter Rees).

2. Anno's father, Titus Hendriks Brandsma, died in Bolsward on October 31,1920, aged 77 years. His mother, Tjitje Annes Postma, died in 1933, at 83 years of age, also in Bolsward. Baukje, the eldest, became a Poor Claire nun with the religious name Sister Maria; she died in Megen in 1939. Apollonia (Plône) became a Franciscan sister known as Sister Maria Barbara; she died in Leeuwarden in 1970. Gatsche Anna married Michiel Jans de Boer, with whom she had two children; she died in Boslward in 1960. Siebrigje entered a convent of the Sisters of the Most Precious Blood and died in Groningen in 1939. Hendrik Antonius became a Franciscan priest; he died in Leeuwarden in 1959. –Translator's note.

3. SU 65, p. 23.

4. Brocardus Meijer, O. Carm. *Titus Brandsma* (Uitgeverij Paul Brand N. V. Bussum, 1951), p. 10 (Hereafter Meijer).

5. *Idem.*

6. In notes for a study of Titus Brandsma, the late Norman Werling, O. Carm., a recognized expert in the field of graphanalysis, describes young Anno at 14 years of age: he is possessed of a "psychological maturity far beyond his fourteen years. He is a tense, strong introvert, bombarded by sense impulses and emotional conflicts, all kept in check by an external discipline that does violence to the body and takes its toll on his health. There is a splendid balance in his obligations to others and to his own self-interests; a balance also to the mental and physical imperatives of his own development." See Norman Werling, O. Carm., *Blessed Titus Brandsma, O. Carm., 1881-1942* (Unpublished notes. Carmelite Provincial Archives, Province of the Most Pure Heart of Mary, Darien, Illinois), pp. 2-8.

Chapter II

Formation

"The Spirit of Carmel Fascinated Me"

The answer came, but not from an expected source.

Anno learned that his mother's first cousin, Casimirus de Boer, who was about to be ordained to the priesthood, was a Carmelite. Without hesitation, Anno contacted him. The two spoke for some time about many things, but finally they got around to the one thing of most interest to Anno: the spirit of the Order to which Casimirus belonged, and about which Anno openly confessed he knew nothing.

His cousin's brief explanations quickly awakened a response in young Brandsma's unsettled, searching spirit. He was fascinated by the unique origin of the Order in the Holy Land, and, attracted by its contemplative charism and its special devotion to the Virgin Mary, already an integral part of the fabric of his own life.

Years later he would describe this first but decisive attraction to Carmel with these words: "The spirituality of Carmel, which is a life of prayer and of tender devotion to Mary, brought me to the happy decision to embrace this life."[1]

On September 17, 1898, five months before his 18th birthday, Anno–now fully convinced–set out for the Carmelite priory at Boxmeer with his father, who was torn between sorrow and joy. There he met two of his companions from school who, possibly influenced by him, had chosen the same order: Willem Cox and Jan van de Staay.

At the turn of the century Carmelites were not well known in the Netherlands. Recently restored in the country, the Order had only three friaries: Boxmeer, Oss, and Zenderen.

Boxmeer, the priory where Anno was going, had been founded in 1652 and was a national monument: its history involves the Counts of Van der Bergh and Hohenzollern, and several works of art are preserved in its cloisters and refectory, giving it a bit of the flavor of a museum. The community was made up of forty religious—priests, students, brothers—devoting themselves to prayer, to study and to apostolic works in the area. The Brandsma parents must have indicated that they were less than overjoyed that their son had chosen an Order so little known, for Anno's animated response countered: "One can be happy anywhere. The names in themselves are not important, but only the spirit that gives life. It is the spirit of Carmel that fascinates me."

A few days later, on September 22, the community invested Anno and five companions with the habit of novices.

Following the ancient ritual of the Order, the prior had asked these young men: "What do you seek?"

"We ask through the mercy of God to make profession of obedience, poverty, and chastity in the membership of your Order."

"May God who has brought you among us," responded the superior, "also grant you to persevere among us."

At the end of the ceremony, as Psalm 133 was being sung, all the members of the community gave a fraternal embrace to each of the new novices: "Behold, how good it is, and how pleasant, where brethren dwell in unity."

According to a venerable custom of the Order, Anno took a religious name: he chose to be known as Titus, in honor of the father for whom he felt such deep affection.

A Time of Testing

Within the venerable walls of the ancient priory at Boxmeer and its ample cloisters of black and white tiles, the six novices painstakingly followed the routine of their new life and experienced, perhaps for the first time, the significance of having given themselves to God, a commitment both joyful and demanding.

The Carmelite novitiate in the Netherlands lasted two years in those days and was designed to be rigorous: the young man who believed he had heard God calling him to Carmel was to be thoroughly tested, "threshed like wheat" as the saying goes. If his was a true vocation, he would meet every challenge and would come through greatly strengthened. On the other hand, if his vocation was only illusory, the product of youthful enthusiasm, it would wither like straw and he would return to the "world."

The first year of novitiate was dedicated exclusively to the novice's spiritual formation; the second–without cutting back on his spiritual development–also included history and sacred eloquence.

During his novitiate Frater[2] Titus devoted himself to learning everything he could about his new life as a religious as well as the history and spirituality of Carmel. With the idealism of his eighteen years he gave himself over not only to studying the foundations of the Order but especially to integrating them into his personal life. Under the guidance of the Master of Novices, Fr. Pius Cox, and of the scholarly prior of Boxmeer, Fr. Gabriel Wessels, the young novice was preparing himself in a practical, down-to-earth way for his final step, religious profession.[3]

The community's day began at midnight with the chanting of matins and lauds in choir. The prayer rose up to the Lord from bodies often shivering due to the cold nordic winter. Only when the river was frozen solid was the schedule relaxed to permit these hours of the Divine Office to be anticipated the previous evening.

Following the midnight hours, the friars slept until five or five-thirty in the morning when the daily activites began: prayer, lectures, manual labor, and recreation.

The Master of Novices provided lessons on religious life, the meaning of the vows, the history and spirituality of the Order, and the life stories of the men and women who had been its bright lights: its saints, literary figures, mystics, theologians, missionaries, martyrs.

The novices were required to learn the Rule of St. Albert by heart and to understand thoroughly each article of the Constitutions, as well as to grasp the significance of the Divine Office, how to pray it correctly and sing it in choir, and how to participate as a community in the celebration of Holy Mass.

Under the direction of their Master they engaged in physical labor: sweeping rooms, corridors, and stairs, caring for the furniture, scrubbing floors, helping in the kitchen, working in the garden, etc. It was the duty of the Novice Master to be available to his charges: both to encourage and to correct them. For their part the novices were to consult him whenever they had problems along the way.

The day ended at nine in the evening with the singing of compline and of the *Salve Regina* before the altar dedicated to the Mother of Carmel. Once the Prior had given his blessing, the community retired until midnight.

Anno's cousin had warned that the first days of the novitiate might be difficult, that he might feel himself abandoned by both God and men, but that afterwards things would change. Frater Titus experienced none of this; he did not have to wait for things to change in order to be happy. He was already happy, confident that he had found his true path.

In one of the earliest lessons on the history of Carmel, Frater Titus learned that during the religious revival that followed the third crusade (1192), a few pilgrims and crusaders, mostly Franks, withdrew to the biblical Mount Carmel near the place named "The Well of Elijah." There they sought to follow the example of the holy Prophet by a life of prayer, silence, and labor. Around 1209, at the request of the hermits living on the mountain, Saint Albert, Patriarch of Jerusalem, wrote them a Rule integrating the ideals of their own way of life. In 1226 this Rule was approved by Pope Honorius III.

These early hermits had located their cells or hermitages around a church honoring the Virgin Mary, Mother of God. They had a sense of being totally dedicated to her, and it was not long before the people were calling them "Brothers of the Blessed Virgin Mary of Mount Carmel." It was through contemplation of the figures of Mary and Elijah the Prophet that Carmel developed its way of life and described it in the Constitutions of the Order. In Mary Carmelites saw the ideal of what they felt called to become: people available to God. From Elijah they inherited a courageous zeal to bear heroic witness to the Presence of the Living God in their world.

Titus Brandsma learned his lesson well. What most drew his youthful attention was the mysterious anonymity with which the Order presented itself to the Church. It was the group as a whole which had experienced the call and took Elijah as their "spiritual Father" and model. No individual hermit took upon himself the title of founder, nor has that title ever been given to anyone.

The original hermits of Mount Carmel spread to various places around the Holy Land. Due to the hostility between Christians and Muslims, however, many of them died as martyrs, others were forced to abandon that sacred soil and return to their native lands: France, England, Italy. With the fall of the Latin Kingdom of Jerusalem, the Order was totally uprooted from the Holy Land and would not return until the 17th century.

The first historical record of the Order in Europe dates from 1235. Frater Titus also learned that, as with all human institutions, during its eight-century existence Carmel had experienced moments of splendor with tremendous numbers of well-known and saintly men and women, but also periods of decline and mediocrity which a few conscientious and determined religious worked to correct.

Thus arose various reforms, such as that of Mantua in 15th century Italy; that of Albi, and that of Touraine in 17th century France. And, above all, the best known and only one still surviving to our own times, the Teresian Reform, begun by Saint Teresa of Jesus in Avila, Spain, in 1562 among the nuns and in 1568 among the friars. Due to this latter reform, eleven years after the death of Saint Teresa, the Discalced Carmelites separated from the ancient Order.[4] Frater Titus was a member of the original branch of the Order of Carmel.

Religious Profession

On October 3, 1899, Frater Titus made his solemn profession,[5] one more stage on his long ascent to the summit of Mount Carmel. It was a journey that would last all his life, a promise, taken under oath, to keep the religious vows as a Brother of the Blessed Virgin Mary of Mount Carmel.

During the solemn community ceremony, the novices were once again asked to affirm their intentions. Then, one by one they made their profession.

It is recalled that Titus pronounced every word clearly:

> I, Frater Titus Brandsma, make my profession and promise obedience, poverty, and chastity to God, to the Blessed Virgin Mary of

Mount Carmel, and to the Most Reverend Ludovico Galli, Prior General of the Order of the Brothers of the same Blessed Virgin Mary and to his successors, according to the Rule of the aforesaid Order, until death.

The Provincial, Fr. Joseph Kerstens, then proclaimed this admonition: "Render unto God a sacrifice of praise." And the community responded: "And fulfill your vows to the Lord."

The newly professed concluded with the words:

> I will offer my vows to God in the presence of all His people, in the courtyards of the House of the Lord. I, Frater Titus, promise moreover to profess literally these Constitutions of the strict observance, confirmed by Pope Innocent X and, with the grace of God, to observe them faithfully.

Each of the newly professed signed a written copy of his vows and placed it in the hands of his superior.

As the entire community listened to the ancient formulas that the newly professed were pronouncing, Titus' father was listening as well, trying his best to hide his emotion; at his side Titus' mother shed tears silently but peacefully.

His novitiate completed, Frater Titus began his study of philosophy in the same priory of Boxmeer, a program that would last two years more. If the truth be known, the few Carmelite friaries in the Netherlands at that time were not centers of intellectual activity. The houses of studies were modest student centers where those matters considered indispensable for carrying out apostolic activity were imparted.

Many clerics, though pious and austere, did not consider philosophy terribly important for their future apostolates. They tended to think of it not so much as a means for honing their minds through mental discipline, but rather as a collection of rather dry principles underlying theology. They had, of course, heard some rumors about the reform of studies being planned in Rome, but Rome was a long way off!

As for Titus, he continued to give his utmost to whatever activity he was assigned. His inexhaustable thirst for knowledge lead him to read every scholarly and spiritual book he could lay his hands on; and with this his superiors were content.

Moreover, he seemed to be losing the shyness that made him do

Professed Carmelite Titus Brandsma at the age of 22 years and a student of theology. *(Photo courtesy of the Nederlands Carmelitaans Instituut)*

poorly whenever he had to speak in public. He began to give talks on both spiritual and literary topics, and to do so with a mature, pleasant voice. He frequently earned sincere compliments.

His efforts, however, did not take his fragile health into account. His chronic stomach pains returned in such an acute form that his superiors obliged him to accept a dispensation from attending certain community activities. In Megen his aches had been passed off as growing pains; in Boxmeer, however, the prior, Fr. Wessels, was wisely unwilling to accept this diagnosis and had forbidden him to attend the midnight Office: "You are to pray the midnight hours during the evening and alone."

Obedience was the only thing that could force this stubborn Frisian to give in and to stay in bed while his confreres, shivering in the cold under their capuches, chanted the divine praises. Throughout his life Titus found such dispensations unwelcome and difficult to accept: not only did they make him feel "singled out," but they deprived him of the joy of praying or working in community. Moreover, they did not seem to have much effect on his delicate constitution.

Nevertheless, Titus learned how to turn necessity into a virtue. In 1900, during one of his long sessions in bed, he prepared a translation from the French of d'Andilly's *Anthology of the Works of Saint Teresa*, a 317 page volume that set forth with great clarity the thought of the great Spanish Carmelite. His work was necessarily imperfect– he was only twenty years old at the time– but it did demonstrate clearly his literary ability.

Master and Friend

Some might say that the philosophy program of the Dutch Carmelites lacked practicality and offered little that bore on the "real world." Nevertheless, Titus, with his clear intelligence and his lively temperament, refused to take it lightly.

It was his good fortune that during his second year in the program a new instructor arrived from Rome. He was a young Carmelite who had completed his doctorate in philosophy brilliantly, and had been named professor of philosophy in Boxmeer. He was Father Hubertus Driessen. Professor Driessen's arrival was like a breath of fresh air in a closed room. At first, however, his students found it difficult to understand him. At this point one of his students became an uninvited mediator: Frater Titus volunteered to take notes in class, to submit them to the professor for approval, and then to distribute them to his fellow students. Fr. Hubertus was moved by this young student's open and determined spirit: he agreed to provide the notes himself, and Titus would see to their distribution. The notes for that single course formed three volumes!

This effort was not to last long. By Christmas of 1901 acute stomach pains, accompanied by hemorrhages, forced Titus to take to his bed for long periods.

Fr. Hubertus spent a great deal of time at Titus' bedside. He talked enthusiastically with his student about the environment of renewal that was taking hold at the Order's headquarters in Rome. This was perhaps the first time that Titus became conscious of belonging to a large family spread around the world. Years later, for Fr. Hubertus' Golden Jubilee of Profession, Titus wrote in the "Book of Friends":

> You came to my bedside and would not allow me to think about my studies, you wouldn't even allow me to talk about philosophy. Rather, you told me about your life in Rome, your difficulties, your disappointments, your efforts, and your battles for love of the Order and its progress. More than a professor, for me you were a father. With all my heart I thank you for the friendship you offered. Ours was a deep friendship founded on a mutual desire to dedicate ourselves to study and to reawaken in Carmel its glorious tradition.

Fr. Hubertus served as professor of philosophy in Boxmeer for only a single year before he was elected Procurator General, then the second highest office in the Order, immediately below that of the Prior General. Consequently, he was required to return to Rome. Titus was proud of his teacher's promotion. Years later he would write:

> I considered your departure a duty. As for me, I prayed a lot since there was nothing else I could do, and, out of my insignificance, I made up my mind to make your proposals understood and loved.

Today Fr. Hubertus is recognized for having understood Titus' spirit, for having given him a hand in the early stages of his development, for having opened up for him the wise and holy horizons he was never to abandon.

One might expect that with Fr. Hubertus' departure, mediocrity would return to dominate Dutch studies. Quite the contrary. The seed had been sown; one had only to wait for it to bear fruit.

In 1902-1903 Frater Titus was sent to Zenderen to study theology. The following year he was transferred to Oss, where he completed the program.

If anyone thinks the life of a professed student boring, he would be mistaken. In Titus' case, it was precisely in these years that he took his first steps toward what was to become one of his chief apos-

Fr. Titus Brandsma, newly ordained priest, (on the right) with his admirable teacher and inseparable friend, Fr. Hubertus Driessen, who would become Procurator General of the Carmelite Order. *(Photo courtesy of the Nederlands Carmelitaans Instituut)*

tolates and, in the end, the reason for his martyrdom: journalism.

Under his leadership a few students organized themselves into study circles and founded a small publication that allowed them to express their concerns. At first it was handwritten under the title *Baptista Mantuanus* in honor of the famous Renaissance Carmelite poet and humanist known as "The Christian Virgil." It was not long, however, before it was published in print under a new name: *Van Neerlands Carmel* (From the Dutch Carmel).

Considering the demands of his studies and the schedule of the community, Titus' own output was phenomenal; more and more he was becoming convinced that the pen was a powerful tool for the apostolate. Those who read his articles would have been hard pressed to suspect that, under the pseudonym "Isebrand," lurked a young student religious.

As editor, Titus did all he could to offer the best contributions from the student journal to publications with greater distribution. Before long the students' efforts were attracting the attention both of the members of the Order and of outsiders. Many offered their collaboration.

In hopes of restoring the old Carmelite Province of Rio de Janeiro, in 1904 the Dutch Carmelites were to establish missions in Brazil. Titus was among the first to volunteer, and he was disappointed when he was not chosen to work in that far-off land; he resolved to do what he could to support the mission through publicity and contributions.

Priesthood

On December 19, 1903, Frater Titus was ordained subdeacon, and on May 28, 1904, deacon. His dream of becoming a priest was about to be fulfilled.

He was 24 years old and had just completed his third year of theology, with a fourth and final year yet ahead. He was as thin and as sickly as ever, but he had acquired considerable spiritual and intellectual maturity.

Rumor had it that following his ordination he was to be sent to Rome to study for a doctorate in philosophy. Titus himself paid no attention to such talk. He would do whatever his superiors wished with the joy and serenity of one who has given his life irrevocably to an ideal superior. On Saturday, June 17, 1905, he was ordained a priest by the laying of hands of Bishop Willen van der Van in the cathedral of Den Bosch. Present were his parents, overcome with emotion; two of his sisters in their religious habits; and his brother Hendrik, a theology student, in his Franciscan habit. Alongside him at the foot of the altar his five companions.

On his remembrance card he had expressed his desire—to fall not too far short of God's plan for him, nor of the hopes that his superiors were placing in him: "Of him who has received much, much will be required."

From that day on Father Titus would examine himself each evening as to whether he had given as he had received. Even in his cell at Scheveningen prison he would return to this thought: "The vocation to the Church and to the priesthood has enriched me with so much consolation and joy that I am prepared to accept whatever may happen to me, however repugnant to my own nature."

Newly ordained, Fr. Titus continued his studies in Oss. He then had to pass a comprehensive examination in theology. This would be the final step in his studies for the priesthood. Two of his classmates were being sent to communities where they were assigned to appropriate ministries; two others were assigned as adjunct professors of theology. To the surprise of everyone, Titus, considered the most talented candidate for a university position, was ordered to remain at Oss as sacristan, a humble position little befitting his intellectual talents. Naturally Titus felt the blow, but never once did he express disappointment; rather, he took up his new duties with his customary calm and good humor: making noting the Masses to be offered, making sure they were offered, and occasionally assisting neighboring pastors.

This development was due apparently to the intervention of one of his professors, Father Eugenius Driessen, a man of great culture (he had received papal honors for his work) but rigidly inflexible. Scrupulously fearful of some possible heresy, he was unwilling to permit any discussion about the content of his courses. Young Titus, on the other hand, was eager to question everything.

Fr. Eugenius viewed his student with suspicion, and—unable to deal with the danger he presumed would be present if Titus were to hold an academic degree and dedicate himself to teaching–he chose to deny him the opportunity.

Once all this was behind him, with great humility Fr. Brandsma was to acknowledge:

> It was very important for me to be put to this test. Father Driessen was right in judging my weaknesses severely because, as my professor, he saw them with greater clarity than anyone else. He gave me valuable advice and he called me to order. I owe him my deepest gratitude. However, at that time there was little understanding between us, because I held opinions that were different from those taught in class, thus causing conflict between him and me. I never considered, of course, this to be wrong since it was all about debatable issues.

Obviously, here was a conflict of ideas, apparently irreconcilable, between professor and student. Result: Titus was held back, and this tested the depth of his virtues.

The rigid Fr. Eugenius was the brother of Titus' best friend, Fr. Hubertus. When the latter returned from Rome he quickly became aware of what was going on. He was astonished. Looking into the matter he arrived at the obvious conclusion: the entire affair reflected nothing more serious than differing points of view on non-essential positions. He requested that the decision be reconsidered.

"Where is Titus?" he asked.

"In Coudewater, taking the place of the hospital chaplain," came the reply.

"Tell him I want to see him as soon as possible," he requested. Titus returned at once and, on October 18, the two were reunited. Titus had scarcely arrived when Hubertus announced, "My dear Titus, you are coming to Rome with me. There is no question but that the new provincial will give his approval; I have already spoken with him. Still it is best that you go to see him and personally remind him of my wishes."

"But what about my 'heretical' tendencies?" asked Titus.

"Just go to see him," the Procurator General repeated with a smile.

And so he went, but not without misgivings; he was sincerely disturbed because he honestly feared that, due to their friendship, Father Hubertus might have judged him more generously than he deserved. He had barely greeted the provincial when, with characteristic simplicity, he blurted:

> Father Provincial, do you have any idea how independent in his opinions is this friar standing here before you? Some of my confreres believe, and with reason, my way of thinking in theological matters is dangerous.

To this the provincial responded: "All the more reason for you to go to Rome."⁶

And so the "Runt" from Frisland accompanied Father Hubertus across Germany and Austria; they spent nights in Cologne and Mainz. Crossing into Italy they stopped in Verona, and finally arrived in Rome one rainy day of October 1906.

On the way to the Carmelite House of Studies they passed in front of St. Peter's Basilica. Like so many who see that wonder for the first time, Titus' entire being was filled with emotion and, right there, he renewed in his heart his profession of that Catholic faith which had been so strongly implanted in his soul from birth.

Doctorate

At the International College of Saint Albert were living–in harmony–Carmelites from many countries: Italy, Spain, Bavaria, Austria, the Netherlands, Malta, the United States, Ireland. Perhaps for the first time Titus became fully conscious of Fr. Hubertus' prestige as Procurator General of an Order with members around the world, and that of another Dutchman, his former Novice Master, Fr. Gabriel Wessels as Assistant General. Yet their high offices did not become an obstacle to their sense of fraternity, and indeed with the community as a whole. There was also another Dutch student at Sant'Alberto, Antoninus van Kerkhoff; like Frs. Hubertus and Gabriel, Antoninus fit the popular conception of the hearty Dutchman. When he was with them Titus felt even smaller than he actually was; he once wrote to his family, tongue in cheek, "We are four Dutchmen in Rome, even though one of us is only half of one." These four greatly enjoyed one another's company and engaged in many a discussion about the concerns of their province.

Students from Sant'Alberto attended classes daily at the Pontifical Gregorian University. Anxious to take full advantage of the oppor-

The Brandsma Family around 1918. Five of the six children are wearing their religious habits: (left to right) Fr. Titus with his Carmelite mantle; Baukje (Sr. Maria) was a Claritian, Apollonia (Sr. Maria Barbara) joined the Precious Blood Sisters, Siebrigje (Sr. Willibrorda) and Hendrik were Franciscans. The only one to marry was Gatsche whose husband, Michiel Jans de Boer, is sitting at the right. The children pictures are from this marriage. *(Photo courtesy of the Nederlands Carmelitaans Instituut)*

tunities offered in Rome, in addition to his full-time program in the Faculty of Philosophy, Titus insisted on enrolling in a course on modern sociology under the tutelage of Monsignor A. Pottier, a noted specialist in the area.

He continued to contribute to *Van Neerlands Carmel*, which since his departure had been languishing. He also committed himself to send frequent reports about Rome and other Italian cities to *Het Katholiek Sociaal Weekblad*; and to provide *Der Voorhoede* with articles on sociological themes and socio-Christian movements in Italy. Moreover he accepted responsibility for the letters to the editors for *Het Centrum*. He even dreamed of beginning a multilingual scholarly journal for the Order.

A fellow student, who was to become the scholarly Fr. Alberto Grammatico, pointed out that his zeal for work was excessive, and that he ought to learn how to pace himself, and how to say "No" to the frequent requests for help that were pouring in from every side. Titus smilingly responded: "But, didn't our Lord do everything He could for us?"

Incapable of saying "No," always punctual for community exercises, ever generous toward those around him and especially with God, he took no time to even think about his failing health. Yet overwork, the Roman climate so little appropriate for him, and the austere nature of conventual life at Sant'Alberto combined to produce a relapse.

The community's day began at five o'clock in the morning. By 5:20 the friars gathered for community prayer both mental and liturgical. Only afterwards did they take a cup of coffee with milk and a piece of bread left over from the day before; at midday there was a plate of spaghetti and some salad, and in the evening an equally frugal supper. With typical humor Titus wrote home: "With the food we have here, I have no difficulty putting into practice the maxim of leaving the table with an appetite for a little more."

His fellow religious did their best to help him. The General himself sent him to spend periods of relaxation in the Italian communities of Albano, Naples, Florence, and even to Vienna and Mainz. Nevertheless, Titus continued in poor health and lost weight.

At the conclusion of the 1907-08 academic year he received his Licentiate in Philosophy. In November, while preparing for his comprehensive examinations, he fainted, writhing in pain. He had barely gotten into bed when his lips reddened with blood. This hemorrhage indicated a serious and painful condition that was to keep him bedridden for three months and brought him to the edge of death.

Titus was fully aware of his condition, but what bothered him most was the fear that he was dashing the hopes placed in him by his superiors. Consequently, with the arrival of spring, he thought he was strong enough to make up for lost time and prepare for his doctoral examination.

Hollow-eyed, thinner than ever, feverish and scarcely able to stand, he took the exam. He failed; he would have to repeat the exam in October. When he learned the results, he shook his head in disappointment and acknowledged what everyone else already knew: "I did all I could."

Four months rest in the Netherlands allowed him to recover his failed energy and to pass his examination brilliantly. On October 25, 1909, he sent a telegram from Rome to the Netherlands: "Examination passed."

ENDNOTES

1. SU. 65, p. 59.

2. The title "Frater" was frequently used among male religious to designate professed clerical students.

3. Meijer, p. 21.

4. Cf. Joachim Smet, O. Carm., *The Carmelites: A History of the Brothers of Our Lady of Mount Carmel* (Darien, Illinois: Carmelite Spiritual Center, 1976-1988). Vols. II & III, passim. Or Joachim Smet, O. Carm., *The Mirror of Carmel: A Brief History of the Carmelite Order*. (Darien, Illinois: Carmelite Media, 2011).

5. Before the promulgation of the Code of Canon Law in 1917, profession was either solemn or perpetual. After 1917 first profession was simple and temporary.

6. Meijer, p. 78.

Chapter III

Plans and Hopes

Educator, Journalist, Author

Doctor Titus Brandsma returned to the Netherlands filled with dreams he was anxious to turn into realities. His academic credentials, which had almost cost him his life, he considered not so much an accomplishment as a launching pad for as yet unperceived worlds to be discovered. He seems to have forgotten, or possibly chose to ignore, the limitations placed on him by his chronically poor health. Almost without pausing to take a breath, he involved himself in a variety of activities: his zeal knew no boundaries.

His first assignment was as professor of Philosophy and Church History in the Carmelite major seminary in Oss. At thirty years of age he was taking the first steps in a career that would lead to a University Chair.

In those years, shortly before World War I, there was a noticeable dearth of vocations to the religious and priestly life; consequently, his classes were not large. Nevertheless, he put his entire heart into his lectures and was as zealous as if he had been dealing with twice as many students.

Along with his duties as teacher, he had also been named Regent of Studies. This position made it possible for him to initiate reforms he had dreamed about since his own student days. Fortunately, Fr. Hubertus, his mentor and friend, recently elected Prior Provincial of the Dutch Carmelites, was supportive of Titus' goals.

As a beginning Titus convinced his superior to send ten professed students to Rome so that, within a few years, the entire Dutch seminary faculty would be renewed. He also insisted that each priest earn a civilly recognized academic degree so that he would be on equal footing with professors in other institutions.

Convinced that the entire formation program would be enhanced if all the students of the province were to live in one community, he persuaded the provincial council to purchase a former Benedictine abbey at Merkelbeek in the southern part of the Netherlands.

Titus' vision was not limited to the formation of Carmelite students. Several of his personal initiatives dating from this period continue to bear fruit: e.g., the library with attached reading room and lecture hall open to the general public that the citizens of Oss still point to with pride. He was a firm believer in Catholic education; indeed he considered it the most important of all apostolates in a country where the majority of the citizens were Protestant. He proposed the establishment of several schools under Carmelite direction and available to all who wished a Catholic education. This was something altogether new to the Order.

First came a Commercial School in Oss, next to the library. In 1919 it would become a complete lyceum and today bears the name "Lyceum Titus Brandsma." A few years later, in 1923, a Classical Lyceum was opened in Oldenzaal.

Both of these institutions were fruits of the so-called "Catholic Battle" waged by Dutch Catholics to obtain government support for their schools. Recognizing the justice of this position, Titus fought hard to achieve it. He even succeeded in having one of his own proposals debated in the Dutch Parliament. In 1926 his efforts were rewarded: the two Carmelite institutions were the first private schools in the Netherlands to receive government support. Even more important, the door had been opened for other secondary schools to receive the same benefits. To encourage them, as early as 1925 Titus had founded a Union of Secondary Schools; he himself served as president of this Union until his death.[1]

Such innovations could not fail to create problems for this young Carmelite. A few of the older religious thought it their duty to protect their province from such dangerous novelties. Father Hubertus, however, continued to support Titus' initiatives. It soon became apparent, moreover, that his ideals were finding broad backing among his brother Carmelites: in the provincial elections of 1912 Titus was chosen as a member of the provincial council, a post he was to retain–except for a single triennium–for the rest of his life.

On most things Hubertus and Titus worked together: Titus prepared the way and garnered support with his reasoned arguments, his practical approach, his sense of humor, his smile, his timely and prudent comments. The provincial let it be known that he was in agreement. Under their technical and tactical guidance, the Dutch Carmel grew in strength and vigor and attracted more and more candidates.

Even with his thorough preparations, Titus' classes failed to absorb all his energy. Consequently, he found "spare" time to dedicate to his apostolate of the pen. In Rome Father Hubertus, mindful of Titus' health, had forbidden him to engage in any kind of journalistic activity until he returned to the Netherlands. But once back in his own country, the young professor was able to give his zeal and generosity free rein–it was "full speed ahead."

His signature, "T.B." was soon to be found in more than twenty periodicals, both national and international: some were well-known publications like *Ons Noorden, De Gelderlander, De Tijd, De Masbode*; others were professional journals like *Het Katholiek Sociaal Weekblad, Revista de Historia, Analecta Ordinis Carmelitarum*. He also wrote for popular religious magazines.

Never one to think small, Titus put forward a detailed plan for the creation of a national scholarly publication in conjunction with the editor of *Het Katholiek Sociaal Weekblad* and future Minister of Social Affairs, Mr. P. J. M. Aalberese. This proposal never materialized.

Undaunted by this setback, Titus turned his attention to another pet project: using the press to make Carmel's voice– silent for so long– heard by his countrymen. *Karmelrozen* first appeared in 1912; only two years later it had attracted more than 13,000 subscribers.

In 1919 he was named editor-in-chief of *De Stad Oss*, a moribund newspaper which he was able to reorganize and revitalize. He held this post until 1923, and during that entire period its eight pages came out regularly, typographically perfect, with pictures and, most important, with accurate information.

Fr. Brandsma's enthusiastic participation in the world of journalism earned him the respect of his fellow journalists. One day it was to lead to his nomination as Ecclesiastical Advisor to the Union of Catholic Journalists (UCIP); this in its turn was to play a major role in his ultimate conflict with the German occupation authorities and to his death.

In the course of his own research, Dr. Brandsma had become painfully aware that there was no Dutch translation of the works of St. Teresa of Avila. This he considered a deplorable lacuna in the area of ascetical and mystical theology. Already as a student he had published an anthology of the works of the saint; now, in 1916, he felt the time had come for a translation, directly from the Spanish, of the complete works of this great Carmelite mystic.

To take on a project of this scope Titus enlisted three collaborators, all Carmelites and all with doctorates to their credit: Athanasius van Rijswijck and the brothers Hubertus and Eugenius Driessen. This team chose Fr. Brandsma as its head, with responsibility for the final revision of the texts and notes. Within a few days, he had presented a detailed plan for the entire seven-volume project to a publisher. It was the most significant and most ambitious program undertaken by the Dutch Carmelites to that time.

The first volume, *The Book of Her Life*, was published in 1918. It was the work of Titus himself, and it was greeted by critics as a promise of even greater things yet to come. Reviewing the volume in Pniel, Dr. C. P. Gunning wrote: "This work, from the pen of the Carmelite scholar of Oss, constitutes an event of exceptional importance." It was not long before a second edition was published.

The following year came *The Book of Her Foundations*, prepared by Fr. Anastasius van Rijswijck. Some years later, in 1924, appeared the third volume, the first part of the Letters, under the care of Fr. Hubertus Driessen. In 1926 the *Interior Castle* and *The Way of Perfection* were published together, a collaboration by Fathers Titus and Anastasius.

Titus had hoped to enjoy a less busy period, with time to finish the entire project, but that never arrived. The reorganization of the Dutch Province, the requirements of new foundations in Brazil, the departure of Fr. Hubertus for Rome, the unexpected call of Titus himself to the Catholic University of Nijmegen, all conspired to put a halt, albeit temporary, to the continuation of the series.

Titus never lost interest in it, however, and he continued studying the doctrine and personality of the Saint of Avila. It is said that he had the *Interior Castle* nearly memorized. To his friend, Fr. Hubertus, he wrote: "There are many things in my life that I certainly regret, but most of all not being able to complete the works of Saint Teresa."[2] It was during this same period that Titus turned his attention toward his tiny native province, Frisland. Its culture, language, and traditions were close to his heart.

Friesland was an almost totally Protestant region. Titus wanted to uncover the area's earlier, pre-Reformation Christian traditions to lay bare the roots he recognized as common to all Frisians. He was not unaware that some Frisian Protestants branded Catholics as being more Roman than Frisian. He wanted to demonstrate that being Catholic was not the same thing as being anti-Frisian. That he was able to accomplish so much speaks volumes about the great sensitivity of his apostolic soul.

In 1917 he, along with other natives of the region, founded the *Roomks Frysk Boun* (Union of Frisian Catholics). For many years Titus served as secretary of the Union. Its goal was to promote the use of the Frisian language and to publicize Frisian culture. Brandsma's dedication to this goal was extensive and intense and perhaps, in the words of Cardinal Johannes de Jong, "somewhat exaggerated."[3] While this evaluation contains more than a grain of truth, it overlooked Titus' apostolic purpose.

The magazine *Der Voorhoede* (*The Vanguard*) occasionally published articles promoting Friesland and the Frisian language. Much of this was due to the encouragement of the poet Jan Rijpma, who had translated the Medieval Latin hymn *Dies irae* into Frisian. Brandsma himself contributed an article on Our Lady of Bolsward which concluded with his hope that "All of Frisia, as one people, pay homage before the throne of the Seat of Wisdom." This article was the first piece in Frisian by a Catholic since the Middle Ages.

Missionary Zeal

Following World War I the Church of the Netherlands experienced a powerful flowering of its missionary spirit. For the Dutch Carmelite province this involved, in 1923, opening missions in Indonesia, today a flourishing and independent Carmelite province. Simultaneously Dutch Carmel sent a good-sized contingent of friars to existing missions in Brazil. Titus himself volunteered for the missions and at one point he had been slated to go to Brazil; however, his superiors decided to keep him in the Netherlands to work on the province's recently revised program of studies.

Although his own hopes of going to the missions had been dashed, Titus did not lose heart. He immediately set about organizing programs to inform the public about the importance of the missions and to encourage popular support for the missionaries. In his "free time" he gathered truck-loads of materials and traveled the length and breadth of the Netherlands to set up expositions and slide shows, and to leave behind brochures and books about the Carmelite missions.

His prior was worried that Titus–not known for strength and stamina–was overextending himself. "Of course not," Titus replied. "Knowing how much our brothers in Brazil need help, how can this possibly be too much for me? How can I stay peacefully and tranquilly at home?"

Actually his zeal did exceed his energy. In addition to his efforts on behalf of the missions, he still had classes to prepare and teach, he was still turning out articles for newspapers and essays for books, and–all these things notwithstanding–he never missed the activities of the common life. To the admiration of his confreres, he was always doing what he was supposed to do and being where he was expected to be. When it was time for prayer, he was the first to arrive at his place in chapel. On the other hand, by the end of the day he was occasionally so exhausted that his prior, himself a strong, robust man, had to help him to his room, at times almost carrying him in his arms. The next morning Titus was again going about his business.

One Sunday, July 3, 1921, he was in Boxmeer directing a weeklong program about the missions. His mother, a widow since the previous year, was taking part. Suddenly Titus was overcome by so much pain that his mother had to take him back to Oss. He had suffered a serious hemorrhage, followed by several smaller ones, which took him once again to the edge of death. It was November before he was able to return to his work.

Fr. Hubertus wrote him from Rome: "This episode was inexcusable. Why do you continue to add new burdens to your

Fr. Titus, on a break from work in 1935, walking in the patio area of the house in Nijmegen smoking his pipe. Smoking in those days did not have the negative connotations it does today and was actually encouraged in the monastery. *(Photo courtesy of the Nederlands Carmelitaans Instituut)*

life?" However, the friendly advice of his friend did little to slow Titus down. His strength restored, his native optimism soon drew him back into all his usual activities, and indeed to a new one he had been thinking about for some time: a national congress on foreign missions. It was to include grand exhibitions in Oss and Rotterdam.

Planned and accomplished: the congress took place in the Spring of 1922. Titus himself welcomed and saw to lodging for several bishops and dozens of missionaries. He set up the program of conferences and gave several himself. He arranged for more than twenty booths for the exhibition, and he even organized an allegorical parade with fourteen carriages.

To everyone's surprise, attendance far exceeded expectations: more than 1,500 of the faithful participated. No one could remember an occasion when there had been such a public manifestation of religious faith. So proud were the people of Oss that, without consulting anyone, a popular subscription was launched to provide a public memorial of this Congress on the Missions: on June 26 of that same year it was dedicated, to the honor of Christ the King. That day Fr. Titus was moved to tears.

One citizen of Oss, who had observed Titus passing back and forth in front of his house day after day on his way to his works, was overheard to say: "If the City of Oss were ever to grant honorary citizenship to any individual, no one would merit it more than Father Brandsma."

Never one to rest on his laurels, Titus worked hard to get funds to establish the first lyceum in Indonesia. Located in the Carmelite Vicariate Apostolic of Malang, Java, its goal was to proclaim the Gospel within the context of Indonesian culture. Its entire program was to be taught in the local language, and the school itself was open to everyone.[4]

Later, when Titus was teaching at the University of Nijmegen, he used his influence to set up an academic chair of Missiology.

Academic Activities

Titus' academic research was earning him something of a name: he had published an important article on the notion of space in a

Central Board of the Apostolate of the Union of Eastern Christians. Fr. Titus at the time was the secretary to the group. He is easily identified sitting with his white cloak. Fr. Brandsma undertook great initiatives in the ecumenical field. *(Photo courtesy of the Nederlands Carmelitaans Instituut)*

prestigious philosophical journal; he had also published an article–unfortunately lost during the war–on the history of philosophy in the Low Countries before the Reformation; and, from his research into Carmelite history, he had made several important contributions to the Monasticon being edited by the noted historian and archivist Dr. Michael Schoengen. With these credentials it was not surprising that he was named a professor in the Commercial School of Oss.

When Father Hubertus heard of this appointment. he wrote to the community of Oss:

> You all complain that he [Titus] works too much, that he cannot go on this way. But when a new position becomes available, you do not hesitate to push him into it. I think he should be in Rome, where he could dedicate himself exclusively to teaching in the Collegio di Sant'Alberto.

Titus seemed pleased with the idea of returning to the Eternal City, but others had quite different plans for him. In mid-June 1923, the prior provincial announced the new assignments for members of the province. One of these was for Father Titus Brandsma.

ENDNOTES

1. INF. 68, p. 17.

2. Rees, p. 70. *Analecta Ordinis Carmelitarum* 4 (1917-1922), 395, and 5 (1923-1926), 563. B. Lurvink, O. Carm., *Carmelo Lusitano* (1984), 174. Four of the seven volumes were published during Titus Brandsma's lifetime; the other three after his death. The series was completed in 1949 through the efforts of Fr. Thomas Keulemans, O. Carm.

3. INF. 68, p. 145.

4. Agencia Internacional *FIDES*, Roma, November, 1985, n° 559.

Chapter IV

At the University

A New Challenge

The creation of a Catholic University in the Netherlands was announced publicly on June 28, 1923. It was to be located in Nijmegen, a city in the southern part of the country where there was a Catholic majority. The university was the fulfillment of a long-held dream sustained by the fervor of Dutch Catholics–hierarchy, clergy, and faithful alike. The Catholic University of Nijmegen (renamed in 2004 as the Radboud University) still stands as a monument to their long battle for religious liberty.

Titus of course was not unaware that the announcement was imminent. The previous April he had received a telegram requesting him to meet with Professor J. H. E. J. Hoogveld, who informed him that the Archbishop of Utrecht had decided that the Catholic University would open its doors at the beginning of the next academic year. Moreover, he told the young Carmelite, Titus himself had been nominated to fill the Chair of Philosophy.

This news caught Titus totally unprepared. At 42 years of age he felt in the prime of life; nevertheless, the offer placed him in a quandary. Prudently he asked for time to consider the offer as well as to consult his superiors, particularly Father Hubertus.

Had the news come a few days later, it may well have come too late. The Carmelite General Council in Rome, preparing to create a General House of Studies for the entire Order, had looked to Dr. Titus Brandsma as an ideal candidate for its faculty.

No doubt the provincial consulted with his Council, and their decision was soon known. At the end of the community meal on June 17, the provincial made Titus' appointment to the new Catholic University public. The community was delighted and broke into spontaneous applause.

Titus' appointment had come as a surprise not only for Titus himself, but also for several of his friends and acquaintances, not because he was a stranger to academic circles, but because several other Carmelites seemed even better qualified: Father Eugenius Driessen and his brother, Titus' good friend Father Hubertus, to mention but two.[1] Titus would have been among the first to acknowledge that there were others more capable than he. He had not sought the appointment but had accepted it as an act of obedience.

No one anticipated that Titus would spend the rest of his life in that position.

Nijmegen

During those final summer months in Oss, Titus worked tirelessly on the arrangements for the official opening of the university. In addition to preparing his own classes, he was called upon to help resolve innumerable difficulties before the fall term. Not least among them were the tremendous financial obligations of the venture, and concerns about whether they could be met, largely through the commitment of the Catholic faithful. A great deal of his time–there are records of at least eight distinct visits–was spent in the offices of the Ministry of Education.

Finally, in September, he left Oss, a city where he had put down deep roots, for Nijmegen. Since there was no Carmelite community there, he rented a room for himself on Spoorstraat. Weekends he returned to Oss in order to enjoy his community and to help out with its many apostolates.

For Titus his position at the university was not simply a job to be done, but rather a challenge to be met anew each day. Extemporaneous presentations were not his style; consequently, he spent several hours each day preparing his classes. Although his natural delivery tended to be somewhat monotonous, he possessed a gift for making his material both interesting and convincing. As a result, his students appreciated the quality of his presentations. His lectures possessed a certain vitality not always found in the halls of academia, a certain passion which came not from his style of presentation but from his own obvious enthusiasm.[2]

Professor Brandsma's day began at six o'clock when he celebrated Mass in the near-by church of the Jesuits. The rest of the morning he spent at the university, where he was lecturing on the history of philosophy, natural philosophy, and natural theology. Later in his career he would also lecture on the history of mysticism. The remainder of the day he worked in his room, busily typing, and occasionally enjoying his pipe.

Yes, like every good Dutchmen in those years, Father Titus smoked. For the Dutch smoking was as much a part of life as breathing. Certainly, it was not considered a vice, especially as he limited himself to a few times a day. And, of course, the health-threatening aspects of an excessive use of nicotine were not yet well known. No doubt Titus was imitating his father: he liked to recall that the elder Brandsma would light his pipe or a cigar immediately on rising and offer the first smoke as a prayer to the Lord.

Professor Brandsma

Professor Brandsma's interests were naturally eclectic: he had little confidence in the "limitations of any one person." Still he was not one of those lecturers who was content simply to list the positions of others. He did his best to explain their thoughts fairly, to indicate their reasoning, and to evaluate their conclusions within their proper context. Titus, moreover, was master of his material and did not hesitate to state his own conclusions clearly.

Fundamental to Titus' thought was his respect for the individual, and he directed his own efforts exclusively to the discovery of truth wherever it might be found. He was convinced that, however revealed, all truth enhances human understanding of the whole of reality. This conviction melded well with his acknowledged talent for synthesis.

In his very first class—on a Saturday morning—he made it quite clear that the study of philosophy has no power to give meaning to one's life if it is isolated from or seen as opposed to God, whose traces are to be found in the depths of every human event. This framework of divine self-giving and human collaboration make up the *Lex Domini in historia* (the Law of God in History). His philosophy was completely theocentric, stamped as it was by his own intense interior life.[3]

The name of Titus Brandsma will not be found among those who have made unique contributions to philosophy. Nor will he be remembered for any great volume of philosophical texts—though he had always hoped for "some months of calm" for philosophical reflection and expression. Nevertheless, among his many philosophical articles his own strong personal convictions about its central issues can be seen.

He was totally convinced of the inter-relatedness of all branches of human knowledge, as well as their relative positions within the hierarchy of truths. He placed special importance on that aspect of philosophy known as *Theodicy* or Natural Theology, and he encouraged his students to seek God in all things, above all within themselves. He hoped in this way they would find there that for which they had been created, the union of the individual with God.

It was obvious that the focal point of his interest was mysticism, and it was the history of mysticism that he presented best in his lectures. Here his intuitions and his vision were most clear. One of his students, the author Godfried Bomans, testified during the process of beatification that his classes on the history of mysticism were "unforgettable" not only for him but for all who attended them.[4] Rightly Titus is credited with the rediscovery of the spirituality of his people.[5]

Students' Friend

Although few would claim he was a brilliant lecturer, little by little he became one of the more popular professors at the Catholic University of Nijmegen. Titus was no learned academic who doubled as a priest on Sundays. He was a priest whose life, wherever he was, bore witness to God. In both his lectures and his homilies he provided a well-blended mixture of academic knowledge and apostolic proclamation.[6]

It was the obvious sincerity of his life that attracted students and it is little wonder that many of them saw him as a father figure as well as an instructor. Others sought him out as a friend. In him they discovered genuine understanding as well as sincere affection. He was "all heart" and the students knew he would welcome them without regard for previously determined office hours. They recognized that such unlimited availability had its source in the inner spring of his love for God.

Titus instinctively took the part of the underdog. As a member of an examining board he took pains to encourage students by formulating his questions clearly and courteously. On the other hand, should one of his colleagues seem to take pleasure in terrorizing a student, Professor Brandsma–a smile hiding behind a few sharp remarks–would attempt to restore calm. The students good-naturedly nicknamed Fr. Brandsma "The Little Professor." When he learned of this, Titus joked with obvious relish that not even the academic regalia of a professor was able to add even an inch to his small stature.

Fr. Titus was filled with love for his Order. Whenever a Carmelite was graduating, Fr. Titus' enthusiasm was boundless. This became so noticeable that one professor, somewhat tongue-in-cheek, warned another: "When that happens, be careful not to offer your congratulations to Brandsma rather than to the student."

It was not only his students who were welcomed by Fr Titus. People of all kinds made their way to his room: rich, poor, Catholics, Protestants, emigrants, etc. He welcomed them all. One of his students noted that Professor Brandsma had time for everyone; no matter how many urgent tasks were clamoring for his attention. During even the most inconvenient visits, he would calmly sit and listen, as though he had nothing in the world more important to do.[7] Even his landlady began to worry about him and advised him not to receive so many visitors; she even offered to tell them that the professor was unavailable or to make excuses for him. Titus would have none of it: "No, don't do that, Madam. Someone might be in urgent need of my help. Just let everyone in who comes to see me. And don't worry about me too much. We are all in God's hands."

Ambitious Plans

Although the university was still in its inaugural year, Professor Brandsma was already numbered among those planning for its future.

During a meeting of the faculty Dr. Josephus Schrijnen, the Rector magnificus, suggested that the university undertake the publication of a series of monographs on various topics. "Who would like to take this on?" he asked. All eyes turned to the Carmelite friar.

Fr. Brandsma raised his hand and asked, "May I give it a try?"

Within a few days he had prepared an outline for the series, suggested a title, *Nijmeegsche Studie-teksten* (Texts and Studies of Nijmegen),[8] and offered it for consideration. His colleagues had no objections.

This was just the beginning. In the Spring of 1926, he began to collaborate with the scholarly journal, *Ons Geestelijk Erf* (Our Spiritual Heritage);[9] He was later to become a member of its editorial board.

From within the university community came a plan to publish a kind of Dutch "Migne" under the title *Bibliotheca Neerlandica Praereformatoria*.[10] One of those called to be in charge was–who else?–Professor Titus Brandsma. A colleague on this project, Professor W. Mulder, S.J., acknowledged: "He is a joy to work with. He always has what you need or knows what you have no idea about. And no matter what he does for you, it is he who will give you his thanks."[11] As though his work as editor were not enough, Titus also authored the first study, on *Devotio moderna*.

Yet another even more ambitious project, was his own brainchild: *Middelnederlandsa Geestelijke Handschriften Biblioteek*.[12] The endeavor involved locating, photocopying, cataloguing and preserving written materials available only in manuscript form. Fr. Titus spent some twelve years on this work and when he left the researchers had brought together 17,000 manuscripts bound into 170 volumes. Today it remains among the most valuable treasures of the university.[13]

Over and above the academic prestige of the university, Titus had plans for its physical plant as well. It was generally recognized that the current facility was inadequate. When Titus was elected president of the Association of Scholars, he called a meeting of the faculty to discuss the acquisition of property for a larger, more dignified campus. Armed with faculty approval, he visited both Amsterdam and Utrecht; on his return he was loaded with plans and designs so grand that, on seeing it, one colleague exclaimed: "If only it were not so magnificent, it might become a reality."

Nevertheless, Titus' dream was realized, although not until after the Second World War.[14]

Native Frisian

In 1924 Titus turned his attention and his energy to his homeland, Frisland. With a group of priests and laymen he visited Dokkum where, in the year 754, St. Boniface, the Apostle of Frisia, had been martyred. They found the site completely abandoned. Titus was determined to restore it. The group set up the National Fraternity of St. Boniface[15] and, with the support of the hierarchy and the Catholic press, was able to acquire land. Not long thereafter a chapel was built on the land, surrounded by the Stations of the Cross. Titus had hoped to convince one of the monastic orders to take charge of the site and to reconstruct its pre-reformation monastery. In this he was not successful.

So much effort and energy was put into this project that some Protestants began to suspect it was a front for a new political movement, and some members of the government feared it might become a separatist movement. They found it hard to believe that the group's sole purpose was to honor the holy man who had brought Christianity to the region.

Slowly the Fraternity was able to revive the practice of pilgrimages–some coming from Scandinavia or from America, others presided over by the Archbishop of Utrecht or by the Bishops of Fulda and Mainz. In 1926 one pilgrimage, with the Archbishop at its head, arrived with more than 2,000 faithful. It was on that day that Fr. Titus gave his first talk in Frisian. Titus was a faithful collaborator with the Fraternity's publication *Ons Noorden* (We Northerners);[16] and he fought resolutely to establish a Chair of Frisian Language and Culture at the Catholic University of Nijmegen.

Such enthusiasm was contagious, and eventually led to several exchanges between Protestants and Catholics in an attempt to bring about a greater understanding of their common heritage.

One fruit of this collaboration was the translation into Frisian of *The Imitation of Christ*, undertaken by Titus and a Protestant friend, A. H. de Vries.[17]

Nijmegen Carmel

Titus had little time to look for a house for the growing Carmelite community in Nijmegen. Yet, with the arrival of several Carmelite clerics to study at the Catholic University of Nijmegen, the rooms rented from the guest house had become totally inadequate. Something had to be done.

Titus and his confreres searched diligently but were unable to find suitable quarters (a member of the provincial council is said to have remarked: "Careful! Titus may be hatching another of his plots"). Finally, there came a breakthrough: a handsome building next to a park on the Kronenburgersingel had became vacant. Without wasting time, Titus rented the property and the nine Carmelites took possession and moved their belongings in a pushcart. The new residence was dedicated to Our Lady of Wisdom, and Titus himself was named its superior from the beginning of the 1927 academic year until 1929.

Still Titus continued searching for a larger, more permanent facility. Unexpectedly, he learned of an enormous structure, formerly a Catholic hospital, that was for sale on the Doddendaal, just across the park. He contacted the administrators and by the spring of 1928 was able to sign the contract. Necessary renovations took a year, but the community was then able to move into an excellent priory with a large internal courtyard.

On the Feast of the Epiphany 1930, the new Carmel was to be blessed by the Bishop of Den Bosch. For its inauguration Titus had wanted more than merely a gathering of friends and colleagues, with a few words of praise that would be forgotten no sooner than spoken. He proposed something more memorable: nothing less than a congress on mysticism. Invited guests included the members of the *Ons Geestelijk Erf* (Our Spiritual Heritage) Association and every expert in the field he could contact. And they came from north and from south: members of various religious orders, diocesan clergy, laymen. Each was warmly received by a hospitable prior who was bursting with joy as he opened the Congress with a lecture on Carmelite Mysticism. Three days were spent celebrating the inauguration of the Nijmegen Carmel: conferences, round tables, studies, dialogues, plans.

Greatly encouraged by the success of this Congress, and convinced of the importance of such meetings, Titus decided to hold others in succeeding years. Before the war put a stop to them, five congresses had been held, each dedicated to a particular theme of Dutch spirituality. Titus' desire to assemble all the materials relative to this theme and to define its boundaries led him to create the Institute for Dutch Mysticism within the university. That Institute, which reflected the ideals of the Journal *Ons Geestelijk Erf*, today bears the name: The Titus Brandsma Institute.

"This Carmel has a special mission," a Jesuit friend of Titus remarked. He compared the Carmelite experience in Nijmegen to a drop of oil on water: first a room in a guesthouse, then a small house, then a proper priory, and finally a parish.

Indeed, the Carmelites had been asked to accept responsibility for the parish of St. Augustin, the church used by the university for its ceremonies. Although it was some distance from the priory, Titus considered it a wonderful opportunity and had no hesitation in recommending that it be accepted. Thus by 1933 the young community, dedicated primarily to study and to prayer, was able to add a parochial apostolate. Fr. Franciscus Willens was named pastor of some three thousand souls.[18]

Trips Outside the Country

Not content with second-hand research, Professor Brandsma took advantage of vacations to visit other countries for study. He was most attracted by Spain, the native land of St. Teresa of Avila. He felt a special attraction for her and her way of living out the spirit of Carmel. During the Easter Break of 1929, and months before the first Congress, he had gone to Spain to study similarities between Spanish and Flemish mysticism. He visited Barcelona, Burgos, Madrid, Toledo, Seville, Jerez de la Frontera, Avila; he spent time in archives, libraries, museums. In some Carmelite friaries he lectured on Carmel's rich heritage; but he also took pains to make contact with the simple faithful whose culture and spirit had contributed so much to the 16th century reform of the Order.[19]

Father Simón Besalduch, a well-known Carmelite scholar and author, accompanied Titus through Catalonia; while there they visited the rector of the University of Barcelona and the Monastery of Montserrat. Recalling this latter visit, Fr. Simón wrote:

We visited the monastery, and the monks put whatever he wanted to see at his disposal. ... He conversed with the Benedictines in Dutch, French, German, Spanish. What tremendous devotion he showed while visiting the church and listening to the Gregorian chant of the monks! ...

Later, as we were strolling along the mountain trails, our dear Father expressed, as though a projection of his inner being, what was in his heart; and he did so with such vitality that it seemed he was dreaming out loud. He spoke of grand proposals that came together in a single ideal: the flourishing of the Order he so dearly loved. We still have so much to do, he said, in order to become what our fathers were. We need to increase vocations. ... We need a comprehensive library that is available to Carmelites of the entire world. ... We need a multi-lingual journal that will publish in all the major languages. ... We need so much, so much, so much.[20]

North American Tour[21]

In 1935 the prior general of the Order, Fr. Hilary Doswald, suggested Titus visit the United States to share his knowledge of the Order's spirituality with the North American Carmelites. Today it is quite normal for a professor to cross the Atlantic for study, but in the 1930s it was possible only for those who were recognized experts.

Titus felt honored, and he wished to prepare himself well. Before departing for North America he spent several weeks in Ireland to perfect his English. He was the guest of the novice master, Fr. Malachy Lynch, and stayed at the novitiate house in Kinsale. Fr. Malachy later recalled that the first thing Titus did on arriving was to make a visit to the Blessed Sacrament. He then visited the sick. He also took special interest in talking with the fishermen of the town. "Fr. Titus," Father Malachy relates, "was the happiest person I have ever known, and moreover a man who was able to spread joy wherever he was." He also knew how to appreciate good things, and therefore, although he had never before tasted Irish whiskey, he pronounced it most satisfactory.[22]

On the high seas en route to America Titus received a cablegram from the Netherlands that informed him that the editors of the *Dutch Catholic Encyclopedia*[23] were urgently awaiting his entry on "Mysticism." Since the idea of publishing the *Encyclopedia* had been his, and since he had already spent a great deal of time on the article, he replied that he would have it ready as soon as possible.

In America he visited the Carmelite foundations in New York, Chicago, Washington, and Niagara Falls in Canada. Not an imposing figure, according to one account: "He was a thin, short (perhaps 5'6"), restless man with nervous energy and a quick walk, wearing thick glasses as he read from his English manuscript."[24] Nevertheless he was welcomed by audiences at various universities and even in theaters with standing room only. Wherever he went he was greeted with crowds and thanked with the warm applause of a public who seemed never to see or hear enough of him.

Wherever he went he spoke about the history of the Carmelite Order and about the way of the mystic. On one occasion he was asked whether mysticism is possible for everyone. "I am sure of it;" he replied; "of course it is a gift of God, but God has made our human nature capable of receiving it and allowing it to develop."

The American Carmelites published his lectures in a small book, *Carmelite Mysticism*;[25] shortly thereafter Titus himself summarized them in an article for the *Dictionnaire de Spiritualité*, an article much praised by the critics.[26]

For his part, Titus took advantage of his brief visit to the United States–a little more than a month–to inform himself about a variety of topics, including journalism. He made it a point to visit Doctor J. Murphy, Professor of Journalism at the Catholic University of America in Washington, to learn about Catholic journalism in America, about public interest in religious themes, and about the education of Catholic journalists. On his return, he reported to his Dutch colleagues: "We cannot complain about America. There they get all they can out of the [secular] press. If here our so-called neutral press were to treat Catholicism with as much dignity, we would have a great deal to celebrate."

A few months before his trip to America, the Union of Catholic Journalists had nominated Professor Titus Brandsma as its Ecclesial Assistant. This nomination was confirmed by the Archbishop of Utrecht.

ENDNOTES

1. Meijer, p. 95.
2. Rees, p. 63.

3. SU 65, p. 110.

4. Rees, p. 59.

5. Josse Alzin, *Un piccolo frate pericoloso: Tito Brandsma* (Collana Pionieri, 32. Edictrice Elle Di Ci., 1985), p. 89. Hereafter, Alzin.

6. Meijer, p. 398.

7. SU 65, pp. 37-38.

8. There were only three publications (1926-1927) in this series. Translator's note.

9. *Ons Geestelijk Erf* is a quarterly journal founded in 1927 and specializing in Dutch spirituality. Translator's note.

10. "Migne" refers to a collection of texts from the early *Fathers of the Church: Patrologia Graeca* with 161 volumes, and *Patrologia Latina* with 221 volumes. The *Bibliotheca Neerlandica Praereformatoria* was based on a marvelous ideal but, unfortunately, was not carried through. Translator's note.

11. Alzin, p. 76.

12. *Middelnederlandsa Geestelijke Handschriften Biblioteek* is a collection of medieval Dutch spiritual manuscripts started by Dr. Brandsma; today it is known as the Brandsma Collection. Dr. Brandsma had unsuccessfully attempted to purchase the manuscripts collected by Dr. Willem de Vreese (Bibliotheca Neerlandica Manuscripta) for the Catholic University of Nijmegen after de Vreese's death. This latter collection is now at the University of Leiden. Translator's note.

13. Meijer, p. 222.

14. Meijer, p. 126.

15. De nationale Bonifatius-Broederschap.

16. This daily newspaper for the northern provinces of the Netherlands was published from 1913-1964. Fr. Titus edited a column in the paper from 1918 until 1938; in 1938 he edited a two or three-page weekly feature called "Frisia Catholica." He contributed some forty articles to this latter section. Translator's note.

17. Rees, p. 62.

18. Meijer, p. 375.

19. Otger Steggink, O. Carm., *La reforma del carmelo español: La visita canónica del general Rubeo y su encuentro con Santa Teresa, 1566-1567* (Textus et studia historica carmelitana, 7. Roma: Institutum Carmelitanum, 1965).

20. Simon Besalduch, O. Carm., *Flos Sanctorum del Carmelo*, (Barcelona, 1951), pp. 827-838. Dr. Brandsma would have welcomed the creation of the Institutum Carmelitanum in Rome under Prior General Kilian Lynch. The Institutum publishes the multi-lingual journal *Carmelus* and its library has the largest collection of books by or about Carmelites in the world. There are also noteworthy Carmelite libraries at Whitefriars Hall, Washington, DC, and at the Carmelite Priory of Boxmeer in the Netherlands. Translator's note.

21. See *Appendix I*.

22. Rees, p. 79.

23. *De Katholicke Encyclopaedie*. In addition to being a contributor, Professor Brandsma served as its censor from 1933-1939. A revised edition was published after the War (1949-1955). Translator's note.

24. Werling, "Journey to Dachau," Ch. 2.

25. A recent edition is available: *Titus Brandsma, O. Carm. Carmelite Mysticism: Historical Sketches*. 50th Anniversary Edition (Darien, Illinois: The Carmelite Press, 1986).

26. See "Carmes," *Dictionnaire de Spiritualité*, Paris, 1935, fasc. VII, Col. 156-171.

Fr. Titus vested in the robes of the Rector Magnificus of the Catholic University of Nijmegen in 1932. The position was for one year. *(Photo courtesy of the Nederlands Carmelitaans Instituut)*

Chapter V

Rector Magnificus of the University

Wise and Efficacious

There were some who felt that Professor Titus Brandsma was too short a man to fill the position of *Rector magnificus*[1] of the Catholic University of the Netherlands. While it is always at the very least imprudent to judge a person's worth by his physical measurements–and today it is at least "politically incorrect" to do so–such judgments frequently come back to haunt those who make them and may occasionally result in truly comical situations. This is exactly what happened to the new *Rector* when, toward the end of 1932, he called at the Vatican in his official capacity.

Among the meetings required by protocol–Pope Pius XI honored him with an audience–one was with the Prefect of the Congregation of Universities and Seminaries. Cardinal Bisleti, a rather corpulent man who happened to be gravely deaf and apparently confused rank with girth. Expecting the *Rector* from Nijmegen to be a typical Dutchman–blond and imposing–whose physical appearance would lend dignity to his high position, he was taken aback when he looked up from his desk and saw a diminutive friar standing in front of him. He immediately concluded he was dealing with some substitute for the *Rector*. "So," he initiated the interview, "the *Rector magnificus* is unable to come personally? Is he sick?"

On entering the august presence Professor Brandsma had introduced himself with his usual quiet voice, but the Cardinal had not heard him. Titus therefore spoke up to present himself again. His Eminence, however, had continued speaking and still did not hear. "What a shame he was unable to come in person."

At this Professor Brandsma, nearly shouting, identified himself a third time. Recognizing his error but still somewhat perplexed, the Cardinal opened wide his eyes and looked the friar over from head to toe and whispered: "You are really he?"

Yes, it was really he, in person. He had been invested in his office on October 17, 1932.

For his inaugural lecture as *Rector magnificus*, marking the tenth anniversary of the university, he had chosen to speak on "The Concept of God,"[2] a theme taken from natural theology. His presentation, although unusual in its content, was accorded high praise and even esteemed as magisterial and ground-breaking.

> Among the many questions I ask myself, none concerns me more than the riddle of why so many educated persons, proud and even haughty about human accomplishments, turn away from God. ...
>
> Why is the image of God so obscured that many of our contemporaries are no longer impressed by it? Is the fault all on their [secularists] side, or is there something we must do to make it once again shine forth more brightly upon the world? Dare we hope that a thorough study of the concept of God will, at the very least, alleviate this most urgent of all our needs? ...

In the lengthy text that followed–more than twenty single-spaced pages–Professor Brandsma traced briefly the history of human attitudes toward God. He then set forth some ideals and goals:

> We must first of all recognize God as the deepest ground of our being,[3] hidden in the most profound depths of our nature, yet able to be seen and contemplated: a God clearly recognized following an initial effort of mental abstraction. Once we have made this way of thinking habitual, we become capable of seeing Him, as it were, intuitively, without any intellectual effort, so that we find ourselves in continual contemplation of God and adoring Him not only within ourselves but also in everything that exists: first of all in our fellow man, but also in nature, in the universe, present everywhere and penetrating all things with the work of his hands. The divine indwelling and operation must not only be the object of intuition, but must reveal themselves in our lives, must find expression in our words and deeds, must radiate from our whole being and appearance. ...

Fr. Brandsma continued to develop his theme and to indicate its consequences:

> Were these ideas–of God's indwelling, of all nature's total dependence on God, of God's guidance and revelation in all things–alive in us, how our words and deeds would have to be changed in order for them to correspond to their character as revelations from God! ...
>
> People must again see God and live in the contemplation of

God. This is called mysticism. So be it. ... Mysticism the further and highest development of that which human nature is potentially. ... Mysticism is in no way opposed to nature; on the contrary, nature is called to see God as the most noble object it can know. It is a pity that this is no longer understood.

Reporting the event in *De Tijd*, the eminent critic Anton van Duinkerken wrote: "The value of Professor Brandsma's presentation has exceeded that of all his predecessors. Never has a lecture on such an occasion been so appropriate." The monthly *De Gemeenschap* (The Community),[4] reflecting the opinion of the general public, stated: "It seems as though, following this talk, our country was freed from a kind of oppressive darkness."

Titus may have felt even greater satisfaction when he learned that a well-known professor of the Protestant school of Theology at Kampen had not only praised the talk highly but had advised his students to study it in detail.

During his term as *Rector*, Titus continued to dedicate himself to being "totally available." He represented the university at no less than eighteen solemn convocations, both within the Netherlands and in other countries; he presided over new programs of study; he acquired new collections of materials considered fundamental for scientific research; he founded a newspaper for the university published under the title *Vox Carolina*; he saw to the development of the library, collecting precious codices and acquiring several Collected Works. It is hardly an exaggeration to claim that, thanks to his work and to his initiatives, the Catholic University earned the admiration both of its own members and of outsiders.

Titus wore the academic gown of the *Rector* gracefully, but nothing could deprive him of his concern for ordinary folk. On one occasion, surrounded by bishops and other dignitaries during a formal procession, he suddenly stopped to shake hands with a little old lady standing at the edge of the sidewalk, an elderly woman who years earlier had helped out in his own home. On another day, standing near a stove and in animated conversation with a pupil, he burned the edge of his scapular. "No matter," he laughed. I'll only have to shorten it a bit. The dignity of a professor ought not be measured by the length of his clothing." For quite some time he was seen wearing a very short scapular.

It was not important to him that his own clothing was simple, or his shoes worn out. But nothing was to be lacking from the university that would detract from its dignity, for it represented the faith of Dutch Catholics. Consequently, he not only offered it his own wisdom, but also his interest in improving it: enlarging the buildings, improving the means for instruction, the libraries, the lecture halls, the assembly rooms, the offices of the professors, etc. He was careful that the needs of both faculty and students received proper attention. He used every means at his disposal to maintain the interest of the public in the university.

Due to his approachable personality, both faculty and students felt they were his friends. To his colleagues he was more a friend than a *Rector*, one sensitive to their needs and concerns. Thus, when a certain Dr. Gerard Brom failed to obtain a chair in the University of Amsterdam, Father Titus went to him immediately and softened the blow to his pride with great delicacy: "Stay here with us. We are very happy to have you here."

Among Titus' best friends was Dr. Hoogveld, a priest and professor. When he was imprisoned in 1940, Titus spared no effort to obtain his release. "We must do everything possible for him," he said with great sorrow. Then, in 1942, when Titus himself was arrested, his friend Fr. Hoogveld was inconsolable and told everyone he met, "The imprisonment of good Fr. Titus is the most serious offense the Germans could commit against Holland."

Another, Professor Josephus Schrijnen, was a shy man due to his homeliness. Yet Titus and he formed a great personal friendship, one that allowed them to express personal observations to one another. Dr. Schrijnen wrote on one occasion, "I thank you with all my heart for all you have done for me. I will never forget it, and I shall ask God to repay you."

It was the same with students. Any one of them could go to the *Rector magnificus* for help at any time: they recognized him as a tactful guide and even as a father.[5] The students knew him well and were aware that in him they had the best of friends, the greatest of protectors.

As *Rector* Titus was constantly on the lookout for scholarships for poor or foreign students, nor did he hesitate to beg help for them even from his own friends. Moreover, when a student graduated, he searched the country, knocking on every possible door, to find a suitable position. He rarely returned empty-handed. All doors were open to the *Rector* who with graceful humility begged bread for his students.

One afternoon in October 1933– the closing of the tenth anniversary of the university– the enthusiasm of the students went beyond the official ceremonies of the program. A large group of students marched to the Carmelite priory with flaming torches to acclaim the *Rector* whose term had ended the previous day. Only with great effort was he able to calm their enthusiasm and their *Vivas*.

Of course, there were also difficulties. Among the ironies of life, the year Fr. Titus was named *Rector* was the same year Hitler became lord and master of Germany; and it was in that very year that the concentration and extermination camp at Dachau was opened.

The sweeping triumph of Nazism had repercussions everywhere. In Nijmegen a group of students sympathetic to the German dictator ran through the cities waving banners. The *Rector* took the news calmly and, contrary to the advice offered by many, refused to punish them publicly. He remained faithful to his principle that one ought not to deal with people as they are, but as they ought to be and could become.

Some days later he explained his position to a meeting of the faculty, expressing firm opposition to taking action against the students. He reserved the right to correct them as they deserved, but without subjecting them to severe disciplinary action. Rather he would attempt to change their perceptions through kindness and understanding.

As might be expected, his decision did not receive unanimous approval. There were some who insisted on drastic steps aimed at ending once and for all every kind of insubordination. Others, with greater experience, were appreciative of the moderate proposal of the *Rector*, especially in times like those when there was a tendency toward extreme radicalism.

A colleague expressed it in this way: "In an environment when every individual holds tenaciously to his opinion, convinced that his is the only valid position, the presence of a conciliatory arbitrator such as Titus is indispensable."[6] In the face of the inevitable conflicts that upset the harmony of any group of human beings, Titus was always on the lookout for points of contact, or reconciliation.

This, of course, was one of Fr. Titus' most characteristic qualities. He was truly a man of peace, but not weak-willed: he was no one's puppet.

At the end of his term as *Rector magnificus*, Titus rendered an account of his stewardship in a memorandum of thirty pages. He did not leave the university with an inheritance of vast volumes, but what he sowed as a man of broad culture, as a consummate organizer and as a holy priest, continues to bear fruit.

In the *Alba amicorum* (*Book of Friends*) honoring him on the fortieth anniversary of his religious profession, we find the following sentiments expressed by both faculty and students: "We admire you as a religious, as a priest, and as a professor. You encourage those who come to you and seek your advice, and you lend a hand to whoever needs it. Your unpretentious, humble labors and your tremendous spirit of self-giving are an inestimable treasure for us."[7]

On All Fronts

When the provincial of the Dutch Carmelites asked each religious to list the work he had accomplished during the year, a confrere, observing Titus' perplexity, said to him, "You should find this very easy. You only have to write: *I have done everything.*"

As a matter of fact, it is not easy to list his many activities. One is astonished at all he accomplished, as though there were no limit to his time or to his concern for others. Titus' motto might have been: "Whatever is good ought to be done." To fail to do something for the sake of recreation or out of laziness he considered selfish.

One of his confreres told him, "Titus, you live as though heaven and earth were on fire. You always have something important to do, and you are always in a hurry."

And this was true. He himself confessed it openly to his brother Hendrik: "One job comes on top of another and sometimes I simply do not know where to begin."

He had left word with the brother who answered the door that he was never to turn away anyone who came looking for him. This was his way of following St. Paul's example of trying to win over as many as possible.[8] He resolved labor problems for workers who consulted him; he corrected copy for a young journalist; he helped those living in slums find decent housing; he gave all the money he had with him to the poor and–at least once–even his own overcoat. He once missed his train to console a mother he found crying on a station platform. For one and all Titus was "the priest with the heart of gold": the woman to whom he gave the blankets from his own bed to cover her children; an illiterate woman for whom he wrote a letter to her son; the students whom he helped make an appointment with a difficult professor; the immigrants for whom he provided words of understanding and faith; the man in need whose confession he heard in the cab of a truck; guests of the community, to whom he gave his own bed, choosing himself to sleep on a sack of straw.

His was a goodness born of deep faith. Titus' secret, like that of all good Carmelites, was to live continually in the presence of God. It was from this intimacy and sense of dependency on God that he found the strength to keep going.

As prior, he reminded the members of his community that it is better to be illiterate but filled with faith than to be a wise man with no heart, because only the person who is closely united with God can be united with his neighbor, only he who feeds on God can give witness to his works. Of him his confreres stated: "Father Titus is calm only in choir and on the train."

His desire was to multiply himself without limit in order to stand in solidarity with those in need. There was no hardship, no work he was unwilling to face. Yet he was always happy, smiling.

His handshakes were proverbial, filled with warmth and energy, the language of a sincere, good heart.

"Our goodness," he said, "ought to be expected and seen by everyone. We should always be looking for ways to help others. Where there is good will, there will always be a way." His life consisted in happiness at being able to help others. Every circumstance, every encounter provided a way leading to God. He was especially pleased when someone invited him to lead a prayer of thanks to

God for some favor.

"Many of the things you do are not your job, Fr. Titus." This was the opinion not only of his superior, but also of his friends and even the people he met casually. There was the old man he helped to push his junk wagon up the hill between the university and the Carmel. Without fuss, Titus had deposited his briefcase on top of the wagon so as to push the better. The poor fellow, moved by a gesture of such kindness, said the same: "Father, this is not work you should be doing." Of course, the man had no way of knowing that the helpful friar straining beside him was the *Rector magnificus* of the university.

"It's not your job!" These were words of well-meaning people who were thinking of the dignity, health, the physical strength of Fr. Brandsma. The only one who didn't let such things bother him was Titus himself; he recognized no occupation as unworthy when it provided an opportunity to help his neighbor. This conviction he put into practice whenever there was need to help someone in the back alleys, or to fill the needs of another, even outside the city. This he put into practice when he visited schools and convents where many religious to whom he was giving spiritual direction awaited him with the affection due a beloved father. He put it into practice too when it was time to console the sorrowing or to rejoice with those who were celebrating. Ever giving, never taking.

Gatske, Titus' sister, recalled: "It was next to impossible for him to refuse anything to anyone.

Once a Dominican friar came to ask him to give a conference. I replied, 'How can you ask this of Fr. Titus, knowing as you do that he already has more than enough to keep him busy.' To this my brother answered: 'I know. But no one seeks alms in a place where none is ever given, but from people who always have something to give.'"

And then there was another woman, a student, who had asked him to give a conference, but then felt ashamed of herself for having asked since she was aware of how overloaded with work he was."[9]

On another evening he called the superior of a convent to ask if he could come to see her. She was agreeable, so he hurried along the wet streets of Nijmegen, then took a ferry; and arrived at the convent an hour later. The superior was not a little surprised to discover that his only reason for the visit was to seek employment for a worker who had been let go. The poor man had explained his situation to Fr. Titus, and he had made the man's concerns his own. Immediately he set about doing whatever he could, even at the cost of losing an evening of his precious time.

On yet another occasion he called at the home of a colleague, Professor Bellon: "I have come to ask you for a loan. It is for a businessman near bankruptcy. Since we are friends I am appealing to your generosity," he explained.

"But I'm no banker," replied Bellon.

"That's not important. I am asking for very little."

"How much?"

"Two hundred florins.[10] That's not much, is it? There is still some hope of saving this poor man from his terrible predicament."

"Some hope, you say! Who is going to pay me back? Or am I to understand that this is a gift?" he asked ironically, knowing only too well Titus' natural goodness.

"Oh, no, by no means. I myself guarantee the loan."

"Very well, I'll do it."

Fr. Titus kept his word and little by little Bellon was paid, until he learned that the one paying him back was none other than Titus himself, who had taken on additional work to do so.

Frequently Titus left the house to bring help and love to his fellow man. This he called "Letting God be God." Actually, he was going in order to find in those he was helping the one whom he already possessed in his own inner being: God.

He gave himself totally to others because he believed that every man was, or should be, a member of the Mystical Body of Christ. He felt deeply his responsibility as a Christian and as a priest. On this point he told his confreres: "May we always remember that hundreds of individuals are brought to the Church daily due to the life and heroic example of a few, but at the same time hundreds of individuals are driven away from the Church due to the scandal, to the un-Christian life style of those who call themselves Christians, and even Catholics.[11]

His prior, Fr. Cyprian Verbeek, worried about his health, advised him: "Fr. Titus, you should go to bed earlier, and you are not obliged to be in choir for community prayer. You may pray the office on your own later in the day."

Titus never liked dispensations. A few days later, when the prior became aware that Titus had worked late into the night, he reproached him seriously: "Is it really necessary for you to be doing so many things?"

"Someone has to do them, Fr. Prior," he responded with a smile.

"True, but not so many. Therefore, I order you to give up a few of them."

"All right, Father. The superiors know better than Titus Brandsma what Titus Brandsma needs to do," he replied. And that is where the affair ended. The following day he was back to his usual activities, and whenever anyone sought his help, he forgot his own needs to provide for them. One day he hurriedly left the house to convince a young lady not to kill herself. Another day he was called by the family of a mentally ill student to convince him to undergo medical treatment.

Not long after, when he felt he had a little time to spare, he went to the prior to let him know that a home for the aged was in need of a chaplain on Sundays; he thought this something he should do, since it would not require any special effort. With his prior's blessing he not only accepted the position, but he kept doing it until his arrest, giving a fervent homily every Sunday and providing great consolation for the elderly guests.

Although he was never a great orator, the sincerity and conviction with which he spoke captivated his hearers, for they listened to him with greater attention than to other, better known preachers of the city. His voice was somewhat monotonous, his gestures a bit too exaggerated for the oratorical style of that time and place. But he knew how to compensate for these defects and became one of the best-known voices of the Netherlands through innumerable conferences, sermons, and radio addresses.

He was also a great spiritual director, both in the confessional and outside it. His too was a great sensitivity for the needs of others, a quality he put into practice each day. Arriving home from a trip too late to congratulate a confrere on his name day personally, he took the trouble to slip a message under his door.[12]

A lay brother of his community acknowledged that "if Titus had not been at my side, my vocation would never have survived. He accepted me as I was and allowed me to become the person I am."

In the area of ecumenism Titus did not limit his attention to his Protestant brethren—then the majority in the Netherlands and especially in his native Frisland. Among them he did have good friends; but he also turned his eyes to the East, to the Orthodox.

During the 1920s we find him participating in the Apostolate for the Reunion with the Eastern Churches, and eventually becoming its Secretary General, as can be seen in a photograph of its central committee. This movement was active in every diocese and parish of the Netherlands. In 1937 it was Titus who provided the spark that gave birth to the creation of the Oriental Institute at the Catholic University of Nijmegen. Eventually it was to provide a program for priests who wished to dedicate themselves to this apostolate. The Carmelite priory frequently hosted Patriarch Terzianus of the Armenians as well as Abbot Nalbandian who was responsible for the Armenian refugees in all Europe. These were days when that nation was being persecuted almost to the point of extinction.[13]

Poor Health

"Why must you be involved in so many things?"

The new prior, Father Arnoldus Wijtemburg, was just as concerned as his predecessor about the health of his most well-known subject. Similar worries were being expressed both by his fellow Carmelites and by his colleagues at the university.

His friend, Professor Brom, accused him ironically:

> You want to engage in battle on every front, and simultaneously to fulfill your duties as professor; and you also want to be an apostle of Frisland, a journalist, a public speaker, and an organizer of expositions; and this does not even include your efforts as architect, nurse, parish priest, friar ...

The result was inevitable.

Finally, in 1937, Titus was forced to admit to his prior: "Father,

I'm afraid something is wrong. My knees are giving out and I can hardly stand. I feel dizzy and have no strength to do anything."

His symptoms seemed to indicate some kind of paralysis. One of his sisters had been a victim of an infection of the spinal marrow, which eventually affected her brain. Was this to be a similar case?

Various specialists were consulted. This required long periods in hospitals as they examined his nervous system, his stomach, his exhausted heart. Finally, they diagnosed an inflammation of the spinal medulla that was affecting his central nervous system. The treatment would be difficult and would require absolute bedrest.[14]

Not until the spring of 1938 did he recover his energy. "Now I'm a new man, guaranteed for ten more years," he announced optimistically. He was mistaken. Only a few months later he told his prior, "Father, I think I had better lie down." This time he was suffering from an inflammation of the bladder and a serious infection of the urinary tract caused by a bacterial infection. "These bacilli," he wrote to his family, "are very treacherous and current: they begin their offensive without an official declaration of war. But I assure you, they have nothing whatsoever to do with the pressure of work."

Though he continued holding his classes and running from one place to another, yet those around him noticed that all was not well with him. His students became aware that at times he was dizzy and had lapses of memory, that occasionally he seemed to leave out significant parts of his lectures. Nevertheless, he was still the popular Professor Brandsma.[15]

In the early weeks of 1940, he was once again hospitalized. From the hospital in Amsterdam he wrote his provincial: "The doctor is very well known and the sisters are wonderful; the only one who leaves a great deal to be desired is this friar."

His medical care, coupled with a prolonged stay in the priory of Merkelbeeck, got him in shape for the opening of the academic year, 1940. By then, however, the university was under the control of the Nazi authorities: Hitler's troops had invaded the Netherlands on May 10.

On the previous August 31, 1939, the birthday of Queen Wilhelmina, the Dutch monarch had decorated Professor Titus Brandsma as a Knight of the Order of Orange-Nassau. Titus wore this decoration on his lapel until it was torn from his coat by the Nazis.[16]

ENDNOTES

1. This is an elected position, that of chairman of the various deans of the university; it is largely ceremonial. Translator's note.

2. *Het Godsbegrip*, 2e druk, Nijmegen, Dekker en van de Vegt, 1932. Rees, p. 74; Fausto Vallainc, *Un giornalista martire: Padre Tito Brandsma* (2ª Edizione. Milano: Editrice Àncora, 1963), p. 106. Hereafter, Vallainc. For an analysis of this talk see John Nijenhuis, O. Carm. "Bl. Titus Brandsma, O. Carm., On the Presence of God." *The Sword* 48:2 (October, 1988), 3-26.

3. "Paul Tillich (1896-1965) popularized this phrase. See a discussion of this point in Nijenhuis, "Bl. Titus Brandsma," pp. 13-14.

4. This monthly was edited by young Catholic writers from 1925-1941. Translator's note.

5. Meijer, p. 161.

6. Vallainc, p.,136.

7. *Idem*.

8. Cf. 1 Cor 9:19.

9. SU 65, p. 110.

10. About US $90. This would have had a far greater purchasing power pre-World War II.

11. Titus Brandsma, O. Carm., *Ejercicios bíblicos con María para llegar a Jesús* (Caudete: CESCA, 1976). p. 18.

12. Told to the author by Fr. Berthold Lurvink, O. Carm.

13. Vallainc, p. 108.

14. Alzin, p. 125.

15. Rees, p. 125.

16. Rees, p. 110.

Fr. Titus at 49 years of age in 1930. His face reflects a great human and spiritual maturity. This photograph was made on the occasion of the 25th anniversary of his ordination to the priesthood. For the previous seven years he had been a professor at the Catholic University of Nijmegen. *(Photo courtesy of the Nederlands Carmelitaans Instituut)*

Chapter VI

Seeking God

Community Life

Cardinal Gasquet once characterized Carmelites as *simplices et sinceri* (single-minded and sincere). "This," commented Titus, "is the most beautiful compliment we can receive. Truly, our mission is not to do great things, but to do little things with greatness."

It was in this spirit that Professor Brandsma learned to combine incredible activity with total fidelity. Completely dedicated to his community, he participated fully in its life down to the least details.

Brother Raphael Tijhuis,[1] who was already a prisoner in Dachau when Titus arrived and who was with him until he was forced to enter the "infirmary," echoed the opinion of most of his confreres: "The spiritual life of Fr. Titus was very intense, yet so interior that it did not cause comment among his fellow Carmelites. His interior life was lived in the full and exact observance of community life. Both in the quiet of the chapel and in the privacy of his room he always sought a closer and more personal contact with God. ... He lived precisely according to the spirit of the Rule of St. Albert. ... Everything required by obedience he did well and wholeheartedly."[2]

The testimony of his brother Carmelites during the Process of Beatification is consistent: there was no place Titus would rather have been than his priory. Once home he could leave his agitated, nearly feverish lifestyle behind and find peace and calm. Titus himself explained: "For me community life is indispensable because it provides the framework for the rest of the day."

Titus' day began in chapel at 5:30 in the morning, even though he may have been working very late or arrived home from one of his many trips well after midnight. He had learned to discipline himself to the extent that he was able to put 'outside' obligations and interests aside and to focus his entire attention on the current moment. Regardless of his professional commitments at the university, or of his many extra-curricular projects, in choir he applied his full attention to the sacred texts.

So deeply did he enter into the prayer of the Church that occasionally he was unaware that he was singing the hymns or chanting the psalms too loudly or that his voice was becoming somewhat strident and even a bit off-key. More than once his prior had taken him aside to admonish him: "Father Titus, it is not necessary to shout; the Lord is not deaf!" And without hesitation Titus would ask pardon: "Oh, I didn't realize I was making such a noise. Thank you for letting me know. I will be more careful." But soon he was once again lost in the depths of his prayer.

Titus felt no desire to live alone with the Lord like a hermit. His was a call to live in community: he considered his small Carmelite community a microcosm of the great human family. To be sure, physical presence is an important aspect of living in community, but it is not absolutely essential. Whether or not he was at home, Titus felt united with his confreres by a spiritual bond, much as St. Paul tells us Christians are joined in the Body of Christ. As a member of his community, he shared in its life, and any good he accomplished was a reflection of his community's dynamism.

Regrettably, he felt, some religious spend far too much time thinking about their personal concerns while giving too little thought to the needs of their community. They easily forget how closely the members of a community are united, each with the others and all with God. Yet, he insisted, it is within this communion that the friars ought to find their worth, their strength and their dignity: "We live in communion with the saints." Community living—whether local or universal—involved loving and serving. "We must force ourselves," he admonished, "to serve one another and so create an environment that will promote our sanctification."[3]

Titus was prior of Nijmegen for several three-year terms. He made every effort to reconcile strict regular observance with an atmosphere of warmth and peace. Although a few of the friars thought him overly rigorous, he was generally successful. His own personality was a major influence within the house: when he was at his place in the refectory, when the clickety-clack of his typewriter was heard coming from his cell, when his hearty laugh resounded through the halls, the priory felt complete; when he was away, it seemed somehow empty.

The daily life of the Nijmegen Carmel was a full one. Generally, the friars rose at five o'clock and were in chapel a half-hour later for the choral recitation of the first part of the Divine Office– matins, lauds and prime– according to the then prevailing practice.

At seven-thirty he celebrated Holy Mass. "This is the best morsel of the day," he used to say. "If I missed this divine food each morning, by noon I would have forgotten about Our Lord." And the faithful who were present were convinced, "Not even the pope celebrates Mass better."

On occasion the sacristan assigned him a different time for Mass– concelebration was unknown in those pre-Vatican II days–which would coincide with a time when some part of the Divine Office was being celebrated. When this happened Titus, who was unwilling to miss any part of the Sacred Liturgy, would try to exchange his assignment with someone who may have been quite content with the overlap.

Following Mass, the community spent a half-hour in mental prayer or meditation.

By nine o'clock each of the friars went about his assigned task. For Dr. Brandsma, this meant going to the university where he would spend the entire morning teaching, receiving students in his office, reading in the library, talking with his colleagues, etc.

At half past twelve the community came together for their midday meal, and afterwards they would enjoy a brief recreation period, usually walking in the cloisters or in the garden.

At three-thirty all returned to the church to celebrate the hour of None. Afterwards each returned to his duty, Titus of course back to his office to be available to the students, who came to talk with him in great numbers, or to attend to one or other of his apostolic efforts.

The workday ended, the community assembled once more for mental prayer, followed by vespers. After supper at seven, there was time for relaxation, and then Titus usually went to his room to prepare for the next day's classes. Shortly after nine the community assembled for an hour's recreation, followed by compline, the solemn singing of the *Salve Regina* and the final blessing of the prior.

By ten o'clock the friars retired to their rooms for the night. Titus' light, however, was rarely turned off until after midnight. There was so much to be done, and the day was so short!

"Tonight, go to bed early," counseled the prior. Well-meaning advice, but difficult for Fr. Brandsma to follow.

Had he so desired, Titus could have cited hundreds of legitimate reasons for requesting a dispensation from the community schedule; not surprisingly, he was unwilling even to discuss such a thing. On the contrary, he was careful not to miss any community activity. Dispensations he abhorred with his entire being.[4]

As a provincial councilor–he held this position for twenty-five years, the eternal "second"–he had participated in numerous discussions about the possibility of exempting university students and school teachers from some community activities. "If the council brings this up," he had stated, "I will oppose it with all my strength. No occupation, however important it may be, will contribute to the growth of the Order if participation in choir diminishes. Other things we do may be more urgent, but hardly more noble. True, certain individuals can and should be dispensed; but this is no reason to establish a general norm. There is only one valid reason for a dispensation: physical impossibility."

Titus' words were the measure of his life.[5]

One evening, for example, when a meeting at the university was lasting longer than scheduled, Titus rose, made his excuses–it was time for community prayer, and he ought to be there–and hurried home. Meetings thereafter tended to begin and end on time; but more importantly, Titus had given witness to the priorities in his own life.

Even during the prolonged periods of his illness, he managed to get by with very little sleep; except when hospitalized he kept right on working.

Occasionally, due to a direct order from his prior, he was obliged to sleep later than the others. But even then, as soon as he noted even a minimal improvement, he would go to his superior with the plea: "Father, it is true that in the afternoon I can do hardly anything, but in the morning, I feel quite able. Please, may I get up at the same time as the others so I can participate in community prayer?"

"What does your doctor say?" the prior would ask.

"I really don't know, but I will call him right away and ask."

A short time later: "Father, the doctor says I can get up at five on condition that I rest for an hour after dinner. Please, allow me to do it."

"All right," responded the prior; "but see to it that no one comes to disturb you during your rest period."

The next morning, he was first in choir. The prior wondered, no doubt, whether he had been too hasty in approving the change, especially as he himself could not detect the improvement Titus was claiming.

Actually, Titus' cell was only a few yards from the choir, but there were times when even that short distance tired him so much that he was forced to sit down immediately, gasping for breath.

Ever Obedient

One of Titus' confreres, a man of somewhat strong opinions, criticized Titus without mincing words: "Fr. Titus is as poor as a church mouse and as pure as a child making his first communion, but when it comes to obedience he is shrewd; he knows exactly what he wants and he goes after it."

To this another friar replied; "Brother, loving what one is required to do is not the same as doing whatever he wants."

To an objective observer, without a doubt the former judgment was both subjective and unwarranted. Titus took all his vows seriously: they served him as the guides as he strove to walk in the footsteps of Christ.[6]

From the very first day of his profession he had been exemplary in the practice of obedience and religious submission. When his superiors allowed him to act freely, he attacked chores with enthusiasm, even when this involved doing things for which he had no heart. When authority asserted itself, he would say: "It's time to change directions."

"Obedience," he held, "is a virtue that is both positive and social.

"What power and vitality there is in an order or congregation whose members are all ready for anything. Unity gives strength. Think of the order of the universe: each and every thing is at the service of everything else. Each one exists in relation to all the others.

"It is in this interdependence that the great strength of religious life is to be found. Each individual is at the service of the great ideal that unites them all. Such unity must be present even in the most trivial and ordinary activities of daily living."

On another occasion he asked, "Of all the things we do, which is the most important?" And he answered himself: "All of them are necessary: important is the work of the one who answers the door, important the work of the cook, important the work of the one who cleans the house, and no less important the work of those who teach."

During a retreat Titus commented:

> Sometimes obedience may deprive an individual of the credit he should be receiving for his efforts, so that others reap the fruit of his work. Sometimes he may not even be thanked. Sometimes no one is aware of what has been accomplished, and no one appreciates it. The religious community is like a mystical body: all the members complement one another, and each is content with his assigned place.
>
> There is no one more unfortunate than an unhappy religious. He is forbidden the pleasures of this world, but at the same time he is unaware of the happiness present in the common life.[7]

Such were the principles by which Titus Brandsma lived: he did what he was told to do as though it were the most natural thing in the world. And when he occasionally asked for an explanation, he did so with complete simplicity and respect. It made no difference who was prior, Titus was obedient, even when the man might be mistaken. When he himself was prior, he counseled obedience; and when he was not prior, he obeyed without resentment.

Those who lived with him have recounted numerous anecdotes about Titus' meticulous obedience.

Among Carmelites at that time it was customary to seek the prior's approval before leaving the house. The departing friar would go first to the prior's cell, where he would state his business and then, kneeling, receive the prior's blessing. Titus' confreres frequently remarked on his humble yet amusing manner of asking permission. "Father Prior," he would say, "is it all right for me to go to the hospital to visit a sick man? and while I'm out, to go by the library, and then to Professor Hoogveld's house to pick up some newspapers, and, if there is any time left, to stop at the bookstore to see what is new?"

If the prior gave his approval, Titus would kneel for his blessing and always say "Thank you."

If, however, for some reason he did not receive permission, then something like the following would take place. He had requested permission to give some money to a large family that was having a difficult time making ends meet. The prior, some twenty years his junior, had demurred: "No, my dear Father. If everyone were like you the poor would be rich and the rich poor. You are poor, and you are supposed to be poor. Let those who are wealthy help these people. There are limits to everything."

Titus was crushed, but quickly recovered his composure to reply, "Very well, Fr Prior." Then totally at peace, he returned to his own room.

On another occasion he went to the prior to obtain approval for a list of periodical subscriptions. Looking them over the prior crossed out several of them, leaving only those that, in reality, were of the least interest to Titus. He looked over the eviscerated list with wonder, lowered his eyes and said, "This is much more practical."[8]

Back in 1915 when his province was looking for friars to send to the missions in Brazil, Titus had volunteered immediately; indeed, his name had been placed on the list of those who would be departing but was later removed. His reaction was noteworthy: "I am happy to remain here, Father Provincial; don't worry about me."

Eight years later, in 1923, when the Dutch Carmelites were opening a mission in Indonesia, once again he was refused permission to go. "I understand," was his reaction; "this is not for me either. I'll be content wherever I am."

Titus was a Frisian, a people noted for its tenacity, for knowing what it wanted and going after it. Titus' flexibility, therefore, represented his victory over his personal inclinations as well as his consciousness that his own satisfaction was to be found in the well-being of his community.

To Give All

Most of Titus' confreres were convinced that he could be assigned to just about any job in the province and do it well. There was, however, one exception: were he put in charge of finances, the money would disappear in a trice. Had he wished, he could have become an excellent lawyer or physician or politician, but he would never have been wealthy. For him the renunciation of material things he had made on the day of his religious profession was insignificant unless it found expression in his daily life; he wanted to be poor in reality. In order to get him to replace a worn-out habit, his prior had to give him an explicit order to go to the tailor.

During a period when the community's economic situation was somewhat less than healthy, he was asked to cut back drastically on the growing list of scholarly journals he was receiving; he consented immediately, even knowing full well how much of his precious time it was going to cost him. Verifying a text needed for one of his articles would require an extra trip to the library.

It took a formal prioral command to make him exchange his wooden bed and straw pallet for a comfortable mattress and springs. Eventually, however, he succeeded in convincing his superior that he really did sleep better on a straw mattress laid on hard wooden planks.

When Titus himself was prior, he taught his friars: "Without poverty a religious is a pharisee, a gentleman of ease pretending to be a poor man. It is like someone who wants only the finer things of life disguising himself in the clothing of the poor. When religious are overly attached to unnecessary possessions, or are always looking for luxuries, then we appear ridiculous before the Lord who received our vows."[9]

Titus made it a point to buy what he could from less prosperous shopkeepers rather than from the well-off, even though the latter might have offered a better price; he was more concerned with helping people than with saving a few cents.

He gave whatever he could to the poor. A frequent theme in his conferences was, "to the extent that one gives up his goods, God will provide for his needs." He instructed the brother who answered the door, "Whenever someone comes seeking alms, give whatever you can. Giving alms is our way of life. It is the alms we receive that provide for our needs, and with our own alms we must provide for those in need. Whatever we give to the poor we give to God."

As for himself, Titus often gave away whatever he had at hand: money, overcoat, even the blankets from his bed. "You know how I dispose of what I have, so why ask me about money?" he remarked to a friend.

His superiors had told him that he was to turn over his salary from the university to the community, but that any other income–from lectures, articles, collaboration with journalists–he could use for his charities. At this Titus remarked with a certain scruple, but with humor, "This almost makes me feel like I have one foot outside the community."

For Titus, money was a tool to be used in the practice of Christian charity; but this did not exclude the use of money for self-improvement. The authentic practice of poverty did not require anyone to shiver from cold in his cell when a bit of heat would enable him to work more efficiently, more productively. It was not true poverty to spend one's vacation at home if he could use the time for learning another language elsewhere. Nor did poverty require anyone to deprive himself of books and journals needed for study. Moreover, whenever there were visitors, they should be offered the best things available: a cup of good coffee, an excellent cigar. One ought not be stingy with the poor: "It is we, not they, who have taken the vow of poverty."[10]

Thus Professor Brandsma had no scruple about asking permission to go to Rome, Paris, Madrid, or Dublin for reason of research or study; but the Frisian friar was incapable of treating himself to even a short trip to visit the attractions of near-by Bergen Dal, or to travel by train in anything other than third class.

Still the economic state of the priory was limited. After Titus' single three-year term as prior, in 1936 the provincial council appointed another, more "circumspect" superior. No one was happier about the change than Titus, who noted, "Fr. Arnold is far more suitable than I for this position."

And when the new prior– a man much younger than Titus– arrived, he greeted him and knelt to receive his first blessing; handing over the seal of the community and the keys he said, "I present you with the keys of a very poorly closed safe."

Healthy Friendships

One of Titus Brandsma's biographers, H. W. F. Aukes, relates hearing the lawyer, M. R. A. L. Houtappel say, "There was something angelic, something pure and sacred that emanated from Titus, and it made no difference where he was, whether in a concentration camp or in his priory." Aukes himself added, "When I visited him for the last time in December, 1941, I found him so totally detached from what was happening around him that there seemed to be a light emanating from him. To me this seemed to be an indication of his personal spirituality and an expression of his union with Christ."

One of Titus' colleagues at the university, Professor Molkenboer, used very similar terminology: "As far as Titus is concerned, I would like to use the expression 'He is as pure as an angel.'"[11]

Sexuality was no tyrant for Fr. Titus; his passion was enthusiasm for work and concern for the welfare of people. Though he was an intellectual, he was not a cold, cerebral person. He loved people with all his heart, but the object of his love was not so much the physical, changeable, visible person but rather his inner beauty. "A humble illiterate is worth more than a heartless savant," he used to say. He was convinced that, deep within themselves, people are– and want to be– much better than what they seem. Hence his tolerance and compassion for everyone, his desire for them to see and love themselves as God sees and loves them. Love was the driving force behind his constant activity.

Titus regretted that the virtue of chastity was too often esteemed and practiced solely under its negative aspect: avoid whatever may begrime you. "Rather," he insisted, "purity must be rooted in the most genuine love of Christ. It has nothing to do with being antisocial, but rather it ennobles and sanctifies our relationships with others. We are called to see the image of Christ in our neighbor, and we are to serve Christ in those with whom we live. The worst enemy of chastity is a purely physical love, whether it be directed toward others or toward ourselves."

During his retreats he pointed out the importance of asceticism for acquiring purity: "Life is a battle, a fight from which there is no escape. Self-control attained through discipline and mortification is essential. Be attentive to the little things: observe custody of the eyes and ears and do so spontaneously–even when there seems to be no real need–if you wish to be strong when there is a danger. Still, we ought not go to extremes with mortification, and we must carefully take pains not to deceive ourselves."[12]

He considered the vow of chastity to be a divine invitation to love every human being: Titus had no enemies. He considered enmity among the greatest of evils: "It is a sin against our sanctified nature," he claimed. Touchiness and bitterness, tendencies to rash judgment, deception and revenge: these need to be overcome through Christian service. In his own relationships, Titus was a cordial, other-oriented person, one who filled his life with healthy friendships.

Guests were frequent in the parlors of the Nijmegen Carmel, especially students drawn by Professor Brandsma's generous hospitality. Titus was pleased that people felt free to call on him, and whenever he was told that he had a visitor, he dropped what he was doing, however important it may have been, and hurried down, visibly delighted. It came to be expected that he would have a box of cigars and a box of candy to celebrate the event.

"Wherever we are," Titus told the members of his community, "we ought to provide a feast for those who are with us and make them feel at ease. We must be all things to all men and look upon everyone with God's eyes so that we love them as He loves them."

It made no difference which member of the community a visitor had come to see; each was welcomed as a guest of the community and the visit became an occasion for community celebration. As prior, Titus would not dream of accepting payment from those who stayed in the priory; and if the guest were a layman he would reserve him a room in a near-by hotel and offer to pay for it. "Hospitality costs us nothing," he said; "it would be humiliating to think of our home as a boarding-house where one has to pay for lodging."[13]

Titus loved his family dearly, as is reflected in the words of his brother, Fr. Hendrik:

> No one wrote warmer letters than Titus. He was interested in everything: the grades of his nieces and nephews, the health of their parents and brothers and sisters, the weather, how the hay was doing, the condition of the livestock. Dad always found him to be a great help. Mom? After Dad's death she went to spend a few days with him in Nijmegen, and they walked around the city arm-in-arm. I too owe him a great deal, as do our sisters." [14]

As long as she was able, Mother Brandsma was welcomed each year for a visit with her famous son. The two walked the streets of the city and visited with friends. Her other children recognized that these visits provided their mother with the happiest days of her year; she seemed to enjoy the time spent at Carmel even more than her visits with them.

The Source of His Strength

If someone were to have asked Titus early in the morning how he had passed the night, he might possibly have heard him mention something about insomnia, which was constant, or a headache, often severe; but during the rest of the day no one would notice any indication that he was not in perfect health.

Aukes, one of his better biographers, attempting to describe Titus Brandsma's fundamental characteristics, wrote: "He was a strong man par excellence, but his strength was totally interior. In spite of his enormous activity he maintained a deep sense of peace and an unvarying stability of character. He was totally balanced. ... His was an openness of spirit that, joined with his simplicity, his goodness and his generosity, explains the charm of his personality."

Like the broad meadows of his native Frisland, his personality was warm and serene, yet vital. Throughout his life, and in spite of his tendency to accept all challenges, he managed to maintain a sense of balance, an internal equilibrium. This became even more evident once he passed his fiftieth year. It was this peaceful vitality that accounted for what many acquaintances described as a special gleam in his eyes, a reflection of the inner fire that burned in the depths of his being.

Titus had taken the "Bookmark of St. Teresa"[15] as a pattern for his life:

> Let nothing disturb you,
> nothing affright you,
> all things pass,
> God alone abides.
> Patience
> obtains all things.
> He who has God
> wants for nothing.
> God alone suffices.

Titus was a true contemplative: undisturbed, calm, master of himself. He was totally Carmelite, the son of an order that appreciates the value of silence, and to this he bore witness by his example–something all the more admirable in one who had difficulty finding a free moment during the day. Yet he was able to maintain consummate balance. Few indeed have achieved this.

On the occasion of the fortieth anniversary of his profession Titus' brother Fr. Hendrik asked him why he had joined the Carmelites rather than the Franciscans like so many of his relatives. Titus replied that "he had wanted to lead a contemplative life rather than one dedicated to the care of souls in a parish."

"A curious response," noted the Franciscan, "because no one ever led a more active life."[16]

Here is one of the paradoxes characteristic of souls close to God: in his own life he achieved a synthesis of the contemplative and the active. In all probability, no one will ever know precisely which element was most responsible for leading Titus to God, contemplation or action. But few will dispute that his activities were products of the inner fire in his soul. "I am convinced," as one of his students, Fr. Borromaeus Tiecke, put it, "that Fr. Titus lived constantly in the presence of God."[17] Neither activities requiring total concentration nor those performed without explicit thought–like smoking his pipe–were able to deprive him of the divine presence.

Titus lived on love. He was totally aware that any effective apostolate is the fruit of prayer, and prayer of the love of God. It is the love of God that is the source, the center and the goal of the entire life of the spirit. Prayer and action follow from and reinforce one another, until finally the difference between them begins to disappear and both are transformed into the one burning flame of love. It is how the heights of Carmel are scaled and the individual loses himself in God, drawing a host of souls in his wake.

Like Elijah the Prophet, who was obliged to leave the solitude of Mount Carmel to call the children of Israel back to Yahweh, Titus too had to leave his Carmel in Nijmegen, compelled by the needs of others or the events of the day. It might be said that it was his willingness to make the needs of others his own that made his intense interior life credible. He never permitted his multiple activities to interfere with his intimacy with God. On the contrary he learned to elevate his efforts into the sphere where he lived alone with God. Recognizing the world as the work and reflection of God, he found his love for creation in no way stood in the way of his love for the Creator.[18]

Titus Brandsma was almost totally reserved with regard to his own interior life. He rarely spoke about himself and–apart from the brief account he wrote while in prison–he kept no autobiographical diary. This is unfortunate because it deprives us of an opportunity to follow the spiritual development of this extraordinary soul more closely.

Nevertheless, it appears safe to say that the dynamic force of his life was his constant search for God, whether in his fellow man or in creation itself, animate and inanimate. His prayer focused on God's love, a consideration that set his own soul on fire with love for God and for his neighbor. It was through prayer that he achieved his inner harmony.

He put it simply: "Prayer is life, not an oasis." He never thought of prayer as simply one more daily duty: prayer was not merely an hour of meditation, or his Holy Mass, or the Liturgy of the Hours. Prayer is not simply another activity; prayer is the heart of life, indeed life itself.

Whether in the priory or away from it, Titus Brandsma was a true contemplative. As a good Carmelite he had taken to heart the advice of St. Albert in the *Rule*: "Let each one remain in his cell, or near it, meditating day and night on the law of the Lord and keeping vigil in prayer."[19] Members of his community, as has been said, have testified that, even though he had innumerable concerns pressing on him, when praying he remained recollected, totally absorbed. Reporting on this witness, Aukes has written: "One had the impression that if a bomb were to explode in the Church, Fr. Titus would not even have noticed it."[20]

For Titus God was not some abstract distant being, but someone, someone he experienced as very close, living in the most profound and intimate part of his soul. Even more, he experienced God as present within himself through grace, and he tirelessly sought an ever more intimate union.

Titus sometimes spoke of "fireplace saints," whose quietistic approach led them to dream about a mysticism brimming over with consolations and sweet idleness. For him, however, the life of the spirit did not involve an abundance of consolations or feelings of well-being; on the contrary, he taught, God Himself, on becoming one with us, did so through suffering, through being despised, through death. In Titus' opinion, prayer requires self-discipline.

Professor of the History of Mysticism that he was, Fr. Titus made use of his vast knowledge of mystical theology and of the great mystical writers for his own spiritual growth. Following the example of several recognized authorities on the spiritual life he liked to compare the soul to a garden that ought to be transformed into a "Carmel" of delights, into a verdant flower garden, where one plants and carefully cultivates a lawn with the grass of humility that everyone has the right to walk on as he pleases. There too one plants lilies and sunflowers.

"Thus we learn that we can seek God with our own faculties. And also that God can make himself known to us in such a way that it is impossible for us not to see him. The sunflower always has its face to the sun, and with its colors it reminds us of it. The purple rose is the symbol of generous love: living, growing, bearing fruit in Jesus Christ. It possesses an enchanting beauty in our eyes; so our presence ought to radiate joy, charm and consolation. Wherever we are, there should be festive joy, just as the rose gives rise to an ambience of festivity and peace."[21]

On one of his retreats Titus stated: "God, who lives in us and in whom we live and move and have our being, is not always hidden.

At times he may exchange his image for reality, and imagination for conscious experience. In the Netherlands too this has taken place ... ."

Whether or not at some point God had revealed himself to Titus Brandsma we will never know, although some biographers assert that it is so. In fact, at one time there was a rumor going around Nijmegen that St. Therese of Lisieux–Fr. Brocardus Meijer, a biographer, says it was St. Teresa of Avila–had appeared to Titus, foretelling the proximate end of the World War. Fr. Hubertus was surprised when he heard about it, even though he could believe that such a thing might have happened to Titus; but when Titus himself learned of the rumor he laughed aloud.[22]

Titus lived the spirituality of Carmel as presented in the documents of the Order: "In the Most Holy Virgin and in St. Elijah the Prophet we learn how one acquires a truly human life only to the extent that he allow God to be truly 'God' within his being."

When his sister, Baukje, a Poor Clare nun, wrote to ask his advice for her personal growth in holiness, he responded with the advice that he doubtless was following in his own life: "Perform perfectly the little, even the insignificant, things you are supposed to do. That's all there is. Follow the Lord as a little child follows its father. As for me, I run after the Lord as best I can, leaving every care in his hands."[23]

Sanctity, even the mystical life, is not something reserved for a few elect souls, but should be the goal of every Christian. In an article published in a Catholic daily newspaper he wrote: "Every Christian has the capacity to be receptive before God. Everyone has a spark which is at once light and fire, which causes true wisdom as well as pure love, which in the soul becomes the beginning of life with God."[24]

Titus was of course aware that no one can see God and live; this, he understood, means that to approach God one must despoil his very self. This he did through the practice of asceticism; as he put it, asceticism "is not so much an effort to avoid something as a practice that frees one's spirit so as to invite Christ to live within us and to cast his divine light on our surroundings."

Titus Brandsma was an ascetic, not, however, the sort who goes about in a long, sour, aloof manner. Observing him, one saw just the opposite. He appeared neither sullen nor gruff, but approachable, kindly, joyful. Those who came in contact with him were usually charmed, and they would never have suspected that this friendly, cheerful Carmelite regularly used both a discipline and a hair shirt, things he normally hid in a corner of his desk. In this way he tried to make his own the first goal of Carmel: "To offer God a pure heart." This is how he set his spirit free in order to be united, even in this life, as intimately as possible with God, and then to make Him known to others.

In his talks Titus frequently referred to the great saints of Carmel, especially to those who suffered–St. Teresa of Avila, St. John of the Cross, St. Mary Magdalen de' Pazzi– because he himself had learned joy through the severe trials with which God had tried him from his infancy. And when he came to the greatest of his torments, when in the concentration camps he was deprived of everything and possessed nothing other than his weakened, painful, infirm body, covered in tatters, even then he was able to rejoice because this too was the gift of God.[25]

Brother of the Virgin Mary

Here is another fundamental ingredient of the charism of Carmel.

From the beginning, according to Jacques de Vitry in his history of the crusades, some crusaders had retired to Mount Carmel where they lived apart in caves "to drink the honey of meditation." The first thing they did once they gathered together as a religious community was build a little chapel honoring the Virgin Mary, Mother of God, the Lady of the Place.

De Vitry's account inspired Titus to invite others to grow in their appreciation of Mary.

> As a Brother of the Blessed Virgin Mary of Mount Carmel," he wrote, "I want to attract into the land of Carmel all those who love and serve Mary as their dear Mother, so that from the hand of this Mother and Beauty of Carmel they may attain the most intimate union with God, the purpose of the contemplative life in Carmel. Jeremiah the Prophet says: 'I have led you into the land of Carmel to enjoy its fruits, the best of them.'[26]

Calling oneself Brother of the Virgin Mary seemed to Titus an enviable privilege– but not one due to vainglory– because he felt it was one of the abundant graces that the Lord was pouring out constantly on his creatures.

> Who can claim," he pointed out, "that do sounds better than sol? I love my Order intensely. It is the way God has shown me to be able to find him. Its charism and history are most dear to me, and I bless him for the beautiful flowering of men and women saints who have filled its cloisters; but I also know that 'In my Father's house there are many mansions,' that, next to the living waters where God has planted Carmel in the garden of the Church, there are other plants just as beautiful.[27]

With pride and joy he wore the habit and white cloak of the Order both inside the priory and outside it. Every Saturday as evening came he hurried to the church in full habit to participate in the singing of the *Salve Regina* and the Litany of the Blessed Virgin Mary before the altar of Our Lady of Mount Carmel, feeling himself in union with Carmelites around the world sharing in that same ritual. Daily, before retiring, they would perform the same rite in a more simple form.

During one celebration a well-known individual, one of Titus' good friends, seeing him wearing his habit and white cloak, remarked: "I thought Carmelites were simple religious, but looking at you wearing your habit so proudly, I am beginning to wonder whether Professor Brandsma really is a good Carmelite!"

"I may well be vain," Titus responded, "but when I am wearing this habit I have absolutely no desire to be so. I wear it with great joy because it is the symbol of Mary's protection. I have full confidence in her motherly aid."

Titus had learned to live "with Mary, for Mary, and in Mary" as a 17th Century Flemish Carmelite– the Venerable Michael of St. Augustine– had written. Titus was aware that for Michael, Mary was like two wings that would lift him up to God.[28] Titus explained: "We experience being led to Jesus through Mary; her arms entrust us to him so that we may love him as she did. Jesus came to us through her. So let us go to Mary, secure in the knowledge that we will find Jesus!"

Titus' love for Mary was contagious.

First of all, it was obvious throughout his academic career. Very few articles came from his pen without some reference to the Mother of God, from the first one in *Katholieke Gids*, through the magazine *Carmelrozen*, which he had founded, and even in the important lecture he delivered on being invested as *Rector magnificus* of the university.

On the occasion of the 15th centenary of the Council of Ephesus, which defined that Mary is *Theotokos*, the Mother of God, the title that is the foundation for all the others, Titus organized a national Marian congress in Nijmegen, August 6-9, 1932. Participants included bishops, academics, representatives of the Dutch government and thousands of the faithful. Many Protestants, however, did not understand such a Marian event; consequently Titus felt obliged to publish an article in the Nijmegen newspaper *Gelderlander*:

> To Jesus through Mary. To Jesus, this is the purpose.
>
> Many people, especially those who are out of touch with the Catholic environment, will no doubt form an idea of our Congress that will not be very precise, and possibly they may think, wrongly, that Catholics exalt Mary too much, placing her on a par with God, or even above God.
>
> Such people are completely in error.
>
> The purpose of this Congress is none other than to achieve a more intimate union with God. Our Congress is a new manifestation of love for God, a new revelation of it. ... If it does not lead us closer to Jesus, it will have failed totally. But I am sure this will not be the case ...
>
> You will see thousands upon thousands of people arriving, some with great sacrifice, joyful sacrifice. And you will see them arriving with holy enthusiasm and with the certainty that the days they are going to spend here will be a powerful stimulus to help them with their lives, a divine aid in their daily difficulties, and a powerful experience of the unity of all in the one Mystical Body of Jesus, which is the Church. No Catholic thinks any differently.

The Congress was a complete success. Afterwards Titus published a commemorative book listing its various events and the studies developed during those four days.

Titus spoke of Mary with great tenderness.

> If we want to be like Mary we must, obviously, be other Marys; we must permit Mary to live within us. ... The purpose of our devotion

to Mary is that we ourselves become other mothers of God; that God may be conceived and brought to birth within us. The mystery of the Incarnation has revealed how intimately God wants to be united with man, how precious man is to him. ... Devotion to Mary is one of the most beautiful flowers in the Garden of Carmel.[29]

His was not a devotion based on sentimentality, but rather a devotion based on his firm conviction of the fundamental truths of our faith. Still, Titus never lost sight of the fact that the Netherlands was a Protestant country and consequently, whenever he spoke about the veneration of Mary, he made it clear that it was based on the truth expressed in the Gospel that Mary is the Mother of God. Moreover, whenever he spoke during popular festivals, he never missed an opportunity to proclaim that in the New Covenant redemption came to mankind first of all through her who is named Mary.[30]

Had Titus given free rein to his love, he would never have tired of speaking about Mary. He was nevertheless constantly aware of the importance of limiting his praises so as not to be misunderstood by his non-Catholic neighbors. This did not prevent him from expressing his love for Mary publicly. Indeed, during the 1932 Marian Congress he had discussed the possibility of reviving an ancient procession in honor of the Virgin Mary through the streets of Nijmegen.

Processions were far from popular in austere Netherlands, but Fr. Titus had been deeply impressed by the fervor of the processions he had witnessed in Seville during a recent visit, and he decided to adapt this public act of faith to his own country. He encountered some opposition, as was to be expected, but eventually the procession was arranged. He was to take responsibility for it: it would take place under his direction, with the collaboration of other devout priests and faithful. As the image of the Virgin to be carried in the procession, he chose a medieval statue of Our Lady of Nijmegen venerated in the Church of St. Canisius.

The procession passed through the streets of the city accompanied by long lines of fervent Catholic faithful, not without arousing the skepticism of a few sophisticated intellectuals who could not comprehend– nor did they wish to do so– such a massive religious demonstration. Titus however considered the devotion of the people more important than the criticism of the few and acted accordingly. Until his death he fervently participated in this Marian Procession each Trinity Sunday. As he walked along and sang, possibly he recalled that centuries earlier similar processions had been held in his native Frisland on this very date.

The success of both the Marian Congress and the Trinity Sunday procession attracted favorable attention; some time later the organizers of an international Marian Congress in Maastricht had no hesitation in choosing Professor Titus Brandsma as president of its preparatory commission. There the study of the Virgin was to focus on the title "Mother of Humility."

Titus' love for the rosary had been instilled in his consciousness from his earliest days. Indeed, he himself acknowledged he could not understand how he could have failed to transfer his rosary to his clerical suit on the day of his arrest; yet even without the beads he continued to pray the rosary on his fingers. In the concentration camp his gratitude knew no bounds when a Protestant pastor was able to provide him with a hand-made rosary. We know that his last act of compassion was to give his rosary to the nurse who was to give him the injection that would end his life.[31]

When all is said and done, Titus' entire life was imbued with the presence of Mary. She was his constant example, and she was the link that united him with God. It was this devotion that would be his tower of strength during the harsh days of his martyrdom.

"He Also Had His Faults"

So stated Fr. Eugenius Driessen as he referred to Titus in a conversation with Fr. Hendrik Brandsma.

The faults of the Saints!

Traditional accounts of the lives of the saints, fortunately in the past, inclined us to think of the saints as persons who had already achieved the goal rather than as those still fighting their way towards it. Today we prefer to know saints as human beings. Displaced from their pedestals, we can recognize their faults, observe the moments when they wavered or possibly even fell. In other words, we prefer to see holiness dressed in flesh and blood, a holiness that is down-to-earth. Possibly it is only by considering their faults, along with their efforts to overcome them, that the example of the saints becomes attractive and stimulating. Perhaps we have come to realize that, in the final analysis, each human life has much in common with the others, and each is distinguished from the others by its own particular gifts and its own way of making use of them. Perhaps we would like to feel that, in similar circumstances and of course with the grace of God, we too might become saints.

Only with great difficulty could a person with as many duties and as many personal relationships as Titus Brandsma present a *curriculum vitae* totally free of imperfections. He was made of the same stuff as other men and had his weaknesses, or at least what passed for weaknesses among those who lived with him. And they are to be seen in the sworn depositions of witnesses during the process of beatification.

Nearly everyone thought of Titus as a friendly, even-tempered man; still, on at least one occasion his native Frisian temper manifested itself. One of his confreres, Fr. Pius van Stegge, had written to complain that because of Titus' negligence the publication of something he had written was being delayed—as *censor librorum* Titus was required to approve the content of each manuscript being submitted by a member of his province before its publication. Titus responded sharply: "You talk about it taking only one hour. Just where am I supposed to find that hour? Yesterday I didn't have even five minutes free all day. I slept barely five hours. Tomorrow will be the same: one obligation after another, each more important than reading your book. You write calmly about one hour. Do you have any idea of what it means to be overworked? Just what do you think I should do, stop taking part in community recreation?"[32]

Like a true Frisian Titus was outspoken. He spoke the truth, pure and unadorned. When required to express an opinion, he did not dissimulate, nor did he try to curry favor through pious platitudes. Whatever the topic under discussion, he expressed himself clearly and without sugar-coating. Yet his interventions were usually cordial and not without a sense of humor.

His brother Hendrik knew him very well: "He had a hot, short temper. He had a difficult time confronting opposition. Occasionally he appeared irritated, even angry. I once saw him lash out at our nephew because he didn't want to listen to his mother."

"Nevertheless," he continued, "he was not authoritarian, but extraordinarily open-hearted, kind and courteous."[33]

Fr. Aloysius van der Staay, who had been with Titus throughout the formation program, recalled: "He was always in good humor, peaceful, reflective, and in control of himself."

Too Many Jobs!

This is the very defect he would most frequently be accused of throughout his life: that he on took on too many jobs. "I am swamped with work," he complained in a letter to his brother Hendrik.[34]

"Why do you take on so many things?" asked his prior. "Wouldn't it be more prudent, and more efficient, to give your attention to fewer things at a time?"

Titus had no defense. He never claimed that others were able to handle a variety of activities all at the same time, and to do them well. Rather he said nothing, perhaps recalling the words of St. Teresa of Avila: "I insist that it is very important, all important, to be completely committed–whatever may come, whatever may happen–not to stop before reaching the goal [perfection]."[35]

Some of Titus' colleagues at the university, a Professor Sassen in particular, accused him of allowing his outside activities to interfere with the time needed to continue his research, or even adequately to prepare his classes. Titus responded: "Professor Sassen does have a point, but he is wrong about the amount of time I spend on other things; it is not as much as he thinks. And on the other hand, why is it that the faculty is continually asking me to take responsibility for everything that comes up?"

Nevertheless, criticism of this kind continued, and it is still not uncommon among those who knew him only superficially. Others defended him. Dr. Borromaeus Tiecke, who had been one of his students, insisted, "He prepared his classes conscientiously;" and several of his confreres testified that he spent at least four hours each day preparing his classes. During the celebration of his fortieth anniversary of First Profession, an article in *De Gelderlander* provided, at least indirectly, a response to his critics: "The time and the assistance of Fr. Titus are constantly in demand, but he has learned well the secret of how to stretch out the day.

It seems that he is able to enlarge it infinitely, not to mention his own energy and love of work as well."

During the Process of Beatification one of the lay brothers testified: "The people consider him a Saint; but we [who lived with him] are not quite so sure."

As prior Titus strove to encourage a harmonious environment through treating all the members of the community with thoughtfulness and respect. Nevertheless, he did require complete obedience to the requirements of regular observance, and he did not hesitate to correct deficiencies, as was his obligation. At times all this required was a glance or a gesture pointing upwards with his index finger, but occasionally something more was required, and this was not always appreciated.

Some of the lay brothers objected to the additional demands Titus' hospitality placed on them—even his brother Hendrik thought him overly hospitable—especially when it cost them extra work. Others particularly disliked his requests for their help outside their normal working hours; they preferred to be left in peace.

There were some who felt their prior lacked respect for their freedom, or even that it was hurting the spirit of the community. One went so far as to ask him, "Have you noticed, Fr. Prior, that when you come into a room certain people leave?" Titus chose not to respond to this observation; another member of the community considered the Prior's self-control on this occasion much to his credit.[36]

Unfortunately, no matter how kindly he said it, a simple though inevitable "No" was not always welcomed. Possibly it was one of these prioral negatives that, when Titus was already in the clutches of the Nazis, occasioned a remark by one member of his community: "I truly regret that he is in a concentration camp, but what a relief it is for him to be away." Years later, when the Cause for his Beatification was being introduced, this same brother remarked: "Better that he be beatified than that he return here."

Finally, we should not forget that Titus Brandsma was a poor manager of money. Under his control, community savings did not last long. This did create a problem for some of his confreres; indeed, some of them complained to the provincial. The latter, along with his council, felt obliged to name another, "more circumspect," prior.

Titus was well aware of his failures in this regard: kneeling before the new prior he had acknowledged: "I present you with the keys of a very poorly closed safe."

Was He a 'Triumphalist'?

Anyone seeking evidence of this would have little trouble: the congresses, exhibitions, processions he organized, the splendor he considered as a normal part of Catholic public life. Nevertheless, he was not a "triumphalist."

Still, Fr. Titus was a man of his age. At that time religious life was flourishing within the Dutch Catholic church. Following the long centuries of open persecution, Catholics were beginning to enjoy a measure of acceptance in society. Indeed, Catholicism was on the march, and there was a well-earned sense of satisfaction with the way things were going.

The Frisian Carmelite was proud of what his people had achieved, and he was eager that Catholic culture be recognized for its positive contributions to the Dutch character. He lived his faith with an obvious enthusiasm that attracted those within its orbit. Still his was not an empty enthusiasm, a merely public display; rather it was the fruit of his inner conviction overflowing into every aspect of his life.

Perhaps the Bishop of Rotterdam, Monsignor Jansens, was correct in affirming: "He was totally genuine. He was a man of exceptional holiness."[37]

ENDNOTES

1. See *Appendix III*.
2. Cf. Raphael Tijhuis, O. Carm., "Dachau Eye-Witness," *Essays on Titus Brandsma*, p. 60.
3. Brandsma, *Ejercicios bíblicos con María para llegar a Jesús*, pp. 17-18.
4. Meijer, p. 321.
5. *Idem*, p. 336.
6. Carmelite Rule, 2.
7. Titus Brandsma, O. Carm., *Jardín cercado, pensamientos para ejercicios espirituales* (Caudete: Cesca, 1978), pp. 15-17.
8. Alzin, p. 98.
9. Brandsma, *Jardín cercado*.

10. SU 65, p. 26.
11. SU 79, p. 152.
12. Brandsma, *Jardín cercado*, pp. 11-13.
13. Meijer, p. 350.
14. Meijer, p. 438.
15. Teresa de Jesús, *Poesías* 30, "Nada te turbe" in *Obras completas*.
16. SU 65, p. 25.
17. SU 65, p. 62.
18. Brandsma, *Ejercicios bíblicos*, pp. 10 and 17 ff.
19. Carmelite Rule, 10.
20. H. W. F. Aukes, *Het leven van Titus Brandsma* (Utrecht: Het Spectrum, 1985), p. 162. Hereafter Aukes.
21. Brandsma, *Jardín cercado*, passim.
22. Rees, p. 87. Cf. SU 79, p. 118.
23. Titus was familiar with the spirituality of St. Thérèse of Lisieux. During his 1935 Lecture Tour of North America, he spoke of her desire to be Jesus' flower, to be plucked by him, to die for him before his eyes, to be strewn on his path and trodden on. Cf. Mary Angela, S.M., "Dachau–That Holy Place," *The Sword* 11 (1947), 34.
24. Redemptus Valabek, O. Carm., "Prayer Is Life, Not an Oasis," *The Beatification of Father Titus Brandsma, Carmelite (1881-1942): Martyr in Dachau*. P. 121. (1881-1942), p. 121.
25. Cf. Brandsma, *Ejercicios bíblicos*, p. 13.
26. Cf. Jer 2:7.
27. Meijer, p. 392.
28. Miguel de San Agustín, O. Carm., *Introducción a la vida interna y práctica fruitiva de la vida mística*, Barcelona 1936, 487-616. Miguel de San Agustín y María de Santa Teresa Petit, *La vida de unión con María*, Madrid, 1957. The Marian spirituality of Michael of St. Augustine (+1684) is frequently compared with that of St. Louis Maria Grignon de Montfort (+1716). However, the terminology of de Montfort stresses the devotee's relationship to Mary as that of a slave to a loving mistress, whereas Michael's terminology emphasizes a filial relationship.
29. Titus Brandsma, O. Carm. *The Brothers of Our Lady*, The Carmelite Press. Faversham, Kent. 1936. pp. 17-20. This booklet was republished by the Carmelites in the U.S.A. in 1980.
30. Vallainc, p. 145.
31. See *Appendix IV*.
32. Meijer, p. 427.
33. SU 65, p. 26.
34. *Idem*.
35. Teresa de Jesús, Camino de perfección 35, 2; in *Obras completas*.
36. SU 65, pp. 91 ff.
37. SU 65, p. 89.

Fr. Titus Brandsma and fellow travellers enjoying the entertainment aboard the ship to the USA. In 1935 Brandsma delivered a series of lectures on Carmelite spirituality in the Provinces of the Most Pure Heart of Mary and St. Elias. *(Photo courtesy of the Nederlands Carmelitaans Instituut)*

Chapter VII

"That Dangerous Little Friar"

Ecclesiastical Assistant for the Press

In the late 1930s Professor Titus Brandsma was one of the most popular people in the Netherlands. For a letter to reach him, it was necessary to write nothing more than his name on the envelope. He was especially well-known among journalists.

Indeed, he was a member of the Union of Catholic Journalists (UCIP) and a card-carrying member of the Fourth Estate: Number 7668.

It was with good reason then that in March 1935, Archbishop de Jong of Utrecht named him Ecclesiastical Assistant of the Union of Catholic Journalists. From that time on Titus dedicated himself more and more to journalism's highest ideals.[1]

The journalists greeted the appointment warmly: "We are well aware of how much Professor Brandsma esteems the Catholic press as well as of his great interest in our problems. It would be difficult to think of anyone more worthy of this position. We welcome him most heartily and we thank him for having accepted this responsibility in spite of his many other important concerns. At the same time we want to congratulate all our colleagues for this nomination and we trust they will appreciate all it entails."

On May 12 he was officially installed in his new position. In a brief response to the introduction by the President of the Union, J. B. Vesters, the new Ecclesiastical Assistant pointed out: "We Catholic journalists must keep in mind that our contributions must be positive, constructive. This is what God requires of those who work for the Catholic cause. Secondly, we must unfailingly practice charity, which is the Lord's desire. Love must shine through the peaceful tone of the Catholic press."

Undertaking this noble yet difficult assignment, Titus Brandsma could not have known what it held in store for him. Nevertheless, when the moment of truth arrived, he would demonstrate with his life the full significance of his words.

The hierarchy was well aware that the man they had chosen would not take his duties lightly. As for the journalists, they welcomed him as a gift from God.

Titus was in a position to work toward a long-cherished goal: that the Catholic press be modern, competitive. capable of earning respect on its own merits in the world of information. Catholic journalists, therefore, would have to be competent, well-educated both in the skills of their profession and in moral principles. With this in mind Professor Brandsma established programs and guidelines that remain valid today.[2]

In 1936 he was named president of a commission made up of members from the Union of Journalists and the Editors of the Catholic Press and charged with studying new developments in the field of journalism. One practical result of the commission's work was a clear statement about how to plan for the future: "New Forms of Journalism."[3] It foresaw how the printed media, radio, cinema, and television–already anticipated–might complement one another. It also predicted that the individual who reads a newspaper for enjoyment rather than for information would soon be watching television instead. And it continued, "The newspaper that stands up for moral principles will not disappear."

Brandsma made a clear statement of his ideals for the Catholic press in two lectures broadcast by the Catholic radio station KRO. His September 22, 1936, presentation was recorded, something of a novelty at that time. In it he stated: "The Catholic Press, if it wants to be faithful to its calling, must provide information of at least the same value and in every area as any other press. The news it provides about business or sports must not be inferior to that provided by other media. This means that its news coverage must be as broad as that of other media, even though this requires greater expenditures. But if this is not the case, Catholic journalists will pay the consequences."

His second lecture–printed in *Ons Noordenof* March 11-14, 1939–makes the point that "A newspaper is like a friend whose opinion we value, whom we enjoy listening to, and whose conclusion we find difficult to escape." He thus preferred publications that provided information, guidelines and illustrations: "If a Catholic periodical does not provide what the public has a right to expect, then there is a danger that the public will consider it as a pitiable thing in need of help but, simultaneously, consider it a waste of money."

Titus, citing Pope Pius XI, called the Catholic press *arma veritatis* (a weapon of truth); he added, "The press is our most powerful arm in our battle for truth." He thus stated the principles on which he was to stand in the confrontations of 1941-1942. "Should the Catholic press abandon this ideal of being a weapon of truth, its very existence would make no sense either for us journalists, or for the Church. It would become worthless. Its steadfast witness to the truth alone constitutes its power and its glory."[4]

To appreciate the importance of Titus' efforts in this sector, we have to keep in mind the size of the Catholic press in the Netherlands. At that time there were 25 daily papers with a total daily run of 1,000,000 copies, representing a third of the total newspaper circulation of the entire country. In addition, there were some hundred periodicals, a news agency, etc.

Titus felt very much at home among journalists. During the national assembly of Catholic journalists he celebrated Mass and gave the homily, recalling "the wonderful right of the Catholic journalist to serve others with the daily bread of the written word." For several years he gave retreats for journalists in the Nijmegen Carmel, focused on practical spirituality. *Gentleness and Humility in Journalism*, *The Apostolate of the Press*, *The Faith of the Journalist* were some of the titles.

He dealt not only with the spiritual difficulties of journalists, but also–given his own broad experience–with technical difficulties and, most especially, with individual ethical, legal, and economic problems.

When he became aware of tensions among individuals, he personally contacted editors or publishers to smooth the way to mutual understanding.

His ability to bring calm to the journalistic environment where curiosity frequently combines with suspicion was tested in 1937 when the Dutch Catholic Party was plagued with factionalism. He signed up for a tour the journalists were making around the country and managed to be assigned a seat next to the chief dissident. By the end of the tour unity had been restored. Journalists themselves often referred to Titus as "the conciliator."

Years later, Mr. H. F. A. Geise, then president of the Union, recalled: "His demeanor, his understanding of opposing opinions, his availability all combined to make it obvious that here was a man who was not thinking of himself but of his mission. ... When Fr. Titus took part in the meetings, everyone was content; when he was absent, we had all kinds of difficulties."

Titus worked to establish a Chair of Journalism at the Catholic University of Nijmegen; it became a reality only in 1948, after his death.

During his Nijmegen years Professor Brandsma was religious censor for the periodical *De Gelderlander* and was also a valued contributor on a variety of topics, both religious and social. One colleague testified: "Fr. Titus was a born journalist, naturally vital and enthusiastic both in his style and his content. He was impeccable, refined, lively, a great storyteller: everyone read him with interest. He loved this great instrument of communication, as well as those who dedicated themselves to it."[5]

He was convinced that regular reading of a periodical had great influence on one's outlook on life. Coincidently so were the officials of National Socialism; but they insisted on choosing the outlook.

Nazi Blacklist

On January 30, 1933, due to the swift growth of the Nazi party rather than to an election, Adolf Hitler assumed the title of Chancellor of the German Reich. Two months later, this time with a majority of votes, Hitler presented the "Law of Total Power" to the Reichstag, thereby dissolving the Reichstag itself and prohibiting political parties. So began the dictatorship that a few years later would force the world into the Second World War. Hitler's core concept was the supremacy of the Germanic or Aryan race. This race was destined to be the leader and inspiration for all others which, little by little, were to be eliminated. Jews and Gypsies were to disappear first, along with communists, invalids, the sick, the retarded; next would come intellectuals and religious groups, especially the clergy, both Catholic and Protestant, who were deemed critical of the "New Order."

The German army, on the other hand, epitomized the ideal, the prototype for society. The German people, intoxicated by constant Nazi propaganda, was swept along by this terrifying nightmare. It was not long before the Nazis, by force of arms, began to conquer other nations. Nazism spread throughout Europe through the powerful arms of the Third Reich, clashing head-on with any individual or group that sought peace through justice. The Catholic church, preaching the equality of all people and the nobility of every race as children of God, was to pay a high price for its audacity.

From the Catholic University of Nijmegen, Titus Brandsma could not remain silent in the face of such nonsense and of the violence being stirred up in Germany. He studied the danger of this racist world-view– one proclaiming the sovereignty of force and race over every other value– from all angles. He then expressed his conclusions through several brief courses in the university. Students appreciated his precise definition of Nazism as well as his forebodings about what it would mean for other countries. He also published articles in the Dutch press about these same dangers.

At least one of his articles came to the attention of the Chancellery of the Third Reich in Berlin. In the autumn of 1935, shortly after the proclamation of the matrimonial laws against Jews, Professor Brandsma and other colleagues protested energetically in a series of articles entitled: "Dutch Voices on the Treatment of the Jews in Germany."[6] In one of these he wrote: "These things being inflicted on the Jews are disgraceful. If their enemies think they can suppress this people with inhuman laws in order to strengthen their own people, they are seriously mistaken. It is self-deception based on weakness." He went on to qualify the Nazi position as cowardice, its followers as cowards.[7]

In Berlin the gauntlet was picked up and, a few days later, the German newspaper *Federicus* responded with an article filled with insults for the Dutch Carmelite, depicted as "A Crafty Professor." Not long after, a small book originating in Germany circulated through Nijmegen; it accused Professor Brandsma and the other professors of being "allies of communism" and included them on its blacklist.[8]

In 1939, during the national pilgrimage to the tomb of St. Boniface, Fr. Brandsma preached: "We are living in a world that actually condemns love, claiming that it is a weakness that must be overcome. 'We want nothing to do with love,' they say, 'but only with the development of one's own strength. Let each individual become as strong as possible and let the weak perish.' They also claim that Christianity has had its day and that it must be replaced by the ancient Germanic powerfulness. Well," he concluded, "although Nazi neo-paganism rejects love, we will overcome this paganism with love."

Under the influence of Nazi principles, some newspapers– e.g., *Volksche Wacht*, *De Knuppel*, and the above mentioned *Federicus*– assailed Dr. Brandsma:

> If the learned professor of Nijmegen believes it is his duty to defend the Jews against the German people, he ought to understand that in Germany Jews are considered rabble, and it is not worth while to fight for rabble. You grab them by the neck, and you beat them–once, twice, three times–and then you throw them out." [9]

"If I were you," his provincial told him, "I would not keep quiet, and I would refute all those calumnies and stupidities."

Titus replied, "there is a Dutch proverb: 'If Barnabas ought to be hanged, then Barnabas must be hanged.' But what can we do against this storm? When this one is over, they will launch another. Still, I doubt that the German authorities consider me a 'Barnabas.'"[10]

Professor Brandsma was wrong.

The Germans Invade the Netherlands

Having occupied Poland and the Scandinavian countries in rapid succession, Germany now turned its sights to the west and its chief enemies: France and England. On the pretext of controlling the North Sea and the English Channel, Hitler ordered the invasion of the Netherlands, Belgium and Luxemburg. Although aware of the neutrality of these countries, the Germans brazenly declared them parties to preparations for an offensive by the Anglo-French army. Consequently, the Nazi army invaded.

At 5:30 in the morning on May 10, 1940, the German army entered the Netherlands. Less than three hours later the Third Reich notified the three governments that, in order to be sure of their neutrality, German troops would take control of their territories.[11] Reprisals would follow should there be any resistance to the "glorious" Nazi armies; on the other hand the greater the cooperation, the less the suffering both at the present time and, most especially, following Germany's inevitable final victory.

Neither the Netherlands nor the other countries accepted these outrageous conditions, especially after having witnessed the invasion; they determined to defend themselves and to resist the German advance, confident that their allies would come to their aid. Their allies, however, had been totally taken by surprise.

The Dutch fought with all the means at their disposal, but within a few days their resistence was utterly broken. On May 13 the government abandoned The Hague; the next day General Winkelman, commander of the Dutch forces, recognizing that the situation was unsustainable, abandoned the fight. Surrender took place on May 15, and by May 19 all of the Netherlands was occupied by German forces.

During the early hours of May 10 when the invasion was just beginning, Titus was celebrating Mass amidst the noise of planes and sirens (the Dutch first line of defense ran along the River Maas from Roermond to Nijmegen). He then went about his daily tasks, interrupting them from time to time to listen to radio reports. At nine he left for the university as usual. The streets were crowded, and the thunder of canons from the banks of the River Waal was continuous. But examinations went on, interrupted from time to time as both students and teachers took shelter in the basement.

Titus spent the afternoon in the basement of Carmel with his confreres. At nightfall the clamor died down and the friars were able to go to their rooms. Four days later there was silence throughout the Netherlands, born of stupor and fear as the Dutch realized that their country had been occupied and disgraced.

During the previous six months Titus had been undergoing a series of medical examinations and exhausting therapeutical treatments; these had forced him to slow down the rhythm of his activities. Now, faced with the conditions imposed by the Nazi occupation, he wrote to his family: "I shall attempt to do only what is most urgent and to remain in my cell working quietly. I have given up my railroad pass."

Toward the end of summer, he wrote again: "My health remains stable, no better, no worse. Fortunately, I can keep busy with just the most urgent matters; as for the rest, I am adapting."

And "I sleep a lot, and consequently do not have time for everything."

Nevertheless, at the beginning of the 1940-1941 academic year his sense of duty took over: he began classes at the university. Forgetting his promises, he was soon taking part in meetings, conferences, seminars, etc.

Political developments, however, were preparing more serious duties for him.

Following their occupation of the Netherlands, the Germans decided to move more slowly so as not to aggravate the Dutch unnecessarily. On May 20 Titus wrote his family: "It seems like the Germans are changing their tactics. Apparently they do not want to make the occupation more difficult than necessary." A few months later, however, he wrote: "We must trust in the Lord. For the rest, everything appears quiet. What worries me most is the press, given the limitations imposed on it [by the government of occupation], and the lies and deceptions being promoted by the Nazis."

More severe restrictions were soon under way. On September 15 he wrote, "Things are not going well for journalists. It is a continual martyrdom. Patience."

Less than a month later the Nazis began to persecute individuals. On October 11, a Carmelite, Fr. Amandus van der Wey, and various professors were detained. Titus wrote, "Although the Nazis have begun to take away some of our own, I can assure you that I am still free." It would not be for long.

The apparent calm of the first period of the Nazi occupation had a simple objective: to give themselves sufficient time to observe the situation in detail, to gather data and to develop a strategy for attaining their goal. In addition to placing the Dutch economy at the service of the Third Reich, there were three targets for Nazi domination: the Jews, Catholic education, and the Catholic press.

The Nazis recognized the faith of Christians as a direct threat to their worldview. Consequently, they were eager to take control of the Christian means of social communication: radio, press, education. The regulations they imposed intended to hasten the conversion of this important sector of the Dutch population to National-Socialism.

They had begun by setting up the usual Nazi youth[12] and labor[13] organizations; since these organizations failed to produce the desired effects quickly enough, the Nazis went on to suppress Catholic organizations.

Nazi anti-religious activity had become so blatant that the bishops felt it necessary to clarify matters lest Catholics fall into the traps set by Nazi propaganda. On Sunday, January 26, 1941, they ordered a pastoral letter– signed by the entire Dutch hierarchy– to be read in every church. It declared that no Catholic was permitted to belong to any Nazi association, and it concluded with this serious admonition: "Catholics who openly support the National-Socialist Movement will be denied the Sacraments, for this movement not only threatens the free development of the Church, but it also constitutes a danger to the Christian life of those who belong to it."[14]

The Fight for Catholic Education

Not unexpectedly, the Nazis retaliated quickly by issuing a series of discriminatory regulations directly affecting Catholic education. On April 20, 1941, the Department of Education issued an order that all religious dedicated to teaching were to receive only 60% of their salary. "Incredible," Titus commented: "this is a disgrace for the authority responsible and will be the ruin of our schools."

He had not yet recovered from this first shock when there was another, yet more serious blow: "As of today and for the future, religious and priests may not be named rectors, deans, or directors of schools and institutions, understood in the broadest sense of the word. Those who are presently holding such positions are to step down on the first day of May."

Father Titus, who had been president of the Union of Catholic Schools for years, was aware he would have to act with extreme caution. It was necessary that all the Catholic associations form a united front and write a letter of protest.

On several occasions Titus himself visited the Secretary General of the Ministry, Professor van Dam, in the hope that he could convince the Secretary to withdraw the order, or at least to modify it. "Mr. Secretary," he pleaded, "many religious men and women have dedicated their entire lives to teaching; from now on they will not have a right to even the minimum living wage."

With his natural goodness, Titus was unable to understand the motives behind this regulation, just as he did not understand how some Dutchmen, even though serving the German government of occupation, would want to bring on themselves the disgust of their own countrymen by obliging them to close their schools. Ingenuously he asked the Secretary to clear up his confusion. With apparent candor the Secretary replied: "We have no motive other than to be sure that the money the State provides for education is not used for other purposes and does not end up in the coffers of the Church."

This preposterous explanation was intended to hide the true objective of this unreasonable decree; however, the truth was made quite clear during an Amsterdam meeting of the "Corporation of Educators," a Nazi organization seeking full control of education throughout the country. Its resolutions were sent to all journalists. One of them stated: "Our goal is five-fold: the education of the entire community; education at the service of the people and of the nation; education following the ideals of the Third Reich; education for national pride based on Germanic culture; education for racial consciousness."

In the face of this situation the Bishops responded with another pastoral on May 1: "Our ancestors fought with every legal means for the fundamental right to free schools. Only Catholic education is adequate for Catholic families. We must defend our invaluable patrimony cost what it may."[15]

A few days later, on May 12, all the Catholic organizations sent a letter of protest to the Secretary General. As Titus had suggested, they presented a united front denouncing the published decrees and calling them "an injustice attacking the rights of individuals, the social welfare, and the Dutch Constitution."[16]

The Ministry's reply was blunt: published decisions were not open to discussion. They were to be followed in every detail.

The affair did produce one positive effect: it was now clear that in dealing with Nazis, talk was useless and argument futile. Each bureaucrat was little more than a tiny gear controlled by a somewhat larger one, the larger one a part of a machine, the machine only one part of a mysterious system totally disinterested in the affairs of its subjects. To make matters worse, the entire mechanism was incapable of reversing itself: it could only continue to advance, crushing whatever lay in its path.

This lesson had to be learned, for the battle would not be soon over.

In his dealings with government officials, Titus learned to distinguish between bureaucrats who were true Nazis–whom he considered traitors to their country–and those who were merely weak, even impotent, with regard to the Nazi forces of occupation. Among the latter he numbered Secretary General van Dam.

Jewish Students

On October 27 Titus wrote: "Following orders, today I was forced to declare that I am not a member of the Jewish race. Obviously, I am pure Frisian. But this is very painful for the Jews. I must stand alongside them."

It was through the Catholic schools that Titus became confronted with yet another of the Nazi goals: elimination of Jews.

Toward the end of August, in spite of previous agreements, the Department of Education decreed that Jewish students were not allowed to attend school, and this included all students of Jewish ancestry, even those who had long ago converted to Christianity. Faced with this regulation– both inherently unjust and totally offensive to Christian doctrine– Titus' could not remain silent. He explored every channel he could think of to permit the young Jews to remain in the Catholic schools. On September 21, 1941, acting with the authorization of the Union of Catholic Schools, he had sent a circular letter to all Catholic schools: "Having consulted with the ecclesiastical authorities and taken notice of the Protestant point of view, it is my duty to assert that the decree obliging schools to reject students who are already enrolled or those who seek instruction in them is a flagrant injustice and a direct attack on the mission of the Church. The Church makes no distinction due to race, sex or nationality."

Aware, however, that the Nazis would not be moved by affirmations of human rights, he went on to propose a practical solution of the problem:

> There are two categories of students who seek our services: one group, converts to our faith, does so out of principle; the other, non-Catholics, acts from secondary and materialistic motives. With regard to the first group, we have no right to expel them for any reason whatsoever; as to the second, there is no reason that obliges us either to accept them or to reject them.[17]

The following week he received a telephone call from the Ministry, informing him that an exception might be made for Jewish students who had been receiving Catholic education before May 1940. He rushed to pass on this welcome news. Before the end of September, however, the Secretary General denied he had made such a concession and reiterated that the regulation was to be meticulously applied.

The Nazi takeover of the Catholic schools was the beginning of a rule of brutality; and it was only the beginning. In the Carmelite schools–in both Oss and Oldenzaal–Jewish students continued to attend classes until a summons came requiring all Jews to go to Amsterdam for deportation.

From that point on it is very difficult to follow Titus' actions since he had to act in complete secrecy. If any record ever existed, the Gestapo would have seized it when he was arrested. We are aware, however, that he was looking into the possibility of sending Jewish students to the Carmelite communities and schools in Brazil.[18]

All the time Titus was worrying about others, he continued to communicate optimism to his family: "Although I have an enormous task, it is not taking all that much out of me. Consequently, I am taking a little better care of myself, sleeping a lot, eating and drinking sufficiently. I am ashamed of myself!"

At the time he was under orders from his doctors to come for check-ups regularly; not surprisingly he simply forgot, for months at a time.

The Battle for the Catholic Press

The defense of Catholic education lead inexorably to the conflict over the Catholic press. It began when the journalists refused to publish the propaganda of the Nazi-sponsored Corporation of Educators.

Titus was not taken by surprise: years before the occupation he had begun to encourage members of the media to prepare themselves for what seemed likely to come. He had asked a colleague, recently named editor of the daily *De Gelderlander*, how he would react should Hitler invade the Netherlands.

"I will know how to do my duty," responded the other.

"Then we are good friends," said Titus.

Once the invasion was a reality, he alerted the personnel of that same newspaper–for which he was the *censor deputatus*: "Before long they will demand that we publish National-Socialist propaganda. Let's not deceive ourselves, my friends, because we will have to fight this together. Everything has its limits."[19]

The excellence of the Catholic press in the Netherlands, both in quantity and in quality, explains why the Nazis were more intent on taking control of it than they were in other invaded countries. By the same token, it also explains the pastoral obligation of the bishops, as well as that of others in positions of responsibility, to defend the press, whatever the cost.

From the very beginning of the occupation the Germans had been sending propaganda supporting Nazi organizations to the editors of all newspapers, with orders for its publication. Many refused to obey, others– fearful that the occupation authorities would remove them from their positions and their livelihood– were less courageous. Not surprisingly the authorities had a plan to replace stubborn editors with others more sympathetic to the new order.

The two organizations representing the press in the Netherlands held a congress in Utrecht on August 10, 1940. The intention was to present a united front before the occupation authorities. Titus was upset when the congress was unable to agree on a clear plan of action. Regretfully he presented his resignation as Assistant for the Press, sending copies both to the president of the congress and to the Archbishop. At the last moment an agreement was reached and the congress agreed to stand up for the rights of the Church as Titus had insisted. Thus, with the full blessing of the Archbishop, he continued in his position. The Nazis, however, had something else in mind.

In less than a month, before the end of August, the Nazi government implemented new and arbitrary regulations that would have transformed the Catholic press from a pillar of truth into a promoter of falsehood. Titus wrote: "The press is not functioning either as they or as we would like. There are many difficulties and there is no clear way to achieve mutual understanding. The press, second only to the churches, is the principal pulpit for teaching truth. It holds the power of the word against the violence of arms."

The bishops could cede no more.

On January 26, 1941, through a pastoral letter read in all the churches, the Bishops had warned that "those Catholics who openly support National-Socialism will be denied the Sacraments."[20]

Now the Bishops repeated their position through the media: "We have been forbidden to take up collections for our cultural and charitable works. The Catholic Radio, which cost so many sacrifices, has been suppressed. And our press has been either liquidated or so limited that one can hardly speak any more of Catholic newspapers.

"Priests and religious have been barred from positions of authority in our schools, not because they lack legal credentials, but simply because they are priests or religious.

"We speak out openly. ... We protest this unheard of violence to consciences which attempts to impose on us a way of life that is contrary to our religious convictions. The situation has become so serious that we have decided to deny the Sacraments to all those who join Nazi organizations."[21]

In response the Nazis accused the Bishops of interfering in politics. To this the Bishops responded with yet another pastoral letter, dated September 8: "We are accused of exercising political power. This has nothing to do with political power, but simply and sincerely with being or not being Christians, ... of preserving our Christian faith and civilization, of saving our souls. These values we will defend to our last breath. No one in public life can place any other foundation than that set in place by Jesus Christ."[22]

The Dutch Bishops were fully aware of the support of Pope Pius

XII who, on various occasions, had stated publicly his appreciation of the firmness of the Dutch Church in proclaiming the Gospel.[23]

In the Service of the Bishops

For Father Titus the pastoral letters of the Dutch hierarchy were a call to battle. He was convinced that the time for action had arrived, and he prepared to fulfill his commitment as Ecclesiastical Assistant for Catholic Journalists without regard for the consequences. "I have the greatest respect for journalists, and I shall never desert them."

One journalist wrote: "The propaganda pieces we were receiving from the Dutch National-Socialists for obligatory publication were nearly all rejected, principally on the advice of Fr. Brandsma. Indeed, he himself wrote the responses we were to send to the authorities." The journalists were caught between a rock and a hard place. On the one hand, the hierarchy had threatened excommunication to those who accepted Nazi propaganda and, they were aware, not only would such periodicals no longer be considered Catholic, but the faithful would be advised to cancel subscriptions. On the other hand, the Nazis had made it perfectly clear that newspapers which rejected their propaganda were running the risk of being suppressed, their editors fired, and their readers left to subscribe to other publications that would support the Nazi ideals.[24]

The situation was serious, but Brandsma was convinced that this was not a time for indecision or double-talk but for unified action.

On August 29, 1941, newspaper editors met in The Hague, and one of the participants was the Nazi-supported Council for the Dutch Press, whose spokesman openly and cynically declared: "Freedom of conscience need not be of concern to anyone. ... no one conviction is more important than another."

It was, of course, useless to point out that when the Nazis spoke of equality, it meant total acceptance of their positions. The only significant moral norm was their own.

Following the meeting at The Hague there were a few days of relative calm. But it was not long before a new deluge of Nazi propaganda flooded the editorial offices. A few examples: "First year students! The National-Socialist Student Front is open to all Dutch students, male and female, who want to help construct a new student society according to National-Socialist principles. Membership in the NSB (the Dutch Nazi Party) not required."

Or this one: "Dutchmen! Your country is in danger. Help eliminate Bolshevism by enrolling in the Waffen SS (army). To enroll and to receive additional information, contact the Waffen SS in The Hague."

Needless to say, both of these Nazi organizations were interdicted by the Dutch hierarchy. "The public," commented one Catholic journalist, "sees a lot, but not everything. It has no idea, for example, how much of the Nazi propaganda we receive never appears in our papers, but for whose omission we are held strictly accountable." Brandsma, as *censor deputatus* of *De Gelderlander*, followed its hardships more closely, but all newspapers faced the same problems. "During the war," stated Mr. G. H. Bodewes, editor of *De Gelderlander*, "nothing was too much to ask our censor. He was at our disposition day and night, always prepared to give us clear, precise advice."

De Gelderlander totally refused to accept the Nazi press releases and propaganda, or the new editor-in-chief they imposed. This occasioned a denunciation by the self-styled "Corporation of Educators"– also Nazi– that the newspaper had thrown its release into the wastebasket. The Chief of the Press Section, wearing the Nazi insignia on his lapel, summoned the editor to The Hague and threatened him with loss of his position if he did not scrupulously obey orders. The editor coolly responded that he was prepared to accept the loss immediately.

The Nazi bureaucrat, who had orders to bark but not to bite, was taken aback and proposed a truce. The editor then returned to Nijmegen to consult with his censor, who dictated a letter sent to The Hague the following day: "We are under the impression that the "Corporation of Educators" is an organization created by National-Socialism with the goal of becoming an official governmental organization. Once it has achieved this status, we may reconsider your demands."

This was not the only letter rejecting senseless regulations sent to The Hague, and the Nazis soon recognized that in the Netherlands they were going to have to deal with a strong, stubborn resistance.[25] But they would not stand for the stubbornness of the Catholic press for long. On December 18, 1941, they directed Communication N° 1.008– with the stamp "Not for publication"– to all newspaper publishers:

> The Ministry of Propaganda and Art informs the Dutch press that it is forbidden to reject the propaganda provided by National-Socialism and its organizations for reasons of principle, so long as it contains nothing damaging to the honor and well-being of individuals or groups and does not attack the reputation of the same. This step has been taken moreover because we believe that nothing should be rejected that promotes the unity of the people of Holland.[26]

It was precisely this unity that was the focus of this attack.

At this point Titus resolved to move from theory to action and assumed the position of intermediary between the hierarchy and the editorial staffs of Catholic periodicals. This was the beginning of the most dangerous activity of his life. It was not his intention to become a "sharp-shooter" but rather a channel for the directives of the Dutch hierarchy. His first step was to visit the Archbishop of Utrecht to be sure that there was agreement on the steps to be taken, and then to contact the most influential newspapers of the country. Both agreed that, at least for the moment, dialogue with the puppet government of the country was useless. Both declared that "In view of the latest shameful regulations, nothing is left for us except our strong determination to resist."

This was the Church's *Non possumus* (We cannot give in) in face of the Nazi challenge.

On December 27 the Archbishop wrote to Titus asking his advice and requesting him to contact the editors of the Catholic press to verify in depth their thoughts about this serious situation. A few days later Titus again consulted with the archbishop. Both agreed that for the moment the bishops should not issue pastoral directives to the editors since the Assistant was to visit and speak with each one personally. He would also visit the other bishops to bring them up-to-date on the thoughts of the journalists. Combining both ventures, it would be less difficult to present a united front.[27]

Years later the archbishop revealed some very interesting details of the interview and of the conversation he had had with the

Ecclesiastical Assistant, Father Brandsma: "It took place on a Saturday afternoon," recalled Monsignor de Jong, "and I had a long talk with him. We had to establish the boundaries within which the journalists could function. Fr. Titus thought it desirable that he speak with the Catholic journalists himself. It seemed to me that this would put him in extreme danger, and I suggested that it would be less risky if the directives, even though prepared by him, were actually sent out by me and the other bishops.

"I told him, 'They will arrest you more easily than me. They will not arrest the bishops.'"

"I am aware of that, Excellency," he replied. "But I can act more freely and more easily than the bishops. I can travel, advise, and personally receive from the journalists assurances of their resolve; that will astonish the Forces of the Occupation."

"I concluded by telling him that, with the grace of God, he could go about this business in peace, and that I would back him with my own authority. I agreed with him and gave him my blessing.

"He wrote up the directives himself and sent them to the various editors."[28]

Titus did write the letter on December 31, 1941; he described the norms to be observed by Catholic journalists. He did not send them by post, however; rather he chose to deliver each one personally so that he could explain the more difficult points. Titus spent the final hours of 1941 making an evening of reflection with his community. The following day, January 1, 1942, he went to a university reception given by the *Rector magnificus*. There he met Mr. Bodewes, editor of *De Gelderlander*, who became the first to know the details of the letter.

A Courageous Letter

Here follows the text of the letter that was to prove decisive in Fr. Titus Brandsma's life. Even today it is greatly admired. With this letter he took up his ministry as intermediary between the Dutch hierarchy and the Catholic journalists. There can be no doubt but that he was aware of the grave consequences it would entail.

Nijmegen, December 31, 1941

Dear Sir:

In view of my appointment as Ecclesiastical Advisor to the Association of Catholic Journalists by His Grace Archbishop de Jong, it is my duty to call your attention to the following:

The Statute for Journalism has formally acknowledged not only the right but also the desirability of the existence of confessional newspapers, as well as those of other factions, in the Netherlands. When the general organization of the press was undertaken, many openly Catholic newspapers maintained their identity, a fact that indicates that our country permitted newspapers inspired by Catholic principles.

Dutch law recognizes the Catholic Church among its great religious associations and also recognizes her right to follow her own principles in her internal organization. Essential to that internal organization is the right of the bishop within his diocese to make definitive decisions regarding faith, morality and ecclesiastical discipline. It is the mission of the bishop to decide what course of action is to be followed by every Catholic of his diocese with regard to faith and morals.

According to her own principles, and according to international law, the Catholic Church recognizes and respects the occupying power; however, in accordance with these same principles, the Dutch hierarchy is obliged to oppose a political movement which attacks her dogmas and fosters principles that are contrary to those of the Church.

For some time now the Dutch press has been receiving communications accompanied by explicit orders for their publication. Whenever these communications are not flagrantly opposed to Catholic principles, the orders have been obeyed; at times however, these communications are so inflammatory that Catholics can hardly read their newspapers without irritation. They are willing to excuse them, however, because they are aware that tremendous pressures are being brought to bear on the publishers. The average reader, however, has no way of knowing just what the invaders are demanding and is unable to judge whether the publisher of the newspaper is printing more than is necessary.

Much to its regret the hierarchy has learned that some Catholic newspapers with a previously stellar reputation today hardly deserve to call themselves Catholic. And it also knows that many others have remained faithful to Catholic principles and have done everything possible to maintain their integrity. The hierarchy is very aware that these publishers and editors find themselves in an extremely difficult situation due to the risks they run in trying to distinguish between what may or may not be tolerated. It also recognizes that those publishers and editors who are trying to maintain the Catholic character of their publications merit their total gratitude and respect.

Yet how very difficult it is to know how far one can go under constraint, when one knows what is at stake! We are well aware that a few days ago the occupation authority issued an order, obedience to which places the publishers and editors of Catholic newspapers in conflict with their adherence to Catholic principles.

That order not only requires the publication of communications of the National-Socialists but it also explicitly forbids their rejection on grounds of principle. And here lies the nucleus of the problem: it is precisely because of principle that Catholic newspapers cannot accept such an order without finding themselves in conflict with the directives of their own bishops who have forbidden support of this movement.

Until now this order from the National-Socialists has not been given officially; it has been delivered only by teletype. Probably it will never have official confirmation. If this is the case, so much the better!

However should the order become official, and should the authorities continue to insist that every communication must be published, then all publishers and editors have the obligation to refuse categorically to accept them—even in the face of threats, fines, temporary or even permanent suspension of publication, even total suppression—if they wish to maintain their status as Catholic.

Even threats of severe penalties cannot be an excuse to conform with the order. There is no other choice. We have reached the limit.

It is not possible to act otherwise. I am sure that in this difficult situation Catholic journalists will know how to live according to their faith and to stand together in defense of the position of the hierarchy. The more united we are, the stronger we shall be.

You are all aware that I write this only after examining the problem from all sides and consulting with other well-informed individuals, and especially with His Grace the Archbishop.

The authorities of the Department of Publicity may freely take notice of our stand. If they do not agree with it, then they will make the existence of the Catholic press impossible.

All who are committed to the Catholic press will take note of these observations. Should they fail to do so and decide to act otherwise, they should be aware that they are forcing the Catholic press into a canyon without exit, thus making its very existence impossible, if not materially then certainly formally. Those who would take that road should know that they will no longer be able to count on the support of their authentically Catholic readers and subscribers, and their publications will disappear in dishonor.

I fully understand that these directives are extremely difficult for those who have been honorably earning their daily bread in the service of the Catholic press for many years; however, they will understand that acting contrary to them would turn them into accomplices of all the evils being put in motion by those who insist, in spite of their protestations to the contrary, on doing violence to consciences.

As yet I do not think that the authorities want to go quite that far. If they do, God will speak the last word, and He will surely reward his faithful servants. Please accept my best wishes for a Happy New Year!

Fr. Titus Brandsma, O. Carm.[29]

"He is to be Arrested Immediately"

On January 2 the Ecclesiastical Assistant, Fr. Titus Brandsma, began his visits to the fifteen principal cities of the Netherlands, one by one. He followed a well-planned itinerary and carried the letters with him.

His first visit was with the Bishop of Haarlem, Monsignor J. P. Huibers. "We were both convinced" reported the Bishop, "that the letter he was carrying would put him in mortal danger. But Father Titus stood up resolutely, asked my blessing, and calmly went on his way. I was deeply impressed by his heroic courage ... I will never forget it."[30]

From Haarlem he went to Amsterdam where he visited two important publishers. The following day he met with the Bishops of Den Bosch and Breda, as well as with several publishers and editors. On January 4 he returned to Nijmegan where a Jesuit called on him to let him know that, in his opinion, the clergy and laity ought to be working together. Titus assured him that he too was of this opinion, and he added that "the priests especially must take up the burden of their serious responsibility."

On January 7 he took a brief respite in the priory at Merkelbeeck, a place he loved. There he participated in the Liturgy of the Hours with that large community of professors and students, and he spoke with a large group of professed students who crowded around him. He especially enjoyed a visit with his friend Fr. Hubertus, who for years had suffered from a partial paralysis.

A few days later he had visited all the bishops and fourteen newspaper publishers and encouraged each to follow the directives of the hierarchy and to keep calm. Strengthened by his visits the journalists, not satisfied with a passive resistance, began to take action. They informed the authorities that they were prepared to follow the directives of the hierarchy, and they requested both the Press Officer of the Commissioner of the Reich, Mr. Janke, and the Propaganda Officer of the National-Socialist Party, Mr. Max Blokzijl, to abrogate the decree of December 18 which was responsible for all the trouble.

While Titus was visiting the bishops and publishers, the Nazi authorities were fully aware of his every move. They also knew that if Professor Brandsma did not obtain the support of a sufficient number of journalists, the Dutch hierarchy would write another pastoral letter advising Catholics to cease supporting publications favorable to the Forces of Occupation.[31]

The publisher of *De Gelderlander* testified: "I suspect that someone within the Catholic press provided information to the authorities about Fr. Titus' comings and goings. The Nazis were fully aware of all our decisions."[32]

Janke, the Press Officer of the Reich, sent a report–marked "Urgent"–to General Commissar F. Schmidt in The Hague. In it he denounced the "excessive" steps the Catholics were planning in order to convince directors of the Catholic press to reject the orders of the Government of Occupation.

"We have been informed," he stated, "that as of January 2, by order of the bishops, the Catholic priest Titus Brandsma of Nijmegen is inviting the editorial officers of the newspapers to participate in this protest. This is sabotage. To prevent this movement of opposition from becoming stronger ... he must be arrested immediately and sent to a concentration camp."[33]

A similar "personal" report was made by a Dutch collaborator, Blokzijl; he included a German translations of Titus letter of December 31.[34]

Unaware of his imminent danger, Titus visited the archbishop on January 10 to bring him up to date on the favorable results of his mission. In Eindhoven a friend of the community, Johannes Vervoot, had heard threats against the Assistant for the Press, and he hastened to Nijmegen to speak with the prior. "He is about to be arrested," he declared. "This is reliable information. I thought it my duty to warm him. Hide him, please."

Fr. Titus himself was not unaware of his danger, but he did not want to discuss it. Weeks earlier his prior had advised him to retire to some out-of-the-way priory and live like a normal religious, even using false I.D. if necessary. No one would know where to look for you. Unconvinced, Titus replied, "That would be agreeable enough for me. I send out the troops [the journalists] to fight the Nazi challenges and then I leave them in the lurch. Does this seem just to you?"

To a friend who asked how things were going he replied, "The Germans are following me and claiming I am sabotaging their orders. They simply refuse to understand. Still I am not afraid. They can arrest me any time they wish."[35] During this period he was aware of two mysterious "students" taking notes of every word the "dangerous professor" was saying.

The Trap Closes

On January 13, 1941, Janke advised the Nazi Department of the Press that General Commissar Schmidt in The Hague had taken note of his January 7 denunciation. Moreover, Schmidt had issued the order to act on the first and third of his recommendations: the first called for the immediate arrest of Professor Brandsma.

On Friday, January 14, someone claiming to be a student called the Nijmegen Carmel from Arnhem to ask whether Professor Brandsma was at home. "No, he is not here," answered the brother porter.

"Would it be possible to speak with him? Where is he?" the student asked politely.

After a moment's hesitation, the brother replied, "Really, I have no idea."

"When is he due back?" the student insisted.

"I don't know that either. Call back on Sunday and perhaps you will have better luck."

Titus was then in Amsterdam where he had gone to request the president of the Union of Catholic Journalists to explain to the Nazis the wishes of both the bishops and the journalists. The official in charge assured the president he had no desire to come into conflict with the Church, and he promised not to require the publication of propaganda. Nevertheless, he added in an aggrieved yet offensive tone: "There is one thing I do not want to see or hear again– Professor Brandsma's activities encouraging sabotage."

That same day Titus returned to Merkelbeeck because his friend, Fr. Hubertus, had sent him a telegram asking him to come as soon as possible. Once there, Hubertus warned him to be careful: "The earth is shifting under your feet. There is no reason to seek martyrdom. Try not to be seen in public in Nijmegen for a time."

Titus was grateful for his fraternal concern, but matters were already taking their course. On his return to Nijmegen he found a letter from the archbishop informing him that the bishops had accepted Titus' draft of the letter and that it would be sent to all the newspapers over their signatures. However, given Janke's promise, they had accepted Titus' advice to wait for a few days before sending it.

On January 15 several journalists informed the archbishop that the Nazis, in total disregard of Janke's promises to the contrary, were again sending their propaganda for publication. The archbishop immediately passed the bad news on to Titus. "Now there is nothing else to do," de Jong told him. The pastoral letter will be published tomorrow."

Titus agreed, and they said their goodbyes. It was the last conversation these two great men would have.

The pastoral was published on January 16. It urged faithful compliance with all the directives of the hierarchy that had been published: "We are fully aware," it stated, "of the new and serious problems being forced on the Catholic press, which has already been dealing with countless others. We would suffer the greatest pain if it now must disappear. But everything has its limits, beyond which we would not be able to recognize as Catholic those newspapers that would publish propaganda favoring a way of life that is diametrically opposed to our Catholic faith. Any periodical that acts in this way will no longer be considered Catholic and this will be made known to the faithful so that they can do what must be done. ... Failure to observe these directives will be considered formal cooperation with the National-Socialist Movement, and those responsible will incur the canonical penalties already announced."In order for this to have uniform application, the hierarchy wishes to receive–through the hands of the Ecclesiastical Assistant, Professor Father Titus Brandsma–a written declaration from the publishers and editors in which they commit themselves to support these directives."

Titus barely had time to verify how the journalists would react. Still, the die had been cast. The Commissar of the Reich would think twice before defying the decisive will of all the bishops. When his friend Fr. Cyrillus Hendriks suggested he not go out in public, he responded with a wink, "Stop worrying. Soon they will be locking me up in a real cell. Finally I am going to become an authentic Carmelite."

On January 17 he returned to Nijmegen, but the following day he left for Oldenzaal to make arrangements for an Armenian orphan who was studying at the Carmelite lyceum but needed a family to adopt him. That same afternoon he went to Utrecht to meet with the archbishop, but he was not at home; he then took a train to Amsterdam. When the archbishop returned and learned that Titus had been there, he was very disappointed.

At that very hour two young men, following the brother porter's advice, called at the Nijmegen Carmel to see Professor Brandsma. Once again, they were unsuccessful.

On Monday, January 19, Titus celebrated Mass in the Church of St. Boniface in the heart of Amsterdam. He had no way of knowing it would be his last Mass. From there he traveled to The Hague to consult with the Department of Education about two appointments: one of a director of secondary education, the other of a rector for the seminary in Sittard. After a light meal he returned to Nijmegen. The train was crowded, so he stood the entire distance. At four o'clock he had his first class at the university. To his students he seemed to be in his usual good humor.

At 5:30 he returned to the priory on Doddendaal and went to his room. Minutes later the doorbell rang.[36]

ENDNOTES

1. SU 65, pp. 60, 110, 127, 142, 151.

2. Christianus Bonetto, "Il giornalismo cattolico secondo Titus Brandsma," *Carmelus* 41 (1994), 127.

3. SU 65, p. 127.

4. Joán Hemels, "Titus Brandsma en de Pers," *National Herdenking Zaligverklaring Titus Brandsma*, 10 Nov. 1985, pp. 16-21.

5. Meijer, p. 507.

6. *Stimmen van Nederlanders over de behandeling der Joden in Duitschland*. Professor Brandsma's contribution is titled "De waan der zwakeheid."

7. Domenico Agasso, "Beato Tito Brandsma," *The Voice of the Martyrs* at www.persecution.com.

8. Rees, p. 98; and Vallainc, p. 152.

9. Meijer, p. 39.

10. *Idem*, p. 540.

11. Information provided by Adrianus Staring, O. Carm. Cf. *Enciclopedia Universal Ilustrada*, 920 ff.

12. The Nazi *Hitler-Jugend* in the Netherlands was known as *Nazionale Jeugdstorm*.

13. The labor group or *arbeidsfront* was intended to press all who were capable into the work force.

14. SU 65, p. 275.

15. SU 65, p. 275; INF 68, p. 42.

16. SU 65, pp. 112, 275; INF 68, p. 42.

17. SU 65, p. 276; INF 68, p. 43.

18. Unfortunately, his hopes were never fulfilled. His proposal did receive support from the Apostolate for the Reunion of the Eastern Churches (as recorded in that organization's minutes of its November 27, 1941, meeting). It was also backed by Sophia van Beckel, a woman who was special advisor to the archbishop on Jewish affairs and who was eventually arrested for providing help to Jews. She died in Sachsenhausen-Oranienburg on Christmas day, 1944. Cf. Leopold G. Glueckert, O. Carm. *Titus Brandsma: Friar Against Fascism* (Darien, Illinois: Carmelite Press, n.d.), p. 10.

19. Meijer, p. 545.

20. INF 68, p. 33.

21. SU 65, p. 270.

22. SU 65, p. 275.

23. Facts have been gathered and documented, articles and books have been written by scholars both Jewish and Christian to demonstrate the solemn and public condemnation of Nazism by the Holy See as early as February 1934. Only biased minds refuse to even look at this evidence. The biography of St. Titus Brandsma is one more confirmation that had the Church spoken out any more forcefully, even more innocent Jewish lives would have been lost.

24. SU 65, p. 131.

25. Vallainc, p. 164.

26. SU 65, p. 280.

27. INF 68, p. 84.

28. SU 65, pp. 86, 147.

29. SU 65, p. 284.

30. SU 68, p. 151.
31. SU 65, p. 302; INF 68, p. 52.
32. SU 65, p. 129.
33. SU 65, p. 288.
34. H. W. F. Aukes, "A Priest Sabotaged," *The Sword* 45:1 (April, 1985) 26-27.
35. SU 65, p. 170.
36. SU 65, pp. 296 ff.

Fr. Titus Brandsma with architects of the new monastery in Nijmegen, located in a former Catholic hospital. The increasing number of Carmelite students in Nijmegen made the relocation from a much smalled building necessary. *(Photo courtesy of the Nederlands Carmelitaans Instituut)*

Chapter VIII

Apologia from Prison

Arrest

The doorbell was ringing insistently as the brother porter hurried to respond. The visitors were two well-built, impatient young men. Greeting them hospitably, the porter asked: "How can I help you, gentlemen?"

"We would like to speak with Professor Brandsma," the younger of the two replied in perfect Dutch. I am the student who has been trying to reach him by telephone, but without success. We are in a hurry. Please let him know."

The other stood silently by, without so much as introducing himself.

The brother showed them into one of the parlors and called Fr. Titus Brandsma, who, as was his custom, came down at once. Entering the room, he greeted his guests with his usual friendliness. He suspected they might be the two unknown "students" who had been taking notes in his lectures.

Then the man who had remained silent spat out in German: "My name is Steffen; I am an agent of the State Security Police. By order of the Security Service you are under arrest. You are to come with me on the 7:35 train to Arnhem. First, however, I must search your personal quarters. Please conduct me to them."

"What is the charge?" asked the Carmelite friar calmly. "If it has to do with my relationship with the press, then it would be better for you to permit me to call the Press Department in The Hague before going any further."

"I have ordered you to show me to your rooms, Professor. Now!" the Gestapo agent responded in clipped tones as he prepared officiously to enter into the monastery. In the face of such rudeness the priest remained calm and led them to his room.

The search of his quarters was careful and thorough: books, letters, papers, furniture—all was examined and strewn about on the floor. Whatever they judged useful they put into a large briefcase: letters from the archbishop, from journalists, from family and friends, private documents, personal notes, etc. Two religious working next door in the office of the secondary school were able to hear everything that was said, all in perfect German; they even observed that one of the officers was trying to find the telephone number for the police in Arnhem, but, possibly due to nervousness, was unable to locate it. "Let me find it," Fr. Titus offered.[1]

The two friars went immediately to the prior to let him know what was happening. Fr. Christobal Verhallen, who had already been made aware of the situation by the brother porter, went immediately to Titus' cell. He waited a moment, then knocked.

As he came in Fr. Titus said: "Father Prior, though you will not believe it, these gentlemen are members of the German police and they have just arrested me." The prior wanted more information and asked why this was being done. The policeman responded with bad grace, almost shouting, "This is none of your business. In any case you already know what is happening, so you can leave." He continued his inspection, taking possession of whatever he pleased.

In the midst of the scattered papers and letters, Titus recognized one that dealt with an appointment for Canisius High School; and feeling it needed immediate attention, he tried to give it to the prior for a reply. "Don't touch anything," he was ordered.

The brother porter opened the door to inform Titus that he was wanted at the door; the exasperated official bellowed angrily, "The professor is not at home, do you have that straight?"

The caller was Mr. Bodewes, editor of *De Gelderlander*, who had come to confer with his Ecclesiastical Advisor and censor. In the meantime, Titus had changed, as ordered, from his Carmelite habit into a black suit. As he normally did when setting out on a trip, he put his breviary into his suitcase, along with a few packages of tobacco.

His office, as well as his personal cell, was closed and sealed by a civil notary who had been summoned. With characteristic good humor, Titus informed his escort sardonically: "Gentlemen, if you want to catch that 7:35 train you will have to hurry. Dutch trains are not in the habit of waiting, even for Germans."

Steffen mumbled something but did not respond. With the Carmelite between them they went down the stairs toward the street.

The entire community had gathered at the entrance to the enclosure of the priory, aware that this was to be goodbye. Fr. Titus shook each one's hand with a firm grip, knelt before the prior and asked his permission to depart. At the threshold he turned and, with a slight smile, whispered "*Memento mei*" (pray for me), and disappeared between the two police agents.[2] It was a very cold night.

Prison at Arnhem

It took only a few minutes to arrive at the station in a police car. Once they had boarded, two women recognized the priest's presence in the compartment reserved for the German military; realizing what was happening, they caught Titus' eye and joined their hands as though in prayer. After a fifteen-minute ride to Arnhem station, they went immediately to the city's jail. As Titus was being processed, he remarked artlessly to Steffen, "It is an honor granted very few to be locked up in jail after sixty years of an honorable life."

The police agent responded: "You should not have accepted the archbishop's order." Titus' first question had finally been answered; he was now sure why he had been arrested.[3] "That I consider an honor; I believe I have done nothing wrong," he responded.

He passed that first night as a prisoner without closing an eye. In his cell–furnished only with a straw bed and a board that served as a table–he felt the darkness and the cold of the Dutch winter in a new way.

He prayed constantly, and remembered everyone: the archbishop, his brother Carmelites, the university community, his family. Above all else, he prayed about his own future. Still he had no misgivings; he felt sure that once the situation had been clarified, and especially in consideration of his poor health, he would be sent back to the priory the following day. The eternal optimist, incapable of thinking evil of anyone, once again was mistaken.

Before dawn, his door was opened and, along with his breakfast, he received the order that on that very day he was to be transferred to the prison at Scheveningen, some ninety miles from Arnhem.

Prison at Scheveningen

Scheveningen, a suburb of The Hague, is said to have the most beautiful beach in all of the Netherlands. It also has an immense prison, reserved at that time for political prisoners. It was frequently referred to as "The Orange Hotel," since the majority of prisoners were loyal to the Queen of the Netherlands, of the royal House of Orange. When Fr. Brandsma arrived wearing the insignia–bestowed by the Queen herself–of a Knight of the Dutch Lion in his lapel, he appeared to be one of themselves.

But this prisoner had been imprisoned because of his fidelity to Christ's Church as well as to his country.

Neither dinner nor bed had been prepared. A bit of bread, a jar of water and two blankets for a bed were his portion. Because it was already dark and the lights had been turned off from outside, cell N° 577 was allowed electricity for a few more moments.

From The Hague, the Nazi judge Paul Hardegen had telephoned, "At nine o'clock tomorrow morning, bring Professor Brandsma to me for interrogation."

Early the next morning a fellow prisoner handed Titus a bedsheet. The priest explained that although he had arrived rather late, he would not be needing the sheet since he expected to be returning home later this same day. His benefactor assured him ironically that he had thought the same thing, many months before.

At 8:30 he was taken by car from the prison to Biennenhof where SS Hauptscharführer (Sergeant-Major of the Special Police) Hardegen was awaiting him.

In order to have even a superficial knowledge of the organization known as the Gestapo (a word formed by the initial syllables of the three elements in the word *Geheimnisstaatspolizei*) or the Secret Police, one has to recognize that it was a kind of state within the Nazi state. It controlled whatever it chose. It was made up of the Security Service, whose charge was the protection of the Third Reich, and the Security Police, which was charged with safeguarding public order.

The Security Service, in turn, was made up of various branches: Group IV-B dealt with relations with the Church, and its chief in the Netherlands was Hardegen, a fanatical Nazi who was one of the individuals responsible for the persecution let loose in the Netherlands in 1940-1942. In 1944 he disappeared on the Russian front.

Actually, it was not within Hardegen's mandate to judge Titus. Another group, III-A-3, headed by E. Oscar Vogel, was responsible for relations with the religious press. In a letter to the Security Service, this latter officer complained that Professor Brandsma's case was being handled by Hardegen in Group IV (relations with the Church), but in Vogel's opinion, it was exclusively a matter of the press and therefore under his jurisdiction.

Vogel's letter proves that those in charge of the Security Service understood Fr. Titus' activity to have been of a purely religious nature.[4] Although at first glance this may not seem of any great importance, it does explain why Fr. Titus' case deserves consideration as a defense of his faith. Had it been assigned to Vogel's Department, this might not have been so clear.

Interrogations

On January 21 Titus underwent a long interrogation by Hardegen. Hardegen was not, strictly speaking, a judge. His objective was to gather as much information as possible. Although Titus had never heard of his inquisitor, he would know him well before long. The Nazi officer concealed his hostility with correct, even courteous behavior. An intelligent man, Hardegen did not follow a conventional script; rather he asked questions flowing logically from the responses of the accused.

The interrogation was divided into two parts. In the first, Titus gave his personal data and explained the origin of the conflict between the Catholic press and the Nazi authorities. In his presentation–which included all the details described to date–he spoke of his meetings with the archbishop, with journalists, and with members of the hierarchy; he detailed the Nazis' failure to keep their promises; he explained the pastoral action taken in defense of Christian principles against the demands imposed by National-Socialist policies.

Toward the end of the first part, Titus declared: "The bishops and I were in agreement that, should any Catholic newspaper consent to publish National-Socialist propaganda, it would be committing suicide." And he pointed out the example of the newspaper *Residentiebode*: within a brief period after publishing this kind of propaganda, because it was no longer considered a Catholic publication, its circulation fell from 40,000 to a little more than 3,000.

On hearing this Hardegen asked, "How can the Church suppress newspapers that are following our orders?"

Without hesitation Titus responded:

> The bishops declared that such newspapers were no longer to be considered Catholic, and consequently they advised the faithful to cancel their subscriptions. Since dialogue had proved to be useless, the bishops decided to instruct the faithful in this way.
>
> This action of the Church was taken in opposition to the Decree of December 18, 1941, issued by the Department of Education and Art; it was necessary because the Church had to protect itself against a law that was in contradiction to Catholic principles. It was the archbishop and I who proposed this line of action.
>
> I am always at your disposal for additional inquiries into this matter. I have given you the facts truthfully. I have nothing more to add.

The second phase of the interrogation began as follows:

> Hardegen: "What was the purpose of your visits to the editorial offices of the newspapers?
>
> Brandsma: "I felt it necessary to state explicitly that we could no longer tolerate the current situation, and that the time had come to draw a line based on principle. Moreover, we needed to know the position and the particular difficulties of each Catholic editor. The bishops needed this information in order to take whatever steps might be required."
>
> Hardegen: "By means of these visits you wanted to have exact knowledge of the position of each editor?"
>
> Brandsma: "That was not my primary purpose, since whatever their positions, the position of the Church would not have changed. It was rather my intention to verify that the majority of the editors would stand behind the directives of the Church."
>
> Hardegen: "Those editors who were undecided were to be encouraged and eventually persuaded to accept the principles of the Church?"
>
> Brandsma: "I have to say that this was not my intention, although it was the final result."
>
> Hardegen: "The editors were being pressured to accept the wishes of the bishops?"

Brandsma: "The Church had already stated clearly that editors who published National-Socialist information would be subject to the previously announced sanctions."

"The archbishop's letter had stated this unequivocally. In the course of the interviews several editors mentioned the danger of economic losses. When the Church is defending her rights, however, she puts spiritual aspects in first place, and only then does she consider material losses that may result from them. I can affirm that for the majority of the publishers the spiritual significance of this affair was decisive."

"The Catholic Church is firm in defense of her faith. In every age there have been men and women who have given their lives to defend it. The Dutch bishops are convinced that when the faithful stand together they have enormous political power. Faith provides spiritual strength that enables the faithful in these uncertain times to make the greatest sacrifices, even material ones."

Hardegen: "Aware of the attitude of its faithful, isn't the Catholic Church trying to sabotage the orders issued by the forces of occupation and by the Dutch government, and so compromising the internal peace of the country and hindering the acceptance of National-Socialistic doctrine?"

Brandsma: "The Catholic Church in the Netherlands does obey the orders of the forces of occupation so long as they do not contradict her own sacred principles. When there is a contradiction, then the Church rejects all collaboration and accepts the consequences that result. If this attitude and its logical application disrupts the inner peace of the country, the Church is the first to regret that outcome, but she does not consider herself responsible for it."

"The Church opposes National-Socialism not for political reasons but because of religious doctrine. It is sad that the forces of occupation support the ideals of National-Socialism, because the Dutch people, and especially the clergy, want nothing to do with it. The Church is obliged to support by her example all the faithful, and especially Catholic leaders."

Hardegen: "Before trying to influence the Catholic journalists, why didn't the Archbishop do everything possible to speak with them, as he did afterwards?"

Brandsma: "I have already stated that there was no intention of directly influencing the personnel of the newspapers, but rather of learning what they were thinking. We had the impression that there was a unified front. We hoped to obtain as many concessions as possible from the Commissar of the Reich once he saw that our unity was not a presumption but a reality."

"Once again I want to insist that the Church obeys the orders of the authorities of the occupation only as long as they are not incompatible with her own fundamental principles. When they are, she is necessarily obliged to reject them."

"I have been told that I must remain in prison until this matter is cleared up. I now declare that the position of the Dutch hierarchy is also my own. "This declaration has been read to me. I know German well enough to have totally understood its meaning. I have spoken the whole truth, and I confirm the accuracy of my words with my signature. Titus Brandsma."

This document is also signed by Sergeant-Major Hardegen and Captain Misiewitz, Chief Assistant for Criminal Affairs.

Behind all Hardegen's questions was but a single objective: to obtain an admission of sabotage. All the activities of the Church, with Fr. Titus as intermediary, the Nazis understood as simple sabotage.

Brandsma concluded that Hardegen's calm was due to his total conviction that he was right and that, whatever the accused might say, he was to be condemned.

Titus' responses had involved precise, factual statements, astonishingly frank. While courteous and by no means defiant, he had made no effort to conceal his opinions. At the same time, he did his best not to aggravate the situation.

Following the interview, Hardegen had no illusions; this frail friar was precisely what he had been led to expect, a formidable defender of the Catholic Church.

It was getting dark as the interrogation ended. Hardegen repeated that Titus' incarceration would last until the affair had been resolved, and he ordered Titus to prepare a written explanation of why the Dutch, and especially Dutch Catholics, opposed National-Socialism. Titus readily undertook this assignment. It provided him an opportunity to state the truth fully, even though it was unlikely to do any good. Nor would he find it difficult insofar as he had already spoken with his students on this very topic. By the following evening he had produced eight pages of closely written text. Hardegen, however, forgot to have them brought to him. Consequently, for lack of other paper, Titus recycled the pages when he wrote out the second part of his daily schedule. Months later Hardegen recalled his request and asked to see the text. Titus then had to copy it anew.

Basically, Professor Brandsma's statement made three points:

> 1. The Nazi ideal was foreign to the Dutch. While it might possibly have provided some benefit in Germany–given that country's particularly decadent circumstances–transplanted into the Netherlands, whose citizens did not feel threatened by decadence, it served no useful purpose.
>
> 2. National-Socialism failed to take into account the Netherlands' deeply rooted religiosity. The Dutch people, especially the Catholics, had made great sacrifices in defense of their faith, not excluding even martyrdom. They would continue along this same road if forced to do so.
>
> 3. The Dutch resented Nazi arrogance. The forces of occupation had taken over all the key positions of public life. Most of their bureaucrats were not only totally inept, but they also trampled on the rights and the beliefs of others. The Dutch scoff at their pretensions and are indignant about their disdain for something as sacred to the Dutch as freedom and independence.

Titus ended his presentation with a prayer: "God bless Germany. God bless Holland. God grant that these two peoples once again find themselves united in knowing and loving him. And may they continue to fight for freedom."[5]

Conviction

A few days later the Security Office of the Reich in Berlin published the official accusation against Professor Brandsma: he had obstructed the plans of the victorious German nation for the Netherlands through his influence on the Catholic press. Providentially, all the documentation of the entire process against Titus Brandsma was preserved.[6]

It concludes:

> The arrest of Professor Brandsma was necessary and it took place on January 19, 1942. The following day he was interrogated in this office concerning his activities. As Brandsma himself admits, Archbishop De Jong and he himself are the individuals principally responsible for the sabotage of the uniform orientation we are attempting to provide for the Dutch people through the press.
>
> The directive for all Catholics to cancel their subscriptions to periodicals that obeyed our orders would have a deleterious effect on the

Dutch people The security measures that we Germans have taken with regard to the press have been systematically sabotaged due to the activity of Professor Brandsma, who has no other purpose than to discredit the German government and Dutch National-Socialism. It is my recommendation that this case result in the prolonged preventive arrest (Schutzhaft) of the Professor.[7]

A harsh verdict, with harsh consequences.

Schutzhaft was a tool the Security Police (Gestapo) used at its own discretion. It required no trial, no formal prosecution, no judge. The use of this tool–totally in violation of human rights–resulted in more than eight million people being taken into custody and sent to the concentration–more realistically, extermination–camps. Of the more than 4,000 Catholic priests killed by the Nazis, only 130 were legally convicted in a court of law; all the rest were victims of "preventive arrest."[8]

In spite of his role in Titus' condemnation, Hardegen appeared to respect him. A few months later Hardegen himself told one of Titus' friends: "He was a real man. He was convinced that he was defending Christianity against National-Socialism." In all probability Hardegen did not realize that he could have given Titus no greater praise; his words confirmed that Titus was worthy of the crown of a Christian martyr.

Hardegen's investigation, not unexpectedly, concluded: "He is a dangerous man, and we have no intention, therefore, of allowing him to go free before the end of the war. Prison is the most appropriate place for him."[9]

This tall blond German was simply one more cog in the Nazi machine. His outward show of courtesy was intended to give the accused a false sense of security, and then to enjoy condemning him. This was party policy; Heinrich Himmler expected no less of his agents. The interrogations, the courtesies–even offering the accused coffee and sweets–were nothing more than façades. Such niceties, however, did not last long. The insignificant friar who had dared to stand against power of Nazi Germany would not escape his just punishment.

Any doubt about why Professor Titus Brandsma was arrested is removed by a document entitled *Jahresberich 1942*, published in *Meldungen aus den Niederlanden* and stamped "Secret." Among other things it states: "The Catholic clergy undertook a grand campaign in the press against Dutch National-Socialism, but the prompt action of the Security Police and the arrest of Professor Brandsma put an end to this effort before it was fully born. The Catholic Church had appointed this competent, well-informed Counselor of the Union of Catholic Journalists to lead this resistance. Once he was arrested it was over."

Writings from Prison

When the interrogation came to an end, Hardegen informed the condemned friar that he was to be jailed *sine die* i.e., indefinitely. He then added with a smirk, "The isolation of prison will not be difficult for you; after all, it should not be very different from life in a monastery."

Like a true Carmelite, Titus took those words to heart. He effectively transformed cell Nº 577 into a hermitage, a setting for contemplation, for serenity, for growth, for holiness. As a remembrance of his 53 days in Scheveningen's prison, he left several precious documents: his personal account of his arrest and interrogation; *The Diary of a Prisoner*–which includes "My Cell" and "My Daily Schedule;" the poem "Before a Picture of Jesus in My Cell;" a few letters; a Way of the Cross; and several chapters of his biography of Saint Teresa.

First Impressions

Titus first jotted down his initial impressions of Scheveningen:

> 'After one night in Arnhem you won't have to spend more than one night here.' That was what someone told me on January 20 when I was locked up in cell Nº 577. The next morning, I was to be ready by 8:30 to begin my interrogation in The Hague. I would probably be done by midday and, considering my health, they would probably allow me to return home.
>
> By the afternoon of the 21st, however, I knew that my detention was to be prolonged while additional investigations were made. Mr. Hardegen, whose interrogation had been quite courteous, encouraged me to make the best of my imprisonment, reminding me that, as I was accustomed to conventual life, it would not be too difficult for me. As a matter of fact, he was right. "Presently I am reminded of some verses by Longfellow memorized during my studies in Me-

gen, words that can be applied to my present situation:

> In his chamber all alone,
> Kneeling on a floor of stone,
> Prayed a monk in deep contrition
> For his sins of indecision;
> Prayed for greater self-denial
> In temptation and in trial.

The "trial" may still come, though in prison life there are already a number of things one has to get used to.

> As Mr. Steffen was locking me in my cell at Arnhem, I remarked, jokingly, that it was certainly unusual for a man to be put in jail at sixty years of age. His reply was comforting: 'You should not have accepted the archbishop's commission.' I was finally sure of the real reason for my arrest. I told him I considered it an honor, and that I did not think what I had done was wrong. This I repeated to Mr. Hardegen: that what I did was a sincere attempt to clarify our differences.
>
> What one side considered standing on principle, the other regarded as resistance to the forces of occupation. I totally reject that accusation, and I insist that my only motivation was to communicate, both to the press and to the Commissioner of the Reich, the Catholic principles set forth by the bishops in response to National-Socialist propaganda.
>
> Likewise, it was my duty to inform the Commissioner of the Reich about the bishops' point of view, whether or not it met with the approval of the Catholic publishers and editors, even though I was confident of their support.
>
> On the very first day of my assignment I had requested an appointment with the Commissioner of the Reich; it was only because of Mr. Schlichting's trip to Rome that we were unable to meet before my interviews with the members of the press.
>
> I am well aware that the position of the bishops as well as that of the press is not looked upon favorably by the forces of occupation, and that they consider the commission I accepted from the archbishop to be resistance, insofar as Catholic principles exclude whatever is incompatible with them.
>
> There is a contradiction between these two sets of principles. In defense of Catholic principles, I am prepared to suffer joyfully whatever is required. My vocation to the Church and the priesthood has enriched my life with so much happiness and has filled me with

so much joy that I will accept with good will whatever lies in store for me, no matter how disagreeable it may be. With Job I can say: 'The Lord gave and the Lord has taken away, blessed be the name of the Lord. ... We accept good things from God; and should we not accept evil?'[10]

Evil, what people call evil, I have not found. And although I have no way of knowing with certainty just how all this is going to end, I know perfectly well that I am in the hands of God; 'Who will separate me from the love of God?'[11]

I am reminded of those well-known verses:

> Take each day as it comes,
> The good with gratitude,
> The harsh with thanksgiving.
> It will soon be morning.

With Gezelle I praise 'my old breviary' which, fortunately, they have permitted me to keep; now I can pray the Hours without haste. What I really miss is Communion and Holy Mass, but God is near me, in me and with me. 'In Him we live and move and have our being.'[12]

God is so near, yet so far; God is always here. The famous bookmark that Saint Teresa kept carefully in her breviary, and that I sent to my colleague Professor Brom when he was in prison, now serves me as a consolation and an encouragement: Let nothing disturb you, nothing affright you, all things pass, God alone abides. Patience obtains all things. He who has God wants for nothing. God alone suffices.[13]

From the Prison of the Police of Scheveningen, January 23, 1942. (On the Feast of the Espousals of the B.V. Mary, my Mother. *Sub tutela Matris*–Under my Mother's Protection.)

"My Cell" [14]

> "*Cella continuata dulcescit!*" (The more one lives in his cell, the more pleasant it becomes.)
>
> Professor van Ginneken has fostered the notion that *The Imitation of Christ* is somewhat pessimistic in tone. I disagree, at least as regards what the author writes about the cell, for there he is truly optimistic. Being a naturally optimistic person, I have personally experienced the joy described by Thomas à Kempis with regard to solitary life.
>
> That much is certain; but when one is locked up in a prison cell for the first time, and it is night, and the door is slammed shut and

secured with locks and chains, he feels rather nonplused for a few moments. Even so, the thought of my having been imprisoned at my advanced age caused laughter rather than tears. So, here I am.

According to prison regulations I arrived late, around 7:30 in the evening, when the day's work had been finished and it was time for bed. My arrival had not been expected, so the cell had not been prepared, even though there was little to prepare: a wash basin with water, a towel and a little piece of cloth, whether intended as a wash cloth or as a napkin I have no idea

They told me they would bring me something to eat, and they did give me a small loaf and a cup of skim milk, which were to serve me for breakfast the next morning as well.

On the table there was a jar of water, and on the bedstead a straw mat and two blankets. One has to adapt to everything. Even though the lights had been turned off at 8:00 in the other cells, I was given an additional half-hour to make my bed.

My cell Nº 577 is by no means a hell. On entering there was no sign above the door declaring "Abandon hope all you who enter here." It doesn't even seem ominous.

When the guard pointed out to the soldier on duty that the cell had not been prepared, he replied, "Since it is only for one night, he does not need sheets."

There is nothing more repugnant to me than the scratching of woolen blankets on my face. Since I had no sheets I had to make do; I folded the clean towel over the tops of the blankets. There were two thin straw mats on the bed, one on top of the other. Normally there are two people to a cell, and when this is so, one of the mats goes on the floor. This I know from experience, because in the cell where I was assigned in Arnhem there was no bed. The straw mats and the blankets without sheets made me shudder. So that first night I went to bed with my socks on.

The next morning, they gave me a sheet and a towel. I explained to the young man who gave them to me– also a prisoner, but one allowed to circulate a bit– that I had arrived late the night before, but now would not be needing them because surely I would be sent home today. He responded sympathetically, "I think you should take them. I thought I would be here only three days, but it'll probably be more like three years." What he said made sense so, since he was far more aware of the situation than I, I took the sheet and the towel.

For a pillow I had only a little sack of straw, rather difficult to shape to my head, but since I had not slept the previous night in Arnhem, I wanted to sleep now in order to be as alert as possible during the

One view of Cell 577 in the Scheveningen Prison (The Hague) where Fr. Titus spent 52 days (January 20-March 11, 1942). The cell, measuring 4x1.90m, had "a wash basin with water, a towel and a little piece of cloth, whether intended as a wash cloth or as a napkin I have no idea ... My cell N° 577 is by no means a hell." It was in this cell that Brandsma wrote his *Diary of a Prisoner* which included "My Cell" as well as the beautiful poem "Before Jesus," a Way of the Cross, half of a biography of St. Teresa of Avila, a defense against National Socialism and two letters. *(Photo courtesy of the Nederlands Carmelitaans Instituut)*

next day's interrogations.

I had brought a sweater with me. I wrapped it around the sack of straw, then covered both with the towel. It began to feel like a nice pillow! Things could have been worse.

This is how I make my bed each day. Since I do not want to wear my socks in bed, I place the other towel at the foot of the bed and so it takes the place of a second sheet. It gets very cold at night, so in addition to the two blankets I spread out my woolen overcoat on top of everything. Then the bed is just right, and that is very important in prison since we go to bed at 8:00 each night and do not get up until 7:00 the following day.

It's not that I sleep all that time, but since they turn out the lights at 8:00 P.M. and don't turn them on again until 7:00 in the morning, where else can one be except in bed?

The cell itself isn't bad. It is a long narrow room, approximately thirteen feet long and six-wide (the bed at the far end takes up the entire width), and nearly as high as it is long. The bottom two-thirds of the walls are brick. Around the bed, for the sake of cleanliness, the walls are coated with concrete. The walls are painted yellow up to the height of the door, with white above. Everything is clean. The door, in the middle of the wall opposite the bed, is painted brown, with a small square window in the center through which the food is passed. Above that is an iron peephole, but I have not yet seen it open.

That first night I didn't think there was a window, but in the morning, I could see that there was quite a large one running the length of the cell, but very high; it is divided into three parts, but only the middle one can be opened. So there is plenty of light, and the ventilation is excellent. I can't see anything through the window except sky and occasionally the flight of a gull.

So far, the panes of glass are covered with the artistry of ice crystals during the entire day, except for brief periods when the winter sun melts them. There are some ten feet of heating pipes, but they don't give any heat, and consequently on the coldest days I shiver constantly; still, so far I am surviving.

The floor is made of large, blue-tinted paving tiles, and in front of the door there was a little mat that I place under the table during the day and beside the bed at night.

The table, if that is what it's called, consists of a few boards fixed into the wall; they form a surface about the size of the opened newspaper used to cover them. The name of the newspaper is *Vaterland* (Fatherland); I can read its large letters from anywhere in the cell.

This cold, naked cell needed a little decoration, so I have made myself

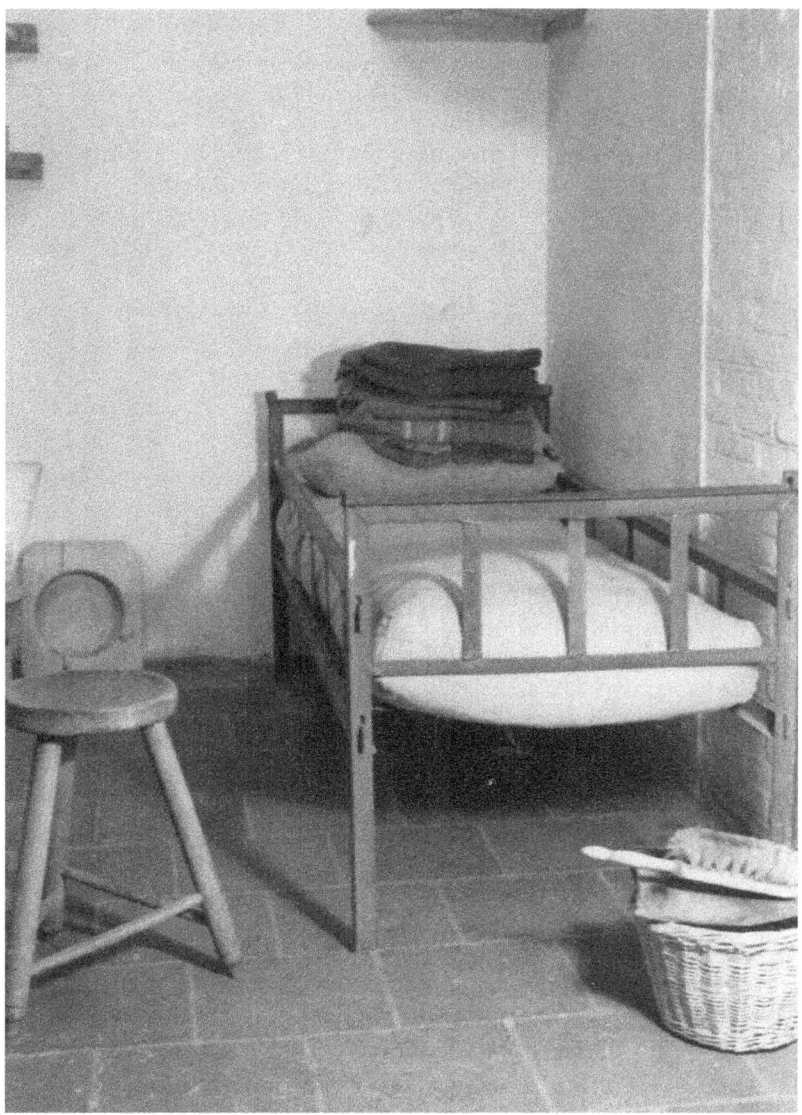

A second view of Cell 577 in the Scheveningen Prison. "For a pillow I had only a little sack of straw ... I had brought a sweater with me. I wrapped it around the sack of straw, then covered both with the towel. It began to feel like a nice pillow! ... I place the other towel at the foot of the bed and so it takes the place of a second sheet. It gets very cold at night, so ... I spread out my woolen overcoat on top of everything. Then the bed is just right ... we go to bed at 8:00 each night and do not get up until 7:00 the following day. It's not that I sleep all that time, but since they turn out the lights at 8:00 P.M. and don't turn them on again until 7:00 in the morning, where else can one be except in bed?" *(Photo courtesy of the Nederlands Carmelitaans Instituut)*

a tiny altar, if you can call it that.

I found a checkerboard with frame in the cell, and since I had no desire to play checkers, I wrapped it in a piece of paper and with a pin—I am not permitted to have a pocket knife or scissors—I made some tiny slits and inserted three holy cards from my breviary in them: "Christ on the Cross" by Fra Angelico in the middle; St. Teresa of Avila with her motto "To suffer or to die" on one side; and on the other St. John of the Cross with his motto "Lord, to suffer and be despised for You."

I also found two pins. I used one to attach a piece of paper beneath the holy cards, and on it I wrote out, in Spanish, the famous "Bookmark" of St. Teresa, Nada te turbe, etc. In the middle I wrote the words "God is so near, yet so far, God is always here." And finally, my own motto: "Take each day as it comes," etc.

"There was no holy card of the Virgin Mary in my breviary, yet her image is obligatory in the cell of every Carmelite; I had to find a solution for this. The volume of the breviary I have with me has a beautiful picture of Our Lady of Mount Carmel by Frein von Oer; since I didn't want to tear it out, I simply opened the breviary on a little corner shelf above my bed to the left. When I am sitting at the table I only have to glance up in order to see her, and when I am in bed my glance falls directly on the Virgin with the star, "The Hope of All Carmelites."

There are no chairs, so a stool is all I have to sit on. When I feel the need of some support for my back— doing nothing is more tiring than toiling— I place the stool between the table and the wall and it serves as a comfortable easy chair.

There is not much more to be said about the furnishings of the cell. There are a broom and a dustpan; a small pail and a floor cloth; a basket for trash; a portable latrine that closes hermetically and which is emptied each day; a blue stone jar with water; a zinc soap-dish, and a hanger with three pegs. The electric light, as I have said, is turned on and off from the outside.

Beata solitudo (Blessed solitude). I feel quite at home in this cell. So far, I have not felt at all bored, indeed quite the contrary. I am alone, it is true, but the Lord is closer to me than ever before. I have an urge to shout aloud for joy because the Lord has willed that I discover Him in His fullness, with no need to be among others and no others able to come to me. He is my only refuge. I am happy. I would be content to stay here always, if that were His will. Rarely have I experienced such joy.

Scheveningen, January 27, 1942; T. B.[15]

"My Daily Schedule"

Nunc lege, nunc ora, nunc cum fervore labora: Sic fiet hora brevis et labor ipse levis. (Now read, now pray, now labor zealously. Thus time passes quickly and work itself more easily.)

> During those first days it was impossible to establish any kind of schedule, but now that I have been here for a week and am getting acquainted with the routine, I have tried to put a little order into my day.
>
> It is not easy to give precise times because here in prison the various daily activities required of prisoners are not always by the clock. In fact it is not easy to find out what the exact time really is.
>
> When I first got here they took my watch. Later they returned it so that I could more easily write my response to the interrogations. But when I got it back, it had stopped, so I had to guess at the time.
>
> Here one never hears the striking of a clock; things done at an exact time in other places here have no fixed order. But my watch is running well; at least I have my own time, independent of Greenwich, Amsterdam, or Berlin.
>
> Sometime between 6:30 and 7:00 we hear the first sounds of the day. That is when the guards awaken the young prisoners on housekeeping detail. Around 6:45 a bell is rung, very softly; then little by little the noise increases and suddenly the bolts are unlocked and the lights go on. This is my signal to get up. I have been in bed since eight o'clock the previous evening!
>
> I first make the Sign of the Cross and then greet the Virgin of Carmel on her corner shelf. I put on my socks and slippers. I kneel and pray three Hail Marys and some other short prayer.
>
> I strip my bed and shake out the sheets and blankets, then fold them carefully. I take the covers off the little sack of straw that serves as my pillow, and, as soon as the door opens, place my urinal there.
>
> Then, still in pajamas–which fortunately I brought with me the day of my arrest–I kneel down on the blankets folded on top of the mat to celebrate my "Mass," to receive Communion, spiritually of course, and to make my thanksgiving. My celebration is much shorter and quite different from what is done at the priory! Still, it is a good beginning to the day. At the priory there is first meditation and then Mass; but here I prefer to have the Mass first, even though I am still in my pajamas.
>
> Finally, the door is opened and they give me my container of water. I wish a "Good day" to the one who brings it, and begin to wash myself. I would like to shave, but this luxury is permitted only on

Wednesdays and Saturdays when the door is opened for ten minutes and we are given a safety razor, soap, and brush. If the razor is not sharp we can ask for another. But, no matter what, we have to hurry.

Around 7:30 they bring coffee. Everyone gets a nice zinc cup with a handle, a plate, and a spoon. At night the cup and the plate are removed and then returned in the morning along with the water.

I break up the bread in the plate and pour coffee on it, and while the bread is softening, I get dressed. So, about 8 o'clock, except for the beard, I am once again a respectable gentleman dressed in black. I sit down on the stool, pray the Angelus and an Our Father and a Hail Mary as is done at the priory; I then have breakfast, much as I did thirty-five years ago in our Bavarian houses where they also break up their bread in coffee and eat it with a spoon. I clean the plate and the spoon, and then begin my morning walk as I smoke my pipe, all the while reviewing all that happened the previous day and thinking about what will happen in the one just beginning.

I repeat the *Memento* of the Mass, remembering all those who are praying for me and trying to be present with each of them through the Communion of Saints.

My walk is not long– three paces in one direction, three paces back. It begins at 8:30 and ends at 9:00 when my pipe goes out. Then I pray matins, lauds and prime, usually still walking. If I get tired going back and forth, I sit on the stool, my back against the wall, and pray peacefully.

I finish about 9:30 when the lights are turned off. Since it is still somewhat dark, I may have to wait a bit until there is more daylight. On Sundays they leave the lights on until 10:00.

At 9:30 I begin my morning meditation, using Cyriel Verschaeve's book *Jezus*, which they allowed me to keep, along with the *Life of Saint Teresa* translated by Kwakman. They had taken these away from me at first, but then they told me they would be returned, and they were.

At 10:00 I write a little. On the first days they ordered me to respond in writing to the question: "Why do the Dutch people, especially Catholics, oppose National-Socialism?" I gave my answer in eight pages.

Presently I am writing my impressions of life in this prison, and also the *Life of Saint Teresa* for the *Spectrum*, something I had promised to do. When I begin to write, I light a cigarette.

At 11:30 I recite Terce, Sext and None, walking up and down. Some mornings my time for writing is interrupted by exercise, which they oblige us to do every day either in the morning or after dinner.

This is amusing. They bring us out of our cells to loud shouts and we stand in the corridor, each with his numbered portable latrine, until everyone is present. Then, leaving our latrines at the end of the corridor, we pass through several more corridors to reach the outdoors. Behind the prison there is a long, narrow space enclosed by a high wall. We form a large circle around the person in charge of the exercise; sometimes he has us walk, sometimes run; then we have to pick up our legs and do calisthenics.

I am not fond of exercising, but I try to do it as best I can. There is one small group that does not participate and simply walks back and forth a little distance away, and there is another that simply sits with their crutches at their sides. But I run and jump with the others. It doesn't last long, ten minutes at most, only five if it is snowing. It is cold outside, and this helps refresh me a bit.

When the other prisoners first saw me–naturally the sight of a clergyman in black with long white hair and the insignia of a Knight of Orange-Nassau in his lapel drew their attention–they greeted me warmly; but here we are all in the same boat and one gets used to just about anything. I am not the first clergyman to be a guest here.

After the exercise we return to our corridor and pick up our cleaned latrines. The doors open and, as soon as we enter, they close. The evils we all share then seem less harsh. To judge by most faces, the prisoners seem resigned to their lot.

Around noon, sometimes earlier, they bring us a covered cylindrical container with our food. On Thursdays there is a kind of thick vegetable soup; Tuesdays bean soup; Fridays a mixture of potatoes, onions and fish. Sometimes we have potatoes with cauliflower and cabbage, or their famous sauerkraut. There has been no meat, not even in pea soup; still everything has been well prepared, even tasty.

The amount of food served is ample, and I usually eat only about a third. Last Friday, if I am not mistaken, they gave us a little container of marmalade, Zwaardenmakers brand, and a slice of butter; I believe this is intended to last us all week, to spread on our bread; however I prefer to put a little of the butter in my soup or pottage and to eat the marmalade like fruit. That's the way I like it.

After eating, I clean my dishes, pray the Angelus, and then kneel down to make my adoration of the Blessed Sacrament, spiritually united with my confreres back at the priory. The *Adoro Te, devote* has become my favorite prayer; frequently I sing it softly and this helps me to make a spiritual Communion.

Afterwards I smoke a pipe and walk or do some other little thing. Yesterday, for example, I rearranged my little altar, and today I filed my nails. Since I have no scissors, I rub them along the cement of the floor or walls. Then I rest a bit, doing nothing at all; but I do not nap because that would keep me from sleeping during the long night.

At two o'clock I pray vespers, compline, and the rosary. This latter I have to do by counting with my fingers because, when I was arrested, in the rush I unfortunately forgot to take it from the pocket of my habit. I can't imagine how I could have done that. But what can I say? The Lord permitted it so I would appreciate its value all the more. After prayer I read the *Life of Saint Teresa*.

During the first days my reading was of a different kind. On Thursday, on returning to my cell after being weighed, I met up with the librarian and his push-cart library. He had left me two books on my table: *The Knock at the Door*[16] by Ina Buodier-Baller, and *De nood der Bariseeles* by Maurits Sabbe. He asked whether I would find those books interesting, and I replied that, frankly, I was not a fan of novels. He then looked about his cart and gave me the third volume of a manual on science, art, and religion, and *The History of Holland* by Dr. H. E. van Gelder. These were more to my liking, so I took them.

I told him I had been given permission to keep two of my own books, the *Jezus* by Verschaeve and the new translation of the biography of Saint Teresa by Kwakman, but that they had never been returned to me. He made note of it and told me that he might find me a life of Saint Teresa because he had many biographies of saints.

He took back the two novels since I am not permitted to have more than two books at a time, and then left. So those first several days I read about art, especially medieval art, and about mathematics, mechanics, astronomy, etc.

Actually, I rather enjoyed those two books; I had read them before, but now I could return to them without haste. Still, what made me really happy was the return of my own two books. This is the kind of reading I find most satisfying in my present circumstances.

I read until four o'clock, lighting my pipe from time to time. At four I kneel to meditate on the life of Jesus and on my own.

At 4:30 they bring bread, some of it for supper, the rest for breakfast the following morning. Until Thursday I had the regular bread, a loaf marked into four parts; on Thursday, however, the doctor visited me in the morning and I told him that I had a stomach problem, that on four different occasions I had suffered severe hemorrhages, and that presently I had a bladder infection caused by *coli bacilli*. I also told him of the medications prescribed by Drs. Woltering, Enneking, Borst and B. van Capelle. Finally, I made him aware that, due to my abnormally low weight and chronic illness, the Office for Food Rationing in Nijmegen had authorized extra food for me.

He told me he would do an analysis of my urine and have me weighed. And he promised to do what he could for me. I weighed 123 pounds, less four for my clothes.

One consequence of the doctor's visit was that they began to bring me bread made with milk and spread with butter. In the evening, instead of the cup of skim milk, they brought me a half-cup of whole milk. The next day they asked for a sample of my urine for analysis, but that's the last I heard of the matter. Basically, my medical consultation resulted in two signs on my door: "Milk" and "White Bread."

This is more appearance than reality. But I am doing all right. As soon as the bread comes, I put it in the milk and eat it; they only give us a very brief time to eat, and then right away we have to put the plate and spoon at the door. By 5:00, or 5:15 at the latest, we must be finished. After that there is no more noise, and nothing goes out or comes into the cell.

After supper I pray the *Angelus* and, spiritually united with my Carmelite brothers at the priory, make my adoration of the Blessed Sacrament; then I light a cigarette and begin my evening walk. Three paces in one direction, three paces back, just as in the morning. From six o'clock until eight I write. I then prepare my bed and recite compline. After that it makes no difference when they turn off the lights. I keep on praying for a while, then get under the blankets until morning.

Scheveningen, January 28, 1942. T. B.

To the above description I want to make a few additions. I should not have said that we are given no meat, because on Wednesdays and Thursdays they do add ground meat to the soup or pottage. Not a lot, but it is meat.

On January 29, Feast of Saint Francis de Sales, patron of journalists, I had just finished cleaning and lighting my pipe for my morning walk when a German soldier came in and told me that I had to give him the tobacco, the cigarettes and the pipe, because I had now been forbidden to smoke.

Fortunately, I recalled the mild-mannered St. Francis de Sales and so made no discourteous reply. I emptied the pipe and gave him what he asked.

The poor guard, totally sympathetic, assured me that he was not the one who had given the order, something I was very well aware of. As a consolation, he told me I could keep the books and the paper I had brought with me. Without a doubt those things were more important to me than the pipe and cigarettes. I crossed out the word "smoke" from my schedule and carried on with the day. I should have expected this, but I truly appreciated having been permitted to smoke during those first days which were so difficult for me.

Scheveningen, January 31, T.B.[17]

Such was the daily prison routine. For the first time in his life Titus had time for everything: measuring his cell, counting the number of bricks, and–lacking scissors–even for filing his nails on cement.

For other prisoners–lacking the spiritual depth of a Titus Brandsma– life was not so agreeable. Only a few weeks after he had been granted the special menu for the sick, an SS officer shouted, "This is not a sanitarium!" The privilege was withdrawn. A fellow-prisoner, Colonel A. S. Fogtelo– not a Catholic– recalling life in the prison and the impression Fr. Titus had made on him, stated:

> The atmosphere of the place was imbued with an aura of sadness. No one was optimistic; all of us moved about with long faces. Once I was assigned to accompany the barber from cell to cell; when I opened the door of one cell, I was astonished to see its occupant rising to greet us with a radiant smile illuminating his entire face.
>
> 'Who the devil is the man in cell Nº 577?' I thought to myself.
>
> I was only able to exchange a word with him, but whenever I saw him, he always appeared to be in good humor: his glance cordial, his personality kindly, his attitude joyful. I can't tell you how deeply this impressed me. In such circumstances, a person who behaves in this way has to possess an extraordinary depth of spirit.
>
> Brandsma was extremely kind and agreeable. His way of accepting people–doubtless due to his priestly formation and his interior life–and his cordial, understanding smile, instilled a measure of self-respect into us who were on the brink of despair. Of all the prisoners I have known, he made the deepest impression. What he did was supernatural. Everyone liked him, even those of us who were not Catholic."[18]

Poetry, Letters

Three weeks after entering prison, Titus expressed his inner peace in a poem he composed before the picture of *Christ Crucified* by Fra Angelico which was the focal point of his "altar." Titus called his poem simply *Aan Jezus*. One of his fellow prisoners obtained a copy of this small piece, and someone else was able to smuggle it outside the prison. From there it went from hand to hand, and soon became famous throughout the Netherlands.[19] There are several translations of this poem into English, each with its own strengths and own weaknesses, as is the case with most translations, especially poetry. The following, by the late Father Gervase Toelle, O. Carm., seems to capture both the meaning and the feeling of the author: a joyful acceptance of suffering uniting him with Christ Jesus.[20]

Before a Picture of Jesus in My Cell

A new awareness of Thy love
Encompasses my heart:
Sweet Jesus, I in Thee and Thou
In me shall never part.

No grief shall fall my way but I
Shall see Thy grief-filled eyes;
The lonely way that Thou once walked
Has made me sorrow-wise.

All trouble is a white-lit joy
That lights my darkest day;
Thy love has turned to brightest light
This night-like way.

If I have Thee alone,
The hours will bless
With still, cold hands of love
My utter loneliness.

Stay with me, Jesus, only stay;
I shall not fear–
If, reaching out my hand,
I feel Thee near.

During the period when Titus was undergoing the long interrogations, writing his prison diary, working on his biography of St. Teresa, composing *Aan Jezus* and the *Way of the Cross*, his confreres and his family had been kept in uncertainty even of his whereabouts. They had had no news of him since the day of his arrest.

The prior had obtained permission for the Brandsma family to write him in care of the Swedish Embassy, or through the General Staff in The Hague, but there was no reply. Not long afterwards a rumor arose that a prisoner who had been released from Scheveningen had seen Professor Brandsma. The prior went to speak with him immediately, and so obtained the first news of their missing confrere.

It was February 18 before the first of the very few letters he was permitted to write from prison was received. It had been written on February 12 and addressed to his provincial, his prior, and community, his brother Hendrik and his sisters, his brother-in-law, nieces, and nephews, and all his friends.

Filled with emotion, the prior read it to the community and then sent copies to everyone to whom it had been addressed. The prior himself took it to the archbishop. After reading it the prelate confessed, "I feel responsible for this entire affair."

Only a few days earlier the archbishop had written to the prior:

> I too regret so very much that Professor Brandsma has been imprisoned. This is due to his actions on behalf of the Catholic press, actions undertaken in the service of the hierarchy. Consequently, he is a victim of his zeal for a good cause, and that is a great consolation. I only hope that his health will hold up. We shall pray for his quick release."[21]

Titus wrote that he felt quite at home in prison. True, he did not have a church, he was unable to offer Mass or receive Holy Communion. He did not see another priest. The world was far away, but he had never before felt so close to God and consequently he was at peace, happy, joyful.

He did make a few requests: he asked for a copy of *The Imitation of Christ*, the next volume of his breviary, a small Carmelite missal, a rosary, some of his clothes, ruled writing tablets and a few other books.[22] He expressed concern lest Archbishop De Jong worry about him or blame himself for his situation. "I suffer joyfully, and I am well and happy."

He included greetings for his family along with best wishes for their Name Days; he expressed concern about his classes, about the examinations, and about other academic matters concerning some of his students. Throughout this letter, even though himself in prison, Titus wanted, perhaps needed, to maintain his spiritual and intellectual connectedness with the outside world. Given his own difficulties, his concern for others is edifying.[23]

Three weeks later, on March 5, he was permitted a second letter, addressed to the same people as the first. Among other things, he wrote:

> Again my greetings from cell 577 where I have been for more than six weeks. I am growing accustomed to it. I am getting along and my health is holding up. On the 21st I had a bit of a temperature along with some pain and I was afraid the bladder and kidney inflammation was returning as it did in December 1939. I asked to see a doctor, but when he showed up the next day, I was already much better. Now I am fine. Mentally I am not suffering: I feel no need for either tears or sighs. Indeed, I even sing a bit, softly of course.[24] The worst thing is the nights: I cannot sleep so many hours and so I lie awake much of the time.

He wrote about his daily schedule, especially about how he is trying to maintain his ties to conventual life. The letter is filled with his own spiritual peace. He expresses his thanks to the prior for having answered his previous letter, though he has not received the items he had requested.[25] He inquires about several of his confreres and colleagues as well as about his family and friends. And he asks for their prayers, with a promise to remember them in his own.[26]

The Biography of Saint Teresa

Around January 27 he had begun working on the biography of Saint Teresa, a project he had promised to *Spectrum* but had never found time to do. When he was sent to prison, he had promised himself, "Now I will finish that *Life* of St. Teresa." He expected to have considerable time on his hands.

At first he used the paper the authorities had permitted him to keep, but when that was gone and they would not provide him with more, he was forced to make do by writing in the blank spaces and between the lines on the pages of *Jezus* by Cyriel Verschaeve. In his letter of March 5, he mentioned that he had written a first draft for six of the twelve chapters he had planned. Although there were days when he was unable to write, in all he wrote 336 pages of very compressed script.

Scheveningen prison was hardly the most ideal place to undertake such a work. The only reference work he had available to him was

Kwakman's translation of *Doctora Mistica* (The Mystical Doctor); thus, he had to rely heavily on his own extensive knowledge of Teresa's history and spirituality. It is not surprising that, given the difficulties of prison life, his literary style grew less and less polished as time went on. Toward the end he was finding it extremely difficult to express himself.[27]

Titus also used his captivity to write on other themes reflecting the Lenten season, e.g., he composed a *Way of the Cross* for the chapel in Dokkum, the site where St. Boniface had been martyred and which he himself had restored. One author has observed: "It is curious that the fourteenth station is missing ... perhaps he wrote it in a different way."[28]

Around that chapel in Dokkum now stand the Stations of the Cross. The twelfth station, dedicated to St. Titus Brandsma, bears the text: "It is an unfathomable mystery, Lord, why you desired to die for us, why you wanted to enter the kingdom of death as though your entire existence had been a failure and an apparent victory for your enemies."

Farewell to Scheveningen

As the extremely cold winter was coming to an end, all of Europe was experiencing apocalyptic terror.

Early on Thursday, March 12, a police officer entered Titus' cell to announce: "In the name of the Supreme Commander of the Security Police I inform you that you are to follow me. You are leaving for the camp in Amersfoort. Transport is waiting."

He had scarcely time to pick up his books, his pen and papers, his pajamas ... Amersfoort! He was already nostalgic as he abandoned his cell-become-hermitage, a place where he had passed hours of intensely spiritual experience. He had barely grabbed his things when a soldier slammed the door behind him.

In the central yard he found at least a hundred prisoners in formation; on command they climbed into canvas covered trucks for the trip to the concentration camp at Amersfoort, in the interior of the Netherlands. The vehicles formed a caravan under the guard of the SS Police. In Titus' van there was soon a heavy cloud of tobacco smoke as the prisoners smoked nervously, down to the very butts of their cigarettes. A friendly student offered him a little package of sugar-candy; at first, he declined, but when the young man insisted he finally accepted. This was the first of many pleasant moments he shared with the youth, named Reef. Taking advantage of the unexpected release from their cells and of the opportunity of companionship, they began to talk to one another, asking, "Does anyone know anything about the camp at Amersfoort?" "How long are we to be kept there?"

One of the prisoners being transported, van Mierlo, recounts: "I was in the same truck as Fr. Gilis, a Redemptorist from s'-Hertogenbosch; Fr. Titus was there as well. We were sitting next to each other. At one point I asked Fr. Gilis if he could hear my confession, for I had been arrested without warning on December 12, 1941. In spite of my repeated requests to make my confession while in Scheveningen, I was never able to do so, and I was filled with very dark visions about what was to happen to us.

"Fr. Gilis thought he could not do this because he lacked faculties for this area. That caused a discussion and someone asked Fr. Titus' opinion. He said that we were all in an emergency situation and that consequently our duty was to help one another. Then he told Fr. Gilis, 'You need have no concern and can hear his confession without scruple.'"

"I was very grateful for those words, and Fr. Titus and I became close friends. That same day, in the camp at Amersfoort, I made a general confession with Fr. Gilis."[29]

ENDNOTES

1. SU 65, p. 106.
2. SU 65, p. 99.
3. SU 65, p. 320.
4. SU 79, pp. 485 ff.
5. SU 79, pp. 464-476.
6. This material is evidence of utmost importance not only as it relates to the life of Father Titus, but also as proof of the anti-religious history of Nazism. The documentation was found under the title "Press" and bears the Identification N° Z-B-78. It includes Hardegen's account of the process and his recommendation for Titus' prolonged detention.
7. SU 79, p. 317.
8. *Explanationes de fama martryrii et martirio, attentis voto Rev.mi Promotoris Generalis Fidei necnon relatione et votis peculiaris Congressus diei 25 maii a. 1971* (Romae, 1973), p. 83.

9. SU 65, p. 155.

10. Job 1:21 and 2:10.

11. Cf Rom 8:35.

12. Acts 17:28.

13. See Chapter VI, note 15.

14. *Mijn Cell en Dagorde van een Gevengene* (My cell and the Diary of a Prisoner.) Remembrances of Fr. Titus Brandsma, written in his cell at the prison in Scheveningen, between January 21 and 31, 1942, with a brief introduction by Fr. Brocardus Meijer, O. Carm. SU 79, pp. 498-500.

15. SU 79, pp. 501-504.

16. *De klop op de deur.*

17. SU 79, pp. 504-509.

18. SU 79, p. 258.

19. Rees, p. 121.

20. The Dutch original in Fr Titus' hand was written February 12-13, 1942 and bears the title *Aan Jezus* (Before Jesus); it was included among the belongings returned to his family after his death. Written in couplets in six stanzas of four lines, each with eight syllables and perfect rhyme, the poem is appreciated more for its content than for its form. The version presented here is taken from *Proper of the Liturgy of the Hours of the Order of the Brothers of the Blessed Virgin Mary of Mount Carmel and of the Order of Discalced Carmelites* (Rome: Institutum Carmelitanum, 1993), p. 455-456. A musical setting has been composed by Fr. James Boyce, O. Carm., and can be found in *The Beatification of Father Titus Brandsma*, Carmelite (1881-1942): Martyr in Dachau. (Rome: Institutum Carmelitanum, 1986), pp. 154-160. Two other English translations appear in *Appendix V* of this volume.

21. SU 79, pp. 134 and 232.

22. Among the books he requested was *Sainte Thérèse écrivain* by A. Hoornaert (Brugge: Desclée).

23. SU 65, p. 251.

24. Here Fr. Titus' sense of humor is displayed, for he is referring to the occasions when he had been corrected by his prior for his overly enthusiastic participation in the Liturgy of the Hours.

25. All those items had been sent but not delivered.

26. SU 65, p. 515.

27. This popular life of St. Teresa was completed by Fr. Brocardus Meijer and published in 1946. Three-fourths of the work had been written by Titus Brandsma. Translator's note.

28. Fernando Millán Romeral, O. Carm., "Campo de concentración de Dachau." *Escapulario del Carmen* 93 (June 1996), 212.

29. SU 79, p. 278.

Chapter IX

An Exceptional Prisoner

The Camp at Amersfoort

At nine o'clock in the morning the convoy pulled into the central square of the concentration camp at Amersfoort. Guards bellowed orders: "Out quickly! Form a line and prepare for inspection!"

There the bedraggled group stood, from nine in the morning until one o'clock that afternoon, buffeted unmercifully by a frigid north wind, their feet covered with a heavy blanket of snow. All prisoners began their stay in Amersfoort standing in formation for hours, sometimes as many as eighteen. This was a practice favored by the Nazis to break the spirit of new arrivals. And it worked. How better impress on these unfortunates that they were worthless, useless dregs of humanity. When their masters finally deigned to remember they existed, it would be only to issue some new command.

On the day of Titus' arrival, the order came at one o'clock: strip, and leave all personal effects aside. Totally naked in the frigid winter air, the prisoners were formed into groups of ten and then continued to wait. Finally, they were ordered to put on the camp's "uniform," rag-tag surplus remnants from the old Dutch army: pants and military jacket, worn years before by youthful, in shape soldiers; the clothing literally swallowed up Titus' slight form. The ensemble was completed by an overcoat, which would be taken away on March 21, the first day of spring, even though in the Netherlands it would still be quite cold, and in 1942 very rainy as well. The prisoners would spend entire days with their clothes and shoes soaked: camp regulations must be followed.

Along with the uniform, each prisoner was given a number–Titus was issued Nº 58–and a colored triangle to be sewn onto the jacket pocket. As a political prisoner, Titus was assigned a red one.

Amersfoort was a camp for transients; from there prisoners were sent to other camps. Officially it was named the *Politzeiliches Durchgangslager Amersfoort,* abbreviated P.D.A. It was a place of forced labor, "a hell on earth, directed by a pack of animals," as Colonel Fogtelo later described it.

During Titus Brandsma's time there the camp population consisted of some 900 prisoners, constantly coming and going. There were several long, narrow barracks, each with four rooms or *Stube.* The prisoners slept on bunks, three deep, each with a straw mat and two blankets whose rips were equaled only by their filth. There were neither sheets nor pillows.

In the center of each *Stube* was a stove. Fed with pine branches it gave off enormous amounts of smoke but very little heat, this in a region where the temperature frequently fell well below zero.[1] Occasionally some of the prisoners were brave enough to steal a few pieces of coal from the guards' well-furnished quarters.

Titus was assigned to the first room of the second barracks.

On the right side of the camp there was another barracks; this building, except for a few rooms reserved for the doctor, served as the camp infirmary and for showers. On the opposite side was a building used as a kitchen; behind that yet another barracks reserved for prisoners suffering from dysentery.

That first afternoon was spent getting acquainted with camp rules and with its SS (*Schutzstaffel*) officers, beginning with Camp Commandant Heinrich and his Chief of Staff Hans Stöver, whom the prisoners called "the Beast"[2] and whose reputation for brutality was unsurpassed. The guards communicated in a single language: insults and hard blows. Violence was their supreme law. Severe penalties were meted out for the most insignificant infractions of camp regulations. Although the staff thought of themselves as members of a superior race, their attitude toward human rights and values demonstrated them to belong to a class that embraced one of the most depraved ideologies of modern times.

Gradually the prisoners got to know one another. They had come from various prisons and represented a broad spectrum of social classes and professions: Protestant ministers, Catholic priests, university professors, journalists, businessmen, laborers, lawyers, students, common criminals, communists, gypsies, homosexuals.

Portrait drawing of Fr. Titus, prisoner at the Amersfoort Camp (The Netherlands) from March 12 - April 28, 1942. The artist, John Dons, captures the complete sadness of a concentration camp: shaved head, baggy military uniform, the fleshy face and hands, the number 58, etc. John Dons saw inside: in the mouth and the eyes of Fr. Titus he found a willing acceptance of pain and a profound interior peace. In very few photographs the innate goodness of Fr. Titus appeared as it does here. *(Photo courtesy of the Nederlands Carmelitaans Instituut)*

They were divided into five categories: 1) political prisoners, with red triangles; 2) hostages, blue; 3) Jews, yellow; 4) "exegetes"– a branch of Jehovah's Witnesses who, Bible in hand, had prophesied Hitler's immanent fall– brown; 5) officers of the Dutch Army, green.

Titus soon became a close friend with a Protestant minister and with the rector, also Protestant, of a school in Amsterdam, with whom he prayed or read the Bible from time to time.

Around six o'clock that first evening they were marched back to the central parade ground where their heads were shaved; immediately afterwards the prisoners, nearly all close to sixty years of age, began their first close-order drill instruction. This activity provided the officers an outlet for their sadism and a means for humiliating others. It was a realistic expression of the camp's values: forcing these prisoners– intellectuals, clergy, and political dissidents– to recognize that they were totally useless, incapable of learning even the most basic drill instruction. Drill over, the prisoners were marched back to their barracks where they were given supper: a chunk of bread that was to serve for both supper and breakfast the next day. Titus was sitting at a bench quietly breaking up his bread when he heard a voice at his side: "How are you, Professor Brandsma?"

"Well, well," he responded without recognizing who was speaking to him. Turning, he saw it was Fr. J. Aalders, the pastor of a church in Enschede for whom he had preached. These old friends chatted, inquiring what had brought each of them to this place. Then Aalders, familiar with the ways of the camp, warned Titus: "Hide your bread well; here we have thieves who steal like magpies."

At that very moment the supervisor of the *Stube* happened to be walking by. Overhearing them he screamed angrily: "Who steals like a magpie here? Get out of here, you piece of filth. You don't belong in this room. Get out, or I'll kick you out!"

Titus, ever the peacemaker, kept repeating, "Easy, my friend; please, be calm. There is no reason for you to be offended." To no avail. The guard grew more and more angry, so the two friends hurried outside.

After several days spent shoveling heavy, wet snow, each prisoner was assigned to a regular work detail. Titus was put with the woodcutters. This group, using hatchets, mattocks and pickaxes, marched to the woods surrounding the camp. The workday lasted as long as there was light, with an hour break at midday. The work was extremely strenuous and ever under the watchful eyes and the hard blows of the guards. Titus' hands trembled from exhaustion.

After a few days a guard shouted, "Get out of here; you are only fit to do the work of the useless." Thus, Titus was reassigned, this time to the potato detail. The hours were the same, but at least he was able to sit on a stool. Shivering from the cold, this crew peeled mounds and mounds of potatoes. Titus reflected, "They may think me useless, but what I am doing now with my hands benefits my companions, while with my mind I am with God."[3]

Cold, hunger, exhaustion: these were the specters of the camp. Some days the prisoners were given no food at all. It was only during the last week of their stay at Amersfoort that they received daily a bit of mashed vegetables, a little margarine, a ration of coffee. The only advantage to the latter was that it was hot; some of the sick, hoping to give it some flavor, even put salt in it. Otherwise the daily ration consisted only of a chunk of bread, a dish of cabbage or carrot soup, and that cup of "dirty water" called coffee. Thus their daily allotment provided only one-fourth of the calories they needed; this for men obliged to work from sun-up to sun-down in freezing weather. Everyone lost weight, as became very obvious when they were obliged to take common showers with cold water. More than a few prisoners died of hunger.[4]

Th. van Mierlo, a fellow prisoner, reported: "With total simplicity Fr. Titus shared everything with his fellow prisoners. The food was inadequate and each of the prisoners in turn was permitted to scrape the kettles used to bring the food from the kitchen. Titus too had his turn; he took off his jacket, rolled up his sleeves, and scraped up everything that remained with his fingers. Like everyone else, he cleaned his pan with his fingers. He was extraordinarily calm while eating or drinking, and he always shared something of the little he had with others, as I myself can bear witness."[5]

Another witness, J. van de Mortel, added: "I never saw him downing his food greedily, even though he suffered from the same hunger as the rest of us. Anyone who has ever experienced true hunger will understand what I am trying to say. But as far as I was aware, Titus did not give food to others since what we received was an absolute minimum, and it was not possible to give it away without doing harm to oneself."

Everything in the camp was programmed to drain the patience and sap the spirit of the prisoners. Some days they were summoned to the parade ground for inspection, then left standing in formation, without explanation, for four or more hours in frigid temperatures. These are things Titus did not mention in either of the two letters he was permitted to write from Amersfoort.

The first is dated March 16, 1942. In it he wrote that the difference between life in the prison and that in the camp was quite significant, as they might guess. In Amersfoort, however, he was finding more companionship and fresh air; he was enjoying contacts with people he knew. He wanted no one to worry about his situation, as it was good enough. He gave instructions about how to write him. He expressed his joy at the prayers being offered, but also his concern for the problems of particular individuals.

Two weeks later, April 1, he wrote again stating that he was getting along reasonably well with at this camp, so different from Scheveningen. Once again he insisted they not worry about him, because the medical attention was better here than in his previous prison, and the authorities more considerate of his health and age. He assured them he could hold out as long as necessary. He was fulfilling his religious exercises as much as possible, and he was deeply aware of his prayerful communion with them all. This letter bears witness to how important a part prayer was playing in his life as a prisoner.[6]

Still his situation at Amersfoort was precarious, as we know from a fellow prisoner. Pastor Leo Siegmund[7] related, "The conditions under which we lived in the camp were unbelievably bad. Sometimes they left us without food for 24 hours. Our clothing and blankets were totally inadequate, especially when the stove went out and the temperature fell below zero."[8]

In spite of everything, Titus seemed to draw strength from his very frailty, strength to keep following in the footsteps of his divine Master.[9] Nor did he lose his sense of humor: he even devised a tongue-in-cheek interpretation for the omnipresent camp logo– P.

D. A. (*Politzeiliches Durchgangslager Amersfoort*)– suggesting it must mean "*Probamur dum amamur*" (we are tried because we are loved).

The Kindest Man in Camp

Titus' chief preoccupation in Amersfoort was the needs of others.

Those brief periods everyone else considered free time were the busiest of all for Fr. Titus. For some prisoners they were the most difficult times of the day: it was then that their thoughts turned to their loved ones at home.

In his own barracks a small group of prisoners began meeting whenever possible in a group they named "The Tilburg Circle;" Titus was of course its driving force. They prayed and meditated together, and they learned how to help each other improve their daily lives. Without exception each of them experienced a growing friendship for the slight Carmelite. Some took advantage of his presence to confess their sins.

Because religious instruction and even the care of souls were forbidden under pain of death, members of the group avoided calling Titus "Father;" instead they agreed among themselves to call him "Uncle Titus."

Every night as they went to their bunks, Titus gave each one a warm handshake as he traced the sign of the cross on their palms–a simple gesture that reminded them of Him who had suffered for all. This gesture became proverbial. Sharing his own inner peace, Titus gave them confidence.

Titus had been in the camp barely two weeks when dysentery struck. The infirmary barracks filled quickly, so that an additional barracks, Nº 4, had to be taken over as a back-up, and it too was quickly filled. While this additional space was being readied, however, many of the sick were left lying on mattresses outside in the freezing weather.[10] On some days as many as seventy-five died.

In the dark before dawn on Saturday, March 21, during roll call in the central square another prisoner failed to respond when his number was called. The SS guard asked sharply: "Who is the swine who did not answer?"

The barracks chief responded immediately: "Brandsma, sir."

On hearing that name, the prisoners' usual lassitude was laid aside and a whisper ran through the formation: "Uncle Titus, is he sick?" A young student who was present claimed that only the name of the camp's most beloved prisoner could have moved those nearly benumbed hearts.

Titus had felt somewhat ill a few days before leaving Scheveningen, but the doctors there were unconcerned with what they thought was only a minor ailment; they had told him it was nothing. But life in Amersfoort– hunger, cold, harsh labor– had worsened his condition. He had not complained; but one day, while sitting on his stool peeling potatoes, he had thought he was dying. He tried to treat himself by eating less.

This time, however, it was more serious. The doctor diagnosed dysentery with hemorrhage and sent him to the infirmary. A fellow prisoner observed that on the way to the infirmary Titus looked like a skeleton. Everyone, himself included, felt that his martyrdom was over. Once again, they were wrong.

Conditions in the infirmary were indescribably bad. The sick were bedded three deep on bunks; in the middle of the ward there were a few portable latrines for the use of all.

Due to the severity of the attacks, the poor victims were forced to climb up and down from bed to latrine every hour or so. This caused sharp spasms for some, constant discomfort for others. They were provided no special diet, and hardly any medication. Titus suffered stomach pains, but he escaped the high fevers attacking most of his fellow-sufferers. He did what he could to help others. Ever the true pastor he dragged himself from bed to bed, comforting, consoling those desperate men without distinction of race or religion. It was not long before they awaited impatiently the visits of "the kindest man in the camp."

He talked and he prayed with them; he smoothed out their blankets and, when someone was dying, he stayed with him until he closed his eyes with one last sign of the cross.

One young Catholic, Jan Hoffmann, he cared for like a mother. He heated stones in the stove to put under his blankets, fed him, encouraged him to keep fighting for life.[11] Pastor Siegmund recalled that it was things like that, things Titus did secretly and out of sight of the guards, that so impressed his fellow sufferers. Everyone loved him because he loved everyone. And everyone sought his support and moral strength to keep on living.

When he witnessed the unlimited love of this Carmelite priest, one communist and former Catholic whose bed was close to Titus' began to pray once again.

Special Communions

But Barracks N° 4 was not given over totally to the victims of dysentery. In *Stube* A there were 160 young Russian prisoners. These unfortunates had been exhibited around Germany as trophies of the Nazi victory over Russia, then sent to die slowly in Amersfoort.

After several months, those still living were stripped completely naked and forced outside in the winter cold; there they died of cold and hunger, some lying against the walls of the barracks, others spread out across the snow-covered ground.

The Nazis forced the Jews to bury them.

The dysentery patients in the next *Stube* knew when each of them died: after dark those who still survived and were able to do so sang, or rather wailed, long dirges that only they understood. The final survivors were deliberately executed.

Fr. Titus' heart was broken when he witnessed such pain but he was unable to do anything but pray and suffer in silence.[12]

Although not totally recovered, Titus was released from the infirmary on March 30, 1942, the Monday of Holy Week that year. He was sent to barracks N° 2 as a convalescent: this permitted him more rest and freed him from strenuous work. He was told that he would have a follow-up medical examination on April 20.

He took advantage of his convalescence to talk with various people, even with some of the guards and especially the overseers; some of them could not help but be touched by his simplicity. Through these contacts he obtained permission to visit his friends in the infirmary, and he spent a good part of each day with them.

When conversations with sick prisoners touched on the guards, they frequently expressed their rage and cursed them. Often Fr. Titus admonished them: "It is precisely because they are not good, as you say, that you must pray for them all the more."

"But that is impossible," they would respond.

"Well," he would insist, "you don't have to pray a lot. A little will do."[13]

Somehow Titus' companions in misfortune were able to obtain a small missal for him, and one of the young men made him a rosary from string and small pieces of wood with a button from a military coat.[14] Today it is preserved as the relic of a martyr. Surprisingly he had also been able to hold on to his copy of *The Imitation of Christ* and the book *Jezus* by Verschaeve; this latter he passed around among the prisoners in sections, except for the pages he had used–writing between the lines–for his biography of St. Teresa.[15]

Each morning when they rose at six o'clock, he joined his group of young friends and shared a brief spiritual reflection. On other occasions he used free moments to pray the rosary or the Way of the Cross with them.[16]

Sundays he celebrated "Mass" and they received "communion"– a very special kind of Mass and communion. After their common shower, a group of five or ten gathered around Fr. Titus– with one of them standing guard. Titus would then read, slowly, the biblical and liturgical texts of the Mass and give a brief but fervent homily.

Obviously it was impossible to consecrate bread and wine, but when the time came for communion, he took each one's hand between his own and, looking directly into his eyes, pronounced the words of the ritual: "May the body of Our Lord Jesus Christ preserve your soul for eternal life. Amen."

Not a sacramental communion certainly, but those who took part affirm unanimously that his glance of faith, his affectionate gesture of taking their hands and the meaningful words that came from his lips gave them a tremendous uplift and produced a psychological effect almost as though they had truly received the Blessed Sacrament. Sometimes, they said, the experience was even more intense than when, as free men, they had received the very Body and Blood of the Lord.

At night, before going to bed, Titus would pass through the barracks taking once again their hands and tracing the sign of the cross on their palms, reminding them of what they had experienced that morning.[17]

Such spiritual "interventions" of "Uncle Titus" took on the significance and power of similar gestures among Christians in the catacombs.

One Could Have Heard a Pin Drop

At that time Amersfoort held some hundred prisoners from Amsterdam, all members of the resistance arrested following an attempted assassination of a high Nazi official. Almost all were members of the educated classes– professors, doctors, architects, etc. They were a strange mixture of ideals and convictions, but united in their resistance to the Nazi aggressor of their country.

In an attempt to make the dismal life of the concentration camp a little more bearable, as well as to cut back on obsessive discussions about hunger, these men sometimes organized lectures or conferences during the evenings following their long workday. Their sessions covered a broad spectrum of subjects, religion being one of the more common until that topic was expressly forbidden.

Good Friday fell on April 3 in 1942. Since various prisoners– each a specialist in his own right– had already spoken, Dr. C. P. Grunning suggested that Fr. Titus speak about his own speciality, the history of mysticism. After some discussion they agreed on a topic: "The Spirituality of Geert Groote and the Brothers of the Common Life." Since the lecture was to deal with Dutch history and literature, it would avoid the prohibition of religious topics.

The first days of Holy Week became more and more unbearable. The guards' violence increased to the extent that on Wednesday, during roll call and inspection, one of the prisoners was kicked so brutally that he died before their eyes.

In addition, members of a special tribunal had arrived to try the members of the resistance. The tribunal had begun its investigation with such exaggerated formalities that the prisoners were well aware something very serious was about to take place. On Good Friday morning the group was interrogated, and that afternoon the members of the tribunal inspected the camp. They arrived at barracks N° 3 just as Fr. Titus had been about to begin his presentation.

It was nearly seven o'clock before the inspectors left and the presentation could begin. Although it was strictly forbidden, several prisoners had come from other barracks–especially from N° 2, Fr. Titus' barracks. In all about a hundred prisoners were present.

Fr. Jan Aalders has provided a description of this most unusual event:

> I remember perfectly the appearance of the barracks that evening. Prisoners were seated everywhere, some reclining on the triple bunks, others lying on the floor. ... The smell of wooden shoes, filthy clothing, and sweat was oppressive. The shaved heads of emaciated men made the scene seem macabre. One heard only the quiet sound of whispered words and the noise of the clogs.
>
> I was sitting between Doctor Max Kohnstamm and Professor Hellema from the University of Amsterdam. Professor Brandsma, that evening's speaker, was directly in front of us, sitting on a potato box. He was dressed in his outlandish, oversized grey uniform which made him seem even smaller than he really was.
>
> That very morning Titus had written an outline of his talk on a scrap of paper– still preserved today– which he held in his hands during his lecture.
>
> He was introduced by Doctor Grunning.
>
> Professor Brandsma began by explaining clearly the importance of Geert Groote in Dutch literature, not revealing that he would get to the matter he wanted to discuss later on.
>
> He then explained the concept of spirituality, the various paths to the mystical life, the different kinds of religious life, etc. Each of his points was carefully calculated to prepare the ground for the topic he really intended to address on this Good Friday: the passion of Jesus as the object of love and contemplation.
>
> At this point he had no need of an outline: his words flowed spontaneously from his heart where his great love for Our Lord was burning. Gradually, imperceptibly, his talk was developing into a profound meditation on the Passion of Jesus, little by little moving each of his listeners.
>
> Today, Good Friday, we enjoy the great good fortune to be commemorating the Passion of Christ in the spirit of those who have gone before us. According to Groote, this gives us the precious right to suffer alongside the Redeemer as well as the consolation of a spiritual union with the Man of Sorrows, with his Cross, with his bleeding wounds. ... Jesus is our example, our strength, the most powerful of all helpers in our own difficulties. On this day an atmosphere of

joyful thanksgiving ought to reign among us, for we are privileged to contemplate the passion of the Lord from within our own pain.

One of those present that Good Friday evening recalled: "He told us that our life in the concentration camp was analogous to the tomb of Christ, and that, like Him, we would be delivered from the darkness."

Fr. Aalders added:

> He went on speaking for more than an hour. One could have heard a pin drop.
>
> Even the communists listened attentively. Had they ever heard anyone preach about love with such fervor? They had been taught how one class hated the other, and here was this tiny friar dressed in grey speaking peacefully about something totally different.
>
> Behind his thick glasses Titus' eyes were so glowing that we forgot his wretched figure, the silence so all-enveloping that you could hear yourself breathing. Within that silence, each of us confronted his own problems, his own misery. ...
>
> When he finished no one dared speak. We returned to our barracks in silence. We felt overcome by the Spirit of God. It was as though some internal music had passed from his soul to ours.[18]

That lecture was an event, one that engendered a spirit of religious enthusiasm and fervor. Years later some of those present recalled clearly what they had experienced around that improvised pulpit.

Following that Good Friday evening Titus appeared exhausted for several days; nevertheless, he spent several hours each day hearing the confessions of those who, moved by the power of his words, requested it. Not a few non-Catholics also wanted to talk with him.

Some asked him to speak again on Easter, this time in his own barracks. As usual, whenever he felt he might do some good, he agreed. This lecture was to be based on Father Brugman, one of the great authorities on the *Devotio moderna*. Deathly tired, exhausted as he was, the talk was not a success: Titus could hardly get the words out of his mouth.

April 20 was Hitler's birthday and the prisoners were required to decorate the SS officers' club, inside and out, with huge pictures of the dictator and other-high ranking Nazis, as well as with swastikas and other ornaments.

To celebrate the event a few members of the resistance movement were to be set free. Titus entrusted one of them with a message for Fr. Schiphorst, pastor of the Church of St. Boniface in Amsterdam, the man with whom he had spent his last afternoon as a free man. In it he mentioned the stomach pains that were bothering him.

The very next day the tribunal published a list with the names of those condemned to be executed. These men were then held in barracks N° 4 under close guard. Before the guard was set, some of the other prisoners– Brandsma among them– attempted to talk with and encourage them. In a letter from Kleve, the prison where he was soon to be sent, Titus told his prior that he had been able to reach one of them, whom he identified with a Latin name, *scintilla*– a word that would identify him to anyone who knew the language but was unlikely to be understood by the camp authorities. He wrote: "Please extend my condolences on the death of Scintilla. The family will be comforted to know that he went to his death with his soul fully prepared, with his mind focused on heaven, and with expressions of deep affection for all his family."[19]

On Saturday the sun was shining brightly. The prisoners were drawn up in formation from 1:30 until 3:30 in the afternoon. Then the seventy condemned men were marched out of their barracks, and the two groups were kept standing under the watchful eyes of 200 SS guards for two more hours, facing each other, and in strict silence. In this way the Nazis had thought to terrorize those who remained, but they were wrong. The silence and the stoicism of those condemned to death moved the remaining prisoners in a very different way: those who were Catholic, with a movement of their eyes, asked for absolution from one of the priests; others looked up to indicate their desire to go quickly to heaven.

On May 3 they were executed at Sachsenhausen-Oranienburg.

Thanks to an informer, Titus, along with his friends Kapteyn and Hoppener, was sentenced to forced labor. Pushing a heavy roller, they were to level a road covered with small boulders. All the prisoners were aghast: his "crime" was his Good Friday talk. Fortunately, however, his 15-day sentence was interrupted by illness which forced the authorities to send him back to the infirmary.

He escaped his full punishment that time, but it would not be for long.

On May 27 a rumor went around the camp that Professor Brandsma's case was being discussed in The Hague, and that he was to be sent to a concentration camp in Germany. "Fr. Titus spent the entire night in prayer," reported a fellow prisoner.

The very next morning one of the *Stube* overseers called several prisoners, Brandsma among them, to inform them that they were being transferred. They were taken to the security closet where they were to leave their prison uniforms and once again put on their own clothes. Titus was no longer N° 58; he was now dressed in his black suit.

That morning he had said, "What lies in my future in Germany is Dachau; from there no one ever returns. They will not treat me gently."

Bidding farewell to his Amersfoort comrades he said: "Courage, brothers, the Lord is with us."

It is Father Aalders who tells us of Titus' final moments at Amersfoort:

> It was early afternoon when I noticed a small group near the infirmary. They got into a small transport. ... I knew by sight several of those being taken away. Among them stood Fr. Titus, dressed in his clericals. I was not able to get closer. I waved to him from where I was, and he made the Sign of the Cross in the air, his last blessing. That was the most wonderful gift I ever received from him, that the camp received from him: his priestly blessing, the blessing of a true, a saintly man.
>
> He got into the truck; it disappeared down the tree-lined road.[20]

"He looks like a little bird, despoiled of everything, but still singing," remarked another prisoner who saw him leave.

But where were they taking him?

ENDNOTES

1. SU 65, p. 192.
2. The term used by the prisoners was "*nelis*," a term signifying a coarse, lumpish person.
3. SU 65, p. 159.
4. SU 65, p. 182.
5. SU 79, p. 275.
6. SU 79, 516.

7. Leo J. F. Th. Siegmund had been arrested in August 1941, because he had translated and distributed sermons of Bishop van Galen of Münster, a man well-known for his courage in speaking publicly in opposition to the Nazi regime. Siegmund was assigned to the same barracks as Professor Brandsma. These two clergymen had known each other previously: Siegmund had been a gym teacher at the Carmel Lyceum in Oldenzaal, Titus a member of the School Board. Siegmund was among those released on April 20, 1942, on the occasion of Hitler's birthday. Cf. Alphons Weiterink in *Tubantia* February 22, 2001. Translator's note.

8. SU 79, 309.

9. Rule of St. Albert, 2.

10. Rees, p. 133.

11. SU 65, p. 197.

12. Meijer, p. 607.

13. SU 65, 213 and 340.

14. See *Appendix IV*.

15. Rees, p. 139.

16. SU 65, pp. 194 ff.

17. SU 65, p. 166.

18. SU 65, p. 179.

19. SU 65, pp. 180-181. This man had fallen away from his religion and had never before given any indication that he intended to return.

20. SU 79, p. 295.

Chapter X

His Final Sentence

Back to Scheveningen

It was 10:00 PM when the transport arrived in The Hague. Without stopping, it left for the suburb of Scheveningen and the prison where Titus had lived during the first months of his detention in cell N° 577. It had now become the fourth station of his long Way of the Cross.

During his first stay he had been held in a one-man cell so he could write his replies to the interrogations, and that period of solitude and peace remained engraved in his spirit. This time, however, he came as one already judged and condemned.

No sooner had they arrived than the guards pushed him into cell N° 632. It was totally dark. Two young men who were already sharing it came awake with a start.

"Who's there?" they asked in alarm.

"I am Titus Brandsma, and I have just arrived from the camp at Amersfoort."

The two youths, Cornelius de Graaf and Willem Oostdijk, jumped off their cot. They were well acquainted with the name of Professor Titus Brandsma, long recognized as one of the great defenders of the Christian faith. They could hardly believe their good fortune, to have him sharing their miserable quarters. Fearing that the famous Carmelite might be taken away the next day, they wanted to take advantage of their opportunity; they questioned him about everything they could think of, and Titus, dead tired as he was, answered them kindly.

Still, total darkness was not conducive to long conversations, so they decided to go back to sleep. They insisted on giving the cell's single cot to their new cellmate while they themselves spread straw mats on the floor.

The next morning the two lads were alarmed to discover that Professor Brandsma looked like a living skeleton, and whispering, they shared their shock with one another. As for Titus, he wished them good day with his usual acceptance of his surroundings as being God's will, and added, "I want you to know how glad I am to find myself with you. The last time I was here I was totally alone in my cell, and I assure you, this is much better."

He soon learned that they were both Protestants. He therefore asked them, "Do you mind if I pray on my knees?"

"Not in the least," they responded.

During their time together, whenever the priest prayed the two young men talked or played cards quietly so as not to disturb him. Sometimes they prayed along with him.

For his part, Titus, trying not to let his asthma disturb their sleep, prayed silently during much of the night. When they got up in the morning, they frequently found him kneeling at the foot of his bed. They wondered how many hours he had spent in this way.

Cornelius shared his impressions of the priest's presence in their cell:

> I talked with him a great deal, and very intimately; this continued for three weeks of tremendous spiritual joy. We two were simple lads, but he enjoyed being with us. ... During that time the Professor talked to us about everything: the origin of the Carmelite Order; Geert Groote; his trips to Italy, Spain and Austria; his visits with Teresa Neumann and Janske van Steenbergen;[1] Teresa of Avila, Francis of Assisi, Thomas à Kempis, Fr. Brugman. ...
>
> Every Sunday we had a kind of spiritual renewal: the professor explained some passage from the Bible, and then we prayed and meditated. On Ascension Day we spoke about the coming of the Holy Spirit. It was an unforgettable experience.
>
> After dinner we used to play cards while the professor knelt and prayed for a long time next to the bed. Sometimes he would pray while walking back and forth. We were aware that he also prayed for quite some time after we went to bed.
>
> One morning at nine o'clock the professor was summoned to an interrogation at the Binnenhof in The Hague; he didn't get back until seven that evening. As usual, he had been given nothing to eat the entire day, but we had saved his rations.
>
> While he was with us the professor wrote on a topic they had assigned

him: "Why he was against the Germans." He made two copies of his response, one he sent to the Security Service, the other he kept for himself.

He was concerned too about our life and faith, and frequently spoke with us about it. ... He always thanked us for the little things we did for him, for example one of us might make his bed or pass him a glass of water. ... He never acted as though he were our better; he was humility personified. He always gave us some of his own food.[2]

Another of his fellow prisoners, H. A. M. van Nieuwenhoven, testified:

> Life in the prison was more bearable than at Amersfoort. The guards were less brutal. Pohl and Katally were vile, but Riszig and Dressel held him in a certain respect. Fr. Titus always gave the impression of being happy.
>
> Riszig, an Austrian member of the SS, came to respect him after a night spent talking with him about spiritual matters. He once remarked, "This man is a saint ... I wouldn't want to confront him: he might start praying and have a cross appear in the heavens and win the war."
>
> He [Riszig] had come to me one evening to talk about some of his problems, and I sent him to Fr. Titus. I don't doubt that he went to confession that night.
>
> What most impressed the guards was the joy that shone through Professor Brandsma's face. I was impressed as well. His eyes held that certain something special. ... I don't think they did anything in the prison to improve his health; there wasn't even a doctor, only a nurse with whom it was just about impossible to talk. They did provide him with some milk though.
>
> When he left for Dachau, I gave him a small package of food for the trip; immediately he gave it to a hungry fellow-traveler. I reproached him for that, and he then gave me back as good as I had given, but kindly.[3]

Nothing to Take Back

Fr. Titus arrived back at the Scheveningen prison on April 28. The next morning, he learned why he had been transferred from Amersfoort: he was to undergo another interrogation by the Gestapo Captain, Hardegen, the same official who had questioned him previously.

It was May 6, however, before the new interrogation took place. It involved ten hours of questioning, from nine in the morning until seven in the evening, without a even break for food. Finally, the Nazi acknowledged that it was useless to continue. He pointed to the telephone, saying, "Call your superior in Nijmegen, and tell him you are about to leave for the concentration camp of Dachau, in Germany."

Shaken by this sudden turn of events, Titus dialed the number but was barely allowed to deliver the message:

> Yes, Father Prior, this is Titus. I am in the office of the Security Service in The Hague. I have been questioned again, and now they have decided to send me to Dachau, one of the largest concentration camps in Germany; that means I will be there until the end of the war. In all probability I will be leaving for Dachau next Saturday; until then I will be held in the prison at Scheveningen. Please send the things I asked for as soon as possible. And don't worry about me; I am fine. I think I will be able to stick it out. My best wishes and regards to everyone. I am not allowed to say more. Good-bye.

The prior quickly tried to assure him that everyone was praying for him, but there was no response. The communication had been cut.[4]

It is now clear that Hardegen's second interrogation had a single purpose: to find out whether Titus' experiences in the various prisons and concentration camps since the previous January had brought this stubborn Dutch Carmelite to see reason. He discovered that, whatever maltreatment this frail old man had suffered, his spirit was as strong as ever. He continued to declare he had nothing to retract. What he had done, he would do again if his superiors, or his conscience, asked it of him. Nothing he had done was political sabotage, as the Germans were insisting. Still, he held no grudge against anyone.

A few days later, back in Scheveningen, Titus added a few details of his interrogation. "In The Hague I was questioned again, especially with reference to certain letters." These were letters he had written about education and about the Jewish students. He was also questioned about his university lectures dealing with National-Socialism, about his activity with regard to a Mr. Noordijk, a supervisor of a school, and about his relationship with a Professor Baader. He was not questioned again about his position with regard to the Catholic press: that was a closed book.[5]

Titus had opposed the nomination of Professor Baader as *Rector magnificus* of the Catholic University of Nijmegen because he was not Dutch but German; he had also opposed the nomination of a Frenchman. His objection was not because he had some ax to grind with regard to either candidate; he opposed both nominations because he did not want to see the university involved in the political conflict then being waged by their respective nations.

It is now known that it was Professor Baader who denounced Titus to the Security Police in The Hague.[6]

Following the interrogation, the Commandant of the Security Police in The Hague sent his report to the Chief of Security of the Reich in Berlin. Along with it he sent the report of the January 21 interrogation, and a letter stating that the Ecclesiastical Assistant of the Catholic Press was still being detained.

With the dispatch of these documents to Berlin, Professor Titus Brandsma's case entered a new phase. It had become no longer simply a problem for Dutch National-Socialism, but one for the Nazi High Command. From this moment on Titus' principles and his very words were understood as being in open opposition to Nazism.[7]

He had a few more days to stay in Scheveningen.

That same day, May 6, Titus wrote a letter– the fifth since his arrest– to his sister, Gatske, and the other members of his family:

> I am back in Scheveningen, but only for a brief time because they have decided to send me to the concentration camp at Dachau, near Munich. I will probably leave for there next Saturday. There too I will find friends, and God is everywhere. My health is good, have no fear for me on that account. I am fortunate since there is little that bothers me. Give my best wishes to the children, to Barbara and to Hendrik [his sister and brother who were religious], and to all the family, as well as to the pastor and his associates. I understand that you are worried about me. I ask all of you, including the children, to pray for me. I am most grateful for your love. Let us remain united in God until we meet again. I will write to Father Prior in Nijmegen from Dachau. You can send your reply through him, just as before. Congratulations to Elena on her birthday, April 25, and to Teresa on hers, May 28. My love to each of you. Your brother in Christ, Titus.

Hardegen recalled that during their first encounter he had asked Professor Brandsma to put in writing his perceptions about why the Dutch did not accept National-Socialism, and that he had never requested the response. Now he wanted it. Titus had only to make a clean copy of what he had written earlier.

Two Gestapo agents, Vorysky and Horacio, questioned the two youths who had shared their cell with Titus as to whether he had talked about his political position. The agents blamed Titus himself for his situation, assuring them that "Professor Brandsma is totally stupid. Had he said one little word of retraction, he would have been set free immediately."[8]

Father Titus, however, was not the kind of man they thought. He had said and done his duty; he had nothing to take back.

Moreover, he had done everything possible to continue living, but he would not bring himself to compromise his principles.

He was in God's hands.

On the morning of May 16 a large group of prisoners was herded into trucks waiting in the prison square to take them to Dachau. Titus was leaving the Netherlands forever; he was entering the immense maw of Nazi Germany.

One more, the final, station of his long and painful road to Calvary.

ENDNOTES

1. Both Teresa Neumann of Könnersreuth, Germany, and Janske Gorissen, of Steenbergen (or Welberg), Netherlands, were said to be stigmatics. Professor Brandsma had visited both in the course of his research. Translator's note.

2. SU 79, pp. 217 ff.

3. SU 79, 324.

4. SU 65, p. 98.

5. SU 79, pp. 251 and 334.

6. For this latter piece of information I am indebted to Father Adrianus Staring, O. Carm. (Cf. the declaration of L. Deimel, SU 79, pp. 334-335.

7. SU 69, pp. 462 ff.

8. SU 65, p. 212.

Chapter XI

A Break Along the Way

Kleve

As night fell that same day, May 16, the prisoners' caravan crossed the frontier between the Netherlands and Germany and stopped in the border city of Kleve.

"Fortunately," Titus wrote some days later, "the trip had to be interrupted. Now we are in the prison at Kleve, and from here we will be sent on to our various destinations." Actually the prison in Kleve, like Amersfoort, was primarily a transit station; men and women from all German-occupied countries were assembled there before being sent to other prisons and concentration camps. Normally the stay in Kleve was brief. Prisoners came and went constantly, as Titus observed in a letter to his brother Hendrik: "Every Saturday a truck with some forty prisoners leaves here for the interior of Germany."[1]

This prison was under the authority of the German Department of Justice rather than that of the Gestapo; nevertheless, the Gestapo maintained jurisdiction over its own prisoners. In general, the regular staff– both administrators and employees– opposed National-Socialism, which they considered to be without legal foundation.

Life in Kleve was relatively tolerable. Only permanent prisoners were placed on work details, and no one was mistreated. Fr. Titus was permitted to wear the black cassock of the diocesan clergy; he was also allowed to keep his breviary, a small missal and a rosary.

While there Brandsma was assigned to two different cells, Nº 69 and Nº 27. One of them he shared with the Protestant pastor Kapteyn, with whom he had already formed a strong friendship, the other with an Italian minor official who constantly complained of being hungry.

The chief discomfort in Kleve was hunger. The food was not only bad, it was scarce: cabbage soup, a chunk of bread with Kwark— a kind of cheese whose fat content had been removed— or occasionally a bit of butter. Titus was allowed the diet for sick prisoners: some kind of vegetable purée and a few cups of herbal tea. He never complained about the food; on the contrary— with possibly an ironic reference to the shortage of food— he wrote to his family, "I have an appetite such as I have never had before."

The doctor no doubt intended the diet he had prescribed for Titus to replace the usual ration for prisoners; not having been told this explicitly, however, Titus, compassionate as always, also got in line for the normal ration, which he gave to his hungry cell-mate, who gobbled it down in an instant. On one occasion he was caught in his charitable game and had to listen to a stream of insults and obscenities— "You damned black-robe" being one of the milder— all of which he humbly accepted.

At Kleve there was a Catholic chapel where the prisoners were permitted to attend Mass on Sundays and even to receive Holy Communion. During the liturgies the prisoners would sing, accompanied by a harmonium, and the altar was adorned with flowers and candles. To Titus this seemed like a dream after so many months of spiritual deprivation. He had begun to think he would never again be able to enjoy such blessings on this earth.

He formed a close friendship with the prison chaplain, Fr. Ludwig Deimel, who has provided the following information:

> I had permission to hear the confessions of the prisoners, and normally I did so in the sacristy; this gave me a chance to talk with them face to face. The guards had no way of knowing, though they probably suspected, that many of them were not precisely going to confession. Then too, since I was part of the prison administration, I had keys to the inside doors. I could enter the cells when I pleased and stay to talk with the prisoners for extended periods of time. Consequently, I was able to spend a good deal of time with Fr. Titus.
>
> When I met him he was wearing a black cassock and had long greying hair; the lines of his face were delicate and spiritual; his movements spry. His demeanor was like that of an ancient sage, very proper and exceptionally cultured, something one could see in his overall deportment. What torture it must have been for him to have been incarcerated without any real reason, often with companions not of the best sort.
>
> He was in full possession of his faculties and we often spoke about

philosophy and theology. I never saw him sad, but always good-natured and in good humor. He was famous for his great humility and equanimity of spirit.[2]

Fr. Deimel told the Vicar General of the Diocese of Münster in 1945, that he had never known any other priest who fit so well the description of holiness; thus long before he was aware of Titus' impending cause, when asked whether he had been aware of anything special about any of the prisoners, he affirmed, "As I recall all those prisoners, I had the impression that in Fr. Titus I had met a saint, a martyr for the faith."[3]

Grateful for the spiritual benefits he had received from his contacts with Titus, the chaplain tried to return the favor to that exceptional prisoner, both by lending him books and by bringing him extra food prepared by his own mother. The only thing Titus asked for was that he obtain permission for him to celebrate Holy Mass. Here the chaplain could do nothing: this was absolutely forbidden to prisoners. He would have to be content with attending Mass and receiving Holy Communion on Sundays. We may presume that Fr. Deimel also brought him Communion on at least some of his many private visits.

The days seemed to be passing peacefully, although not without difficulties. One day Titus was caught talking to another prisoner during the morning exercise period and was thrown out of the group. Another day, during an inspection of cell N° 69, the jailers found a paper cross pinned to the door as a focal point for prayer. "What the devil is this all about?" screamed the guard as he ripped the offending paper from the door.

Still, Titus was well aware that this peace was temporary. All it would take was a Nazi voice calling his name, and it would all come suddenly to an end. He already knew his final destination was Dachau. What he was experiencing during this peaceful interlude was like the joy of Holy Viaticum.

House Arrest?

During their conversations Fr. Deimel had brought up the possibility of the Dutch friar's being held under house arrest. "Given the poor state of your health," he had suggested, "the Nazi authorities might possibly authorize your being held in some German priory; you would of course not be permitted to take part in any public service and would be obliged to remain under the supervision of the Nazi authorities. There is some precedent, e.g., the parish priest Fr. Augustinus Bulters, a Franciscan. Why don't you investigate this?"

The German authorities permitted a family or legitimate superior to request such an arrangement on behalf of the interested party, but it was always considered an extraordinary concession. Hence, as the chaplain explained, "The Carmelites in Nijmegen have to be informed, since it is up to them to make the first move. I myself can do nothing."

Fr. Deimel later explained what took place: "A tool merchant in Kleve, Jan van Herik, acted as intermediary between the Carmelites and me. He possessed a special permit for importing tools for the Wehrmacht, and this allowed him to cross the frontier freely.

"What I asked of him was two-fold, one oral, the other written. This latter was typed on extremely light paper and hidden at the bottom of a package of cigars.

"Jan van Herik returned disheartened after his first visit. Fearing a trap, the Nijmegen Carmelites had received him coldly. Only on his third visit was he able to convince them to seek a meeting with the Gestapo commander in The Hague and to look up the official named Hardegen. When he returned after his fourth visit, van Herik brought good news."

The prior of Nijmegen, accompanied by a lawyer whom the Nazis trusted (Asuerus Brandsma, a relative of Titus), traveled to The Hague on June 2 to talk with Hardegen, a man with whom he had already had some contact. At the same time they had also written to the prior of the German Carmelite priory in Bamberg; unfortunately he was temporarily in a rest-house in Bohemia due to poor health.

Contrary to their expectations, Hardegen received the prior and the lawyer immediately. They explained why they were seeking the privilege of "house arrest" for Professor Brandsma.[4] Hardegen, of course, knew very well that Brandsma could not be considered a mere criminal, nor even an anti-German; he was a convinced anti-National-Socialist, and he made no secret of it. This could not be tolerated.

After a lengthy discussion Hardegen stated the situation clearly:

> Professor Brandsma not only refused to retract his statements, but he reasserted totally what he had said in his previous statement. He is a hardhead. Under the German system one can believe whatever he wishes, but he may not give voice to it. Professor Brandsma is not quite the type of man who is able to keep his ideas about the Jews, about the Catholic press, or his other ideas conflicting with National-Socialism to himself.
>
> He is a dangerous person. If we were to set him free he would return to his activities, and the Security Service is not about to tolerate that. We have learned that when we give Dutch officials their freedom, rather than being grateful for our generosity, they set about sabotaging our plans with venomous propaganda. No, the Security Service has no need of further corroboration of this ...
>
> We are aware that Professor Brandsma is sick, but he should have taken that into consideration before attacking our great country. In his own correspondence, the professor himself states that he is well. No hospital could give him better care than this prison. As to Dachau, I can honestly assure you that no one is sent there unless the authorities are sure that he has sufficient strength to endure the life of the camp. And as to medical attention, treatment is free in that institution of human solidarity.
>
> Consequently, for these and other reasons, Professor Brandsma will find no better place than Dachau, a place Heinrich Himmler himself has established for the welfare of political prisoners.[5]

The Nazi official put an end to the meeting–and to his monologue–raising his right arm and shouting, "Heil Hitler!" He then turned on his heel and left them alone.

If the above statements had not been made by a Nazi, their cynicism would be unbelievable. The entire world was becoming aware of the horrors hidden under the name of Dachau and other Nazi extermination camps.

After spending a half-hour trying to make Hardegen listen to reason, the prior and the lawyer made their way back to the station with only one conclusion: "We have not accomplished a single thing. We may as well not have come. Still we have learned something we will never forget: for people like these, a man's life has no value whatsoever."

Two Letters

A few days earlier, on May 28, Titus had written to the prior of Nijmegen. In this letter, following the advice of Chaplain Deimel, Titus described what the prior might do, things his confreres and friends had already been doing for some time.

> So far the date for my departure to Dachau is not known. I have been questioned again at The Hague, in particular with regard to some of my letters. When leaving Amersfoort, I was told I was being held in preventive detention because of my anti-German sentiments and because they were afraid that if I were released, I would abuse my freedom by working against Germany. Being sent to Dachau means I will be imprisoned there until the end of the war. Dachau is near Munich and has several subsidiary prisons. I will let you know to which I will be assigned, presuming that the sentence will be unchanged.
>
> Father Provincial might try to get the German authorities to commute my sentence to house arrest in some German priory– e.g., Mainz, Vienna, Bamberg, Straubing– of course with great restrictions on my freedom of movement as well as on my work, and with the obligation of remaining in that city, or even within the priory, and to report to the authorities regularly, to have no correspondence with the Netherlands, etc. Father Bulters of The Hague was granted his freedom on the condition that he move to Venray.
>
> In my opinion, the most promising tactic is to go to the Provincial Office of the German Security Police, Binnenhof 7, in The Hague and to speak with Mr. Hardegen, Office 137. He is the official who always interrogated me; he is also the one who told me that the lawyer from Zwolle, Brandsma, had been asking about me, and the one who turned over my large suitcase to him. I don't think he [he lawyer] was able to do me any good, but I am grateful to him for his interest.
>
> He might return as a follow up, either alone or with Father Provincial or with someone the Provincial may designate. This appears to be a good idea to me, but I leave the decision up to you.

He then continues writing about his life in his previous prison in Amersfoort and about other matters dealing with academic affairs, the work of his confreres, and especially about the works of Saint Teresa.[6]

On June 3, unaware of the negative outcome of the previous day, he wrote his seventh letter from prison, this one addressed to his Franciscan brother, Father Hendrik, to congratulate him on his 60th birthday:

> Who would have thought I would be writing to you on your sixtieth birthday from prison! How many things have happened during those sixty years! In these sad times it is enjoyable to recall the past. Still, those good times will return, and I hope it will be soon. Right now, various ones are trying to find some way for me to be interned in a German priory of our Order, similar to what was done for Father Bulters. But we will just have to wait and see whether they can do anything for me. I have put the entire matter into the hands of St. Joseph who took the Virgin and the Infant Jesus into Egypt. Like Jesus and the Virgin, I trust in his powerful protection. Please join me in this prayer.
>
> I am well enough, given the circumstances. You'll see how I come out of this, and afterwards make up for lost time.

He continued, writing about family matters and giving some advice with regard to the Way of the Cross for the Shrine of St. Boniface in Dokkum. Finally, he asked his brother to give his best wishes to everyone.

"I cannot write each of them personally; indeed, they made an exception permitting me to write to you. While they are very courteous and kind here, it is still a prison."[7]

The Attempt to Set Him Free

In all his letters Titus affirmed that he was all right and that no one should worry about him. Those who were familiar with him and who had heard others talking about the concentration camps, knew this could not be quite accurate. Consequently, a group of his friends was redoubling their efforts–especially during the time when he was about to be sent to Dachau–to spare him at least that, aware as they were that Dachau would mean his death.

Gratefully, though without much confidence, Titus did not discourage these efforts, and he even accepted the advice of those who thought he should take a more active part in their efforts to save his life.

In the meantime, the chaplain, Fr. Deimel, tried a different approach as well: he asked that Titus be examined and evaluated by a doctor from Cologne (he had little confidence to those assigned to the prison, since he was aware that at least some of them were themselves Nazis). A Dr. Steffes, Professor from Münster, aware both of Titus' poor state of health and of the reputation of Dachau where he was to be sent, also appealed on Professor Brandsma's behalf.

The chaplain next recommended that Titus appeal personally to the German authorities with an explanation of his health problems. And again Titus– ever seeking God's will– followed the advice of his confreres and his friends. On June 12 he addressed an appeal to the Security Service in The Hague through the prior of Nijmegen.

Both the content and the tone of this document are quite different from those of his letters. This is not surprising, since in his letters he was trying to assuage the concerns of his family and friends, whereas in his appeal he was attempting to impress the seriousness of his medical problems on the Nazi authorities, just as he had been advised to do.

In his appeal Titus declared that he had suffered four serious stomach hemorrhages; that, neither in prison nor in the camps had he ever been allowed to follow the special diets the doctors had ordered; that he suffered from a chronic urinary infection that required regular medical treatment and that caused him to get up several times each night; that he suffered from serious dysentery. He also asserted that he suffered from insomnia and that he frequently lay awake by one or two o'clock in the morning.

He suffered memory lapses and at times was unable to concentrate. He sometimes experienced hallucination– for example he would hear the ringing of church bells and could not get this out of his mind. Whenever he played checkers the squares on the board remained intensely engraved in his mind to the extent that for days afterward he would see the floor of his cell as though it were divided into different colored squares.

He complained that he was deathly tired throughout the day, and that after even the lightest work he would have to sit down, overcome by exhaustion. He enumerated certain hypogastric organs that were functioning improperly.

He summarized as follows: "The undersigned is of the opinion that although what he has described might permit a temporary stay in a prison or camp without deleterious effects, a long-term incarceration would be life-threatening, and if it were very long, fatal." He concluded by indicating several Carmelite friaries where he might be sent under conditions to be determined by the authorities: Nijmegen and Merkelbeeck in the Netherlands; Mainz, Bamberg and Straubing in Germany; Vienna in Austria.[8]

The end result of his efforts, as well as those of his brother Carmelites and friends, was absolutely nothing.

That Titus took this step is not surprising, nor is it incompatible with his stated willingness to accept whatever lay in store for him.[9] At no time did he make a statement that was false, or even an exaggeration, in order to petition the limited freedom his friends were fighting for; every detail stated in his appeal was confirmed by his fellow prisoners after the war.[10] Moreover, the defense of one's life is an inalienable right of every human being, so long as he does not betray his conscience.[11]

Some of his biographers– including Fr. Brocardus Meijer, who has been cited frequently in these pages– have suggested that during the period Titus spent in Kleve he suffered some serious spiritual distress. They suspect that he suffered doubts with regard to his activity on behalf of Catholic journalists, as well as about God's plan for his life, doubts that became his "dark night" engulfing him with an agonizing breakdown.

There is nothing, however, in the voluminous acts of the process of beatification that provides a foundation for such an assertion, although there is no lack of reasons why it might not have been the case. Fr. Adrianus Staring, who as Vice-Postulator of the Cause was the individual most familiar with the documentation on Titus Brandsma, expressed his conviction that statements of this sort are pure speculation. Moreover, the prison chaplain, Fr. Deimel, testified from personal observation that "when all efforts to set him free had failed, Fr. Titus showed no surprise, no dejection, no despondency, no despair. On the contrary, he remained peaceful, joyous, full of confidence in God."[12] And he concluded, "Those who have participated in these affairs in a Nazi prison are aware of how draining they are."

Titus confided in a young man, "I knew this [the activities leading to his arrest] meant that I was signing my own death warrant, but that certainty did not prevent me from doing my duty." His fellow prisoners recall how often he repeated, "We are in the hands of God."

On June 12, Titus was told that, along with other prisoners, he would be leaving Kleve for Dachau the following day.

"The Lord Is with Me"

The next morning forty prisoners were lined up in front of the prison, chained two by two, awaiting the order to march to the station and board the train that would take them to Dachau. His eyes clouded by tears, the chaplain kept his eyes fixed on Titus, who appeared full of some inner fortitude and suffused with an inner light. As the Carmelite passed close to him, he heard him say, without looking at him directly, "Goodbye, my good friend. Nothing bad can happen to me, because the Lord is with me."

The previous evening Fr. Deimel had brought Titus Holy Communion. Now Titus would imitate the great Patriarch of Carmel, the Prophet Elijah, who– persecuted for his defense of the true religion, exhausted and on the point of collapse– with the strength of bread provided by an angel, was able to walk forty days and forty nights to the Mountain of God.[13] Titus, strengthened by the Eucharist, set out along the final stretch of his Way of the Cross.

Chained to his friend, the Protestant pastor Kapteyn, Titus set out for Dachau.

In the city of Gladbach they had to wait for a train coming from Belgium with another shipment of prisoners destined for Dachau. Among them was a large contingent of Catholic priests.

From Gladbach they traveled through Cologne, where there was another long delay: due to a recent air raid the tracks were blocked with rubble.

On June 15 they arrived in Frankfurt and were immediately transferred to a prison. There Titus met another priest, Heinrich Rupieper, who was to become a close friend. Because of his experiences in various camps, Fr. Rupieper was able to give Titus valuable advice about life in Dachau.

In one of their conversations during the trip, Titus had said, "It was necessary for these things to happen, so that mankind would open its eyes and recognize the anti-Christ."[14]

The following day the journey continued. Several clergymen were assigned to the same compartment as Professor Brandsma: the pastor, Fr. J. Delcourt, a Belgian Jesuit L. de Coninck, the above-mentioned Fr. Rupieper, another Catholic priest, Fr. G. Redeke, and Titus' friend Pastor Kapteyn. They were one in their love for Christ and in the suffering they shared.

They traveled through Mainz and then to Nürnberg. There, due to the allied bombardments, they stayed three days in a large gymnasium. On the day of their arrival they were given nothing whatever to eat. The next morning, they received a small chunk of bread and something called coffee; for the remainder of that day there was nothing else.

The air in the gymnasium was asphyxiating. There was a water fountain in one corner, and several casks that served as toilets– a hundred men to each– in various places.

The prisoners were not told the reason for this long stop-over, nor anything else that was going on. Titus, however, remained peaceful and resigned. "This will soon be over. Our Lord's providence will fit it all into its proper place."

After three days the stench in the gymnasium was so bad, the air so unbreathable, that the prisoners breathed a sigh of relief as they returned to the train.

Before boarding they were again chained, two by two.[15]

ENDNOTES

1. SU 65, p. 324.
2. SU 79, pp. 331 ff.
3. SU 79, p. 337.
4. SU 79, pp. 332 ff.
5. Meijer, p. 637; SU 69, pp. 138 ff and 251 ff.
6. SU 79, pp. 528 ff.
7. SU 79, p. 530.
8. SU 79, pp. 532 ff.
9. A parallel can be drawn with Paul's statement in Phil 1:21-23.
10. Meijer, p. 337.
11. SU 79, pp. 337 and 532.

12. SU 79, pp. 532 ff.
13. Cf. 1 Kgs 19:8.
14. SU 79, p. 348.
15. SU 65, p. 230.

Chapter XII

Dachau Concentration Camp

Dachau

The trainload of prisoners made its way across the magnificent Bavarian countryside and came to a stop in the Dachau station at five o'clock, the evening of June 19, 1942.

Immediately the SS shouted orders to detrain, punctuated with blows and kicks. Divided into groups of thirty, the prisoners were herded into covered transport trucks for the drive to the camp, some two and a half miles outside the town. On arrival they were marched to an open area in front of the administration building, the *Jourhaus*. There they were looked over by SS officers, proud in their high boots, flaunting the skull insignia on their military hats, armed with pistols and whips.

They had entered the notorious, infamous concentration camp of Dachau.

Walking in the footsteps of this Dutch Carmelite confrere, known in his own country as Professor Titus Brandsma but to me as my brother Titus, I visited the concentration camp of Dachau. It was a pilgrimage filled with emotion.

It was only a twenty-minute train ride from Munich. Dachau is a city of 30,000 inhabitants, about two miles north of the Bavarian capital. It has become all too well-known for the concentration camp built there by the Nazis in 1932.

Since it was still nearly an hour before the camp would open at ten, I decided to walk from the station to the camp.

As I left the station platform, I walked under the huge station identification sign; merely reading that name– DACHAU– sent a shiver of anxiety through my body. Two ladies were standing in a small square, apparently waiting for a bus. "Excuse me," I asked, "Can you point out the road to the *Konzentrationslager*?" I seemed to sense sadness, perhaps shame, in their eyes when they heard that name. They indicated the road to the camp.

After a brisk forty-minute walk, I left the main road. As I turned to the left toward the camp and saw its watch towers, I felt a chill.

I had read and thought so much about the camp that my emotions ran away with me and I felt I had forgotten everything I had learned. I bought a map in the shop and went into the camp proper as though I were entering sacred space.

For a moment I was disoriented: the entrance for tourists is not the same as the one used by the prisoners. Quickly I recovered my sense of direction and found the *Jourhaus*, a disappointingly small building whose ground floor was protected by a large wrought iron fence and gate with the inscription *Arbeit macht frei* (Work brings freedom). It was through that very gate that every prisoner had entered. Fr. Titus never came back.

The camp is rectangular, about 2,000 feet by 1,000.

Inside the great iron gate, Titus would have seen an enormous building, nearly 700 feet long, and with two wings of approximately 200 feet each. This was the old Administration Building; the central area contained offices as well as the clothes-lockers, laundry, and the feared "baths" where prisoners were tortured. Today the entire structure is used for the camp museum. Behind this installation were the "bunkers" where punishment cells for special prisoners were located. In between was the area where executions and severe punishments took place: there prisoners, tied to a post or hanging from a wall, were flogged.

In front of the Administration building was a large, unpaved parade ground, the *Apellplatz*, where prisoners were assembled for roll call morning and evening. It could hold between 40,000 and 50,000 men.

Northwards from the center of the parade ground was the so-called *Lagerstrasse*, the "main street" of the camp, nearly 1000 feet long and bordered by poplar trees planted by the prisoners. It separated the two rows of the camp's 34 barracks. These were constructed at right angles to the *Lagerstrasse* and separated from one another by smaller passages known as *Blockstrassen*.

As one left the parade-ground, the first two barracks were designated by the letters B-C and D-E. In theory they housed recent arrivals, the infirmary, a canteen, a library, and shops. In practice they never served such humanitarian purposes.

Then came the prisoners' barracks, numbered from 1-30, odd numbers to the right, even to the left.[1] They were built of wood on cement slabs and were approximately 300 X 30 feet. Barracks Numbers 26, 28, and 30 were reserved for clergy: No 26 for Germans, the other two for foreigners, mostly Poles.

The barracks was divided into four sections or *Stuben*, each with a living/eating area and a dormitory. Between each two *Stuben* there was a single common service area that served as both lavatory and privy.

According to the original plan, each *Stube* was intended to house 52 prisoners, or 208 for each of the barracks. Due to the tremendous expansion of the Reich, however, by the time Titus arrived each building held 1,600 prisoners. When there was no more room in the dormitories the overflow slept in the living area or even in the streets.[2]

At the entrance of the service areas– the first thing one saw on entering the barracks– there were shelves where the prisoners were required to leave their wooden work-shoes. In the eating area there was a row of tiny cupboards, one for each prisoner.

The camp security system was intended to prevent escape. Between the rows of barracks and the outside wall there was first of all a street; on the far side of the street was a border of grass about six feet wide– a "no man's land"– posted with signs bearing skulls and a warning that anyone stepping onto it would be shot without warning.

Beyond the grass strip was a trench some six feet deep; next was a barbed wire barrier at ground level and then a second concave one some ten feet high. On the other side of the barbed wire was a road, and finally a high wall topped with an electric fence. There were seven watchtowers on the wall, each manned by two sentries with machine guns trained on the camp and ready to fire; they were so placed that every area of the camp was covered.

To the left of the camp and outside the wall were the crematories and, behind them, the common pits where remaining ashes and bones were thrown.³

The supreme authority for all Nazi concentration camps was Heinrich Himmler. Under his command were the two most powerful arms of the internal politics of the Third Reich: the Gestapo and the SS, neither responsible to any other authority. The former supplied prisoners for the camps, the latter guarded and exploited them. Both were created to enforce Hitler's ideals and were natural developments of his totalitarian mentality. Members dressed ostentatiously in black military uniforms, insignia on their helmets and lapels. On their cuffs appeared the words: *Totenkopf* (Death's Head).

The officer in charge of the camp was the *Lagerführer* (Camp Chief), with sub-officials responsible for each section.

The prisoners were divided into "commands." In 1940 a position called *Lagerälteste* or Dean of the Camp was created. He was to serve as the link between the authorities and the prisoners. He issued orders through the Deans of the Barracks and the Deans of the *Stuben*. In charge of work details were the *Kapos* and their seconds who were usually common criminals, big and brutal, with unlimited authority.

The SS officers were trained to deal with "human refuse," i.e., the prisoners. They had but one duty: to exploit the prisoners to the maximum and at the least possible expense until they died. This was the purpose of the camp: death.

Dachau was efficient. The prisoners, shackled, entered the camp by way of the *Jourhaus*; they lived wretchedly in overcrowded barracks; they were forced to perform inhumanly hard labor; they were plagued by hunger and physical abuse; when no longer fit for work they were transferred to the 'infirmary' where they served as guinea-pigs; and finally they left the camp as puffs of smoke from the crematory and little piles of charred bones to be thrown into a common pit or used to fill up potholes in the road.

Some 206,200 men were registered as prisoners in that somber camp; of these far more than the official count of 31,951 died there. Indeed, countless prisoners were never registered; others were taken there only for execution, and many were transferred to other auxiliary camps to be eliminated in gas chambers.

Dachau! The very name produces a shiver of horror in decent people. It has become a symbolic of the monstrosities men have invented for the torture of their fellows. There Hitlerian fanaticism descended to the level of lurid sadism. At war's end when some of the atrocities committed at these "model institutions"– as the Nazis referred to their concentration and extermination camps– were revealed, both the world at large and the German people themselves were horrified.

Number 30492

Fr. Titus Brandsma arrived in Dachau at five o'clock in the evening June 19, 1942. Along with his fellow prisoners, he was submitted to a series of formalities, known as *Aufnahme* or reception: they were required to provide their personal data, which was then compared with records forwarded by the Gestapo. The prisoners were asked why they had been arrested; those who said they didn't know were abused.

The SS filled out complicated forms, and each prisoner was required to respond in writing to a long list of questions about his life– following a master outline on a large placard posted on a wall. These documents would become the first pages of a camp record for each prisoner, one that would continue to grow as long as he was there.

Titus was photographed, front and side, and then fingerprinted. Each prisoner had to sit on a chair beneath a large reflector in front of a camera. The Nazis amused themselves by releasing a needle hidden in the chair just as the picture was being shot, causing the prisoner to jump. The condemned man's photo would then show his face contracted due to the unexpected pain; this would provide indisputable evidence of his depravity!

The prisoners were then marched, military style, to the *Jourhaus* where the *Raportsführer*, a subaltern in charge of registration, would list them. Most of the older prisoners were unable to keep up the pace, which earned them both insults and blows. Heinrich Rupieper, a fellow prisoner, reports that Titus was one of those targeted for beating by the Dean of the Camp, Karl Kapp.

Next they were marched to the bath house where they were forced to submit to a series of indignities from the guards. One man shaved every bit of hair from their bodies, a very painful procedure due not only to the lack of expertise and the brutality of the "barber," but also to the condition of the razors which, rather than cutting, pulled out the hair. The resulting cuts and scratches caused considerable pain because the prisoners were immediately forced into a bath filled with a strong, caustic disinfectant.

Using the butts of their guns, the guards compelled the prisoners to submerge themselves completely, thus irritating their eyes, noses and the more delicate parts of their bodies. For the SS, this was a form of recreation as well as an occasion for obscene jokes.

Following this torture, the prisoners were sent to the showers, more than 600 men at a time. The water was controlled by the SS who enjoyed alternating water temperatures from nearly boiling to icy cold.

Next they were marched, completely naked, into the *Effectenkammer* or clothes-room, where they turned over their personal effects and received their prison uniform: pants and jacket– white with grey or blue vertical stripes– a jersey, a cap, wooden shoes, a number and a colored triangle which they were to sew onto their jackets. The clothing was distributed without regard to size: if it was too small the one in charge would joke, "Don't worry about it; in four weeks it will fit you perfectly." They were provided only one outfit; consequently, when it rained, they were forced to spend the entire day and night in wet clothing even in that frigid climate. Professor Brandsma was given the number 30492 and a red triangle: political prisoner.

Such was the situation in normal times; in "busy" periods, as when Titus arrived, those in charge of the new arrivals were overwhelmed, and at times the prisoners had to wait for several hours, occasionally for several days, before being processed. And they waited again, naked, in all kinds of weather, for their issue of clothing and utensils.

Registration formalities also included a medical examination, with yet another form to be filled out. Special attention was paid to the teeth; it was well known that the SS would recover the gold from the mouths of dead prisoners.

New arrivals were then sent to quarantine in barracks N° 24,

Konzentrationslager (KZ) Dachau (Dachau Concentration Camp) and its surroundings towards the end of the war. Now only two barracks remain to visitors to see. The camp measured 600x300 meters. Thirty-four barracks, located on both sides of the Lagerstrasse, held over 12,000 prisoners at any time. In 12 years, over 206,000 prisoners were at the camp and at least 31,951 died. *(Photo courtesy of the Nederlands Carmelitaans Instituut)*

Gate at the entrance of the Dachau Concentration Camp (Jourhaus) with the saying *Arbeit macht frei* (Work will make you free). The open area is the *Appellplatz* (Roll Call Square) where 40,000-50,000 prisoners would assemble, sometimes for an entire day, for review. *(Photo courtesy of the Nederlands Carmelitaans Instituut)*

separated from the rest of the camp by a barbed wire fence. There they normally spent two or three weeks. This practice was due in part to fear of contagion, but it also served as a kind of boot camp to prepare the prisoners for life in the camp. There they were instructed in the various formalities of military drill: how to salute properly–Prussian, Berliner, etc.; and how to distinguish the different ranks of the SS and of the *Kapos*, something they were never to forget or confuse. They were also taught the required procedures for maintaining their quarters and their cupboards; special emphasis was placed on cleanliness– one of the obsessions of the Deans. While in quarantine they were also taught Nazi songs. Singing in the camps was a matter of utmost seriousness: the "Dachau Anthem" was thought to move the hearts of the most hardened criminals; "Die Morsoldaten," and the "Blauer Dragoner" were common sounds in every Nazi camp.

Of course, they were also taught their own place in the camp's hierarchy: "Get a move on, you clerical swine. We have a lot to teach you here!" the jailers would scream with an air of superiority.

Titus was quarantined for only ten days. Brother Raphael Tijhuis,[4] a fellow Dutch Carmelite, provides some details:

> Once I was able to get close to where Fr. Titus was being held [i.e., to the quarantine barracks], but at first he did not recognize me. When his ten days there were over and he was assigned to our barracks, he said, 'Thank God I am out of that hell. At least now I am with you. It is impossible to live in the new arrivals' barracks.'
>
> We laughed at that and warned him that the worst was just beginning.
>
> He replied, "I'll do my best to stay in the background and not to aggravate any of those gentlemen [the Kapos]."

Titus had been assigned to barracks Nº 28, third *Stube*. It was there that he met Brother Raphael. In barracks Nº 30 were five Polish Carmelites, four priests and one seminarian.[5] "We have a priory all our own," commented Fr. Titus.[6] He was not far wrong: Dachau may indeed have been the largest religious house in the world, at times holding as many as 3,000 clerics.

In barracks Nº 28 each prisoner was assigned a straw mat, less than two feet wide, for his bunk; the bunks themselves were stacked three deep and stood side by side with no space between. Each man was also assigned a cupboard for his personal utensils: a mess-plate, a spoon, a knife, a towel, a napkin.

The Camp Schedule

Prisoners lost all rights on entering the camp. From their first moment in the quarantine barracks they were made aware of this.

The fundamental rule of that bizarre world was: avoid calling attention to yourself, try to be invisible, never become intrusive. Even more important was hearing and seeing nothing, for the SS and their cronies, the *Kapos*, could do no wrong: there was nothing to prevent them from eliminating possible future witnesses. Every prisoner was at the mercy of anyone wearing a uniform.

Woe to anyone who dared make a comment or ask a question! Of course, if they were asked something, then any response was better than none, and every response was to be made in a loud voice, after the fashion used by the SS.

The camp schedule was deliberately arranged in such a way that the prisoners had no time to become bored, no time to think about themselves, no time to experience nostalgia for their families or their freedom.

The daily schedule was sacred:

```
SUMMER
4:00                Rise
5:15                Roll call
6:00 –12:00         Work
12:00 –13:00        Dinner (including going back and forth
from work)
13:00 –18:00        Work
19:00               Roll call
20:45               Everyone in the barracks
21:00               Everyone in bed
Lights out

WINTER
5:00                             Rise
Sun-up to Sun-down               Work
Everything else as in summer.[7]
```

The day began with the sound of wailing sirens. Barely awake the men began their day to the sound of curses, insults, threats, and to unwarranted cudgel blows from the Dean of the *Stube*.

Once, after having received more than a few of those blows, Titus commented humorously, "I am beginning to think that this is his morning prayer."

They had one hour to get ready: wash, dress, straighten their bunk and cupboard, drink their coffee and swallow the bit of bread left from the night before, and make use of the latrine. This might seem adequate; but even the most dexterous needed at least ten minutes to straighten his bunk to the satisfaction of the *Kapos*: the mat had to be absolutely smooth and form a perfect rectangle with its folds sharp; the cover had to have its corners perfectly aligned both horizontally and vertically. The *Kapos* used a carpenter's square to see that the edges and corners of mat and cover were precise.

Since the bunks were three-high and one next to the other, the men had to coordinate their efforts. It was nearly impossible to make up an upper bunk without disturbing the one below, consequently the latter had to wait and could easily become impatient. This in turn caused daily arguments and fights.

It did no good to get up early in order to gain time: first, this was forbidden, and second, there was no light. For fear of punishment for a bed poorly made, some prisoners slept on the floor, but this too was forbidden.

After the beds came the cupboards. These too were rigorously regulated, with a certain place for each item: towel, clothing, eating utensils, etc.

Fr. Titus had never been dexterous. At 61 years of age he was in no condition to take care of all these details within the allotted time; consequently, he was frequently the target of blows. Fortunately, there was usually some kind soul, such as Brother Raphael, to lend him a hand. Strict standards for personal hygiene were clearly justified, but impossible to maintain due both to the brevity of time allowed and to the lack of sufficient facilities. At times the situation was catastrophic and the stench in the washrooms was indescribable. Once a week they were marched to the showers, something that gave them the impression of well-being. The shower, along with bread and bed became Dachau's three "B"s: Bed, Bread and Bath (in German, *Bett, Brot, Bad*).

As soon as the siren sounded again the prisoners were marched, military fashion, to roll call on the parade ground. This took place twice each day. The morning roll took place at 5:00 and was completed by 5:45, because work was waiting. But the evening roll call, scheduled for seven o'clock, was another matter altogether: at that hour the SS had nothing for the prisoners to do, so it could last as long as the SS wanted and be conducted any way they pleased. Evening roll call was the most difficult of all camp activities. After a long day of hard labor, the prisoners were kept in formation for long periods, often as many as four hours, sometimes throughout an entire night, and occasionally, if someone was missing, all the following day.

It was at times such as these that prisoners experienced the reality of their situation: totally at the mercy of a crowd of bullies who allowed them to do nothing but breathe, and that not too loudly. It was a scene no survivor would ever forget: lined up in snow, or rain, or icy mist, under powerful spotlights and with machine guns being trained on them from the watch-towers.

For the SS this was recreation; they watched from their windows through field glasses. Nor did the SS lack in imagination for new ways of annoying or causing pain. If the "show" was not to their satisfaction, they might order it repeated amid insults and blows.

At the evening roll call everyone whose name was on the morning list had to be present, living or dead. If someone died during work, his fellow prisoners had to return his body. Even the sick or disabled were required to appear, unless they had already been sent to the infirmary.

Not infrequently those calling roll discovered that someone was missing. In that case the entire prison body had to remain in formation until the missing man was found. Often he would be discovered in some corner of the camp dead from cold or hunger, or possibly asleep from exhaustion, or hiding in order to kill himself. If he were really trying to escape– no one ever succeeded– his return was inevitable and quick, and ended with his immediate public execution, usually by hanging.

The march to and from roll call was always accompanied by the singing of German songs, and those who did not know the words had to sing along anyway with a "la, la, la." But woe to the person who did not sing! Sometimes the camp band would play, and then the prisoners had to keep up with the rhythm of the march.

If the assembly ended quickly, there was a very brief time for supper: some greens or potatoes in a broth and a hunk of bread. Half of the bread was to be saved for breakfast the following morning.

After supper came "free" time, unless they were assigned some additional task or had housekeeping to take care of, e.g., kitchen duty, cleaning, etc. When possible, the prisoners used this time to wash themselves, especially their feet: when the signal came to enter the dormitory, their feet would be inspected.

Finally, the signal was given to return to their barracks—8:45 PM, 7:00 in winter. Twenty minutes later the lights were turned off and everyone had to be in bed or run the risk of severe punishment.

Totally exhausted, their stomachs never really filled, these poor men prepared to pass the night; they hoped to sleep and so forget, at least for a few hours, their miserable existence. Often this was not easy to accomplish: frequently some drunken SS officers would awaken them and demand that everyone get up, on the excuse that they were making sure that the prisoners were wearing the proper night attire. Occasionally these nocturnal visitors required the men to leave the barracks and go out into the frigid weather for however long it pleased their guards.

Night was the time when prisoners were most aware of their wretched situation. They had survived one more day, but another was soon to begin. Would it be like the last one? They lived in perpetual uncertainty, ever at the mercy of countless imponderables, knowing that anything could happen at any moment.

Life in Dachau was one long unimaginable sadness. "Here," the officer in charge of the roll call would say, "no one is permitted to laugh. The only one allowed to laugh is the devil, and I am the devil."

In the camp prisoners could be punished for anything at all: dirty clothes, a jacket incorrectly buttoned, a button missing, dirty shoes or sandals, turning up one's collar to avoid the cold, putting their hands into their pockets to warm them. Prisoners, of course, were never right. Should a prisoner be required to speak to a guard or to a member of the SS, he had to stand at attention at a distance of ten feet–otherwise the officer might think he was being threatened.

The prisoner was obliged to remove his hat and address the superior formally, e.g., " Prisoner Nº XXXXX respectfully requests of (here he was required to give the complete name of the superior with all his titles, without any error) that ...."

Food was the most critical problem in the camp. The prisoners' daily allotment was totally inadequate, both in quantity and in quality. Hunger was the main topic of daily conversation among the prisoners.

The daily ration in Dachau came to fewer than 600 calories, almost entirely carbohydrates: a soup with perhaps a slice of potato, turnip or cabbage. Sometimes it contained a few bits of horsemeat. There was also a bit of bread, but certainly not made of wheat. It was essential that each one receive exactly the same amount; and, thanks to the prisoners themselves, this was in fact the norm.

Some of the SS threw food on the ground and ordered the hungry prisoners to get down on all fours and eat it without using their hands. Other prisoners were ordered to grunt like pigs, or to eat out of their superiors' hands like dogs.

Hunger brought a few to shameful actions: some would risk their lives for a little bit extra, others fought for a scrap of bread, still others stole from their fellow prisoners. Some collected and ate worms. There were even some cases of cannibalism: on November 14, 1942, in a train bound for Danzig, some corpses were found showing signs that parts had been eaten. It was during that summer that many prisoners starved to death.[8]

Worked to Death

In spite of his extreme weakness, Titus was declared to be in "good health." This meant he was required to do hard labor from sun-up to sun-down. This was not entirely a bad thing; it was far worse to be considered useless for work and classified as an invalid. The SS imposed all kinds of indignities on those unfortunates, and they were in danger of being loaded onto a "death train" at any time.

Dachau was a camp whose motto was *Arbeit macht frei* (Work sets one free). Himmler had given the SS the word: "We need money to finance our ultimate goal: One Reich for all Teutons. We will get the money by forcing this human refuse ... to hard labor. It is a crime against our race to worry about them."[9]

A decree issued on April 30, 1942, announced:
> The war has brought about an obvious change in the purpose of the concentration camps and in the way we must make use of the detainees. Holding prisoners for reasons of security, reeducation or making examples of them is no longer of primary importance. Our new direction must be toward economics, and this means that we must take steps to convert the camps into economically productive entities.

From that time on, the Nazi authorities directed their efforts first toward increasing the population of the camps, and second toward increasing their productivity. The new order meant "Death through work."[10]

The organization of work groups was under the control of the *Arbeitseinsatz* (a subaltern for labor details) who, under the command of an SS officer, was responsible for the make-up of the various groups that were to work within the camp; those who were to work outside the camp were under the control of the *Kapos*. In general, the organization was chaotic. There were no adequate tools, no transportation. Human beings took the place of both machines and beasts of burden.

Productivity was far below average, and could hardly have been otherwise. The prisoners were poorly fed, poorly dressed, and often suffered from untreated wounds. Moreover, they had no desire to contribute to the victory of the Reich.

Titus was always assigned to one of the details working on the farm, the *Liebhof* (Garden of Love). This was one of the more difficult details: they worked from six o'clock in the morning–as soon as the roll call was over–until the evening roll, thirteen hours a day, with no days off. There were more than 200 acres in the *Liebhof*. The work detail left the camp each morning around 5:30, singing Nazi songs and marching in formation in their wooden shoes for a half-hour under the strict vigilance of the SS and their guard dogs. Each detail was made up of between 100 and 120 men; 90% of them would be dead or seriously ill within the first month. Among themselves the prisoners dubbed the *Liebhof* the *Friedhof* or cemetery; during some periods 23 or more of those working there would die each day.[11]

The entire day was spent in the fields weeding, throwing out stones and rubble, pulling heavy disks or plows, loading wagons. All this under the watchful eyes of the *Kapos* who forbade the workers even to stand upright. The Nazis called this work "planting medicinal herbs," but the prisoners, keeping the same initial letters (HKK), renamed it "no blows today."

At noon they retraced their morning march to eat. Since they had not been permitted so much as a drink of water all morning, they had been fasting since breakfast. Now they received a plate of broth with a bit of cabbage or beet. Happy the man who was served a potato, with its peeling!

By one o'clock, after washing their dishes– which hardly needed cleaning– they were again marching off to work until seven in the evening.

Following their thirteen-hour day, dead tired and drawn up in formation for roll call, they received instructions and orders to the shouts of "Attention, you filthy swine" and similar terms of endearment. Once, when the roll call went on and on–which happened with discouraging frequency–Brother Raphael asked Titus in a whisper, "Now what" To which Titus replied, "We'll just have to wait and see; we have lots of time."[12]

Titus was a thin, sick man, more accustomed to intellectual than to physical labor. Many a time when other prisoners found little difficulty performing a task, or getting out of a jam, he was caught and punished with the heavy boots of the SS. The dean of his barracks, Fritz Becker, and the dean of the *Stube*, Walter Thiel, for some reason could not stand the sight of Brandsma and continually called him "you stupid Dutchman" and beat him even when he had said or done nothing to make them angry.

"I am amazed," confessed his friend H. Rupieper, "how he could put up with all that with such patience, without animosity or resentment. He even rejected the advice that I, a veteran prisoner, gave him: that he should report it to the camp commandant. His response was that everything was in God's providence."[13]

"When in the living area," commented Brother Raphael, "it was astonishing how calm and peaceful he appeared in spite of the continual noise and disturbances that were normal there. I would tell him to hurry up, but he did not want to give the guards any reason to get angry. If I finished before he did, I would try to help by getting him out of the way of the *Stube* dean. The last ones finished were usually treated to pushes and kicks and blows. When Fr. Titus went through the doorway, that brute of a dean would use his bludgeon to beat noisily on the top of the doorway just above his head."[14]

Each day he forced himself to march off to work wearing wooden shoes that bruised his feet terribly; it was forbidden to take them off until they reached the *Liebhof.* There they could exchange them for sandals or go barefoot.

It was not easy for Titus to keep up with the military pace set by his fellow-unfortunates. One day he lost a shoe. The *Kapo*, Schultz, forced him to continue marching, barefoot, while being kicked on his heels until they bled.[15]

Sometimes two Polish Carmelites,[16] Fr. Januszewski and Fr. Urbanski, themselves walking skeletons, helped him by hiding him between themselves or forcing him to the ground to escape a harsh ow. They were not always successful, among other reasons, because Titus himself was not aware of what they were doing.

Titus had never had much of an appetite, and in other camps he had shared portions of his food with fellow prisoners. In Dachau he generally licked up the very last sliver of food. At times, however, he would gather a few traces on a piece of paper and give them away saying, "Here, my friend, you need this more than I."

The mortality rate in the camp was enormous, which caused the SS to be concerned about preserving the labor force. The worst period was between June and September of 1942 when, on average, 150 prisoners died daily, including at least five each day from barracks N° 28. On returning from work, the prisoners would ask one another how many had died that day.

He Was Always Praying

While teaching at the university Professor Brandsma had not infrequently reminded his students, "We should have great respect for pain, because there is something sacred about suffering." Now he was teaching this same lesson with his life.

In Dachau suffering was endemic. Titus was not simply resigned to accepting it; he was learning to embrace it as his way to walk in the footsteps of Jesus. He refused to be just one more number within that mass of humanity destined for degradation and death; he accepted fully the challenge to minister to others without counting the cost to himself. He said as much in a conversation with one of his fellow prisoners, Fr. Joseph Kentenich, later the founder of the Schönstadt apostolic movement: "Now," the diminutive Carmelite remarked: "I have to put in practice what I used to teach others."[17]

For Titus, living his convictions and preaching with actions as well as with words was a source of inner consolation.

For much of his time in Dachau Titus ran a constant fever. His legs were swollen, and his feet had open sores so deep that they affected his very bones and caused atrocious pain. In normal circumstances his condition would have required total bed rest and a well-controlled diet. But this was Dachau where prisoners were forced to dig in frozen earth, to scour floors, and– each in turn– to carry the heavy kettles of food for the entire barracks, not to mention to undergo kicks and blows without end.

It was not long before his legs began to fail because of excessive fluid. He could barely get his feet into his wooden shoes; they became instruments of torture. At times his fellow prisoners had to support him while marching to the fields for work.[18] Twice each day he was marched to the *Liebhof* and back, and twice a day he stood in formation for roll call. He had neither time nor supplies to care for his feet. It was useless to seek help in the infirmary; most of the "nurses" were carpenters or woodcutters, uneducated people whose chief interest was serving their time in the hope of getting extra food, sometimes even stealing it from their patients. Should anyone dare to complain, these "angels of mercy" would scream: "Shut your mouth, you son of a bitch!"

Brother Raphael helped all he could. He had Titus sit on the floor during some free moments so he could clean his sores with a piece of paper and bandage them with a scrap of old toweling–no one knew where he found it. "Does it hurt a lot, Father?" the Brother would ask. "No, Brother," Titus would reply. "It feels much better now." Ever gracious, Titus would thank him for his concern and declare it had done a lot of good. "Now I feel like a new man again!"[19]

Titus had been in barracks N° 28 barely a week when he received his first beating. When the prisoners returned from work that evening, they found a sign indicating that the door to their quarters had been painted and that they were to use a different entrance. Titus forgot, and went through the forbidden door. The dean of the *Stube* caught him and, furious, began hitting and kicking the unfortunate old priest until he was floored; even then he continued to express his rage.

A few days later Titus received an even worse beating. Brother Raphael gives some detail:

> We all had to leave our quarters whenever they were being cleaned, except for those who were doing the cleaning. On one of those occasions we had all gone out when Fr. Titus noticed he had left his glasses inside and wanted to go in and get them. Knowing he would run into the dean and suffer the consequences, I tried to stop him.
>
> "But, Brother, without them I can't do anything," he responded.
>
> I told him I would get them, but he would not hear of it, and before I knew what he was doing, he had already gone inside. The dean saw him right away and shouted, "Brandsma, what do you think you're doing?"
>
> "I forgot my glasses, Sir," he replied as he tried to escape the approaching storm. But before he could reach the door, he got such a blow that he went down.
>
> "I'll teach you to forget your glasses!" the dean shouted. By the time Titus was able to get back on his feet, he was bleeding from his nose and his mouth, and he had several broken teeth. His glasses had fallen to the ground; I picked them up, broken. I asked him if he was in much pain.
>
> "No, Brother, it's over and done now. If you had gone in, you would have been the one to be hit. The broken lens is the real problem: without my glasses I cannot see."
>
> Everyone gathered around and some Dutchmen asked what had happened, but he simply told them, "Nothing, nothing worth talking about."
>
> Once again he had forgiven and immediately put the incident out of his mind. His forgiveness, his peace, in spite of the beatings he received, were so obvious that, on at least one occasion, even one of the guards asked his forgiveness."[20]

"One of the most annoying things," recounted Brother Raphael, "was the foot inspection."

> Every night before going to bed we had to wash our feet and then they were inspected minutely by the dean of the *Stube*. Once Fr. Titus' feet did not pass muster and he was made to stand apart until the inspection was over. Then the dean began to shout, "I'll teach you what cleanliness and order is all about!" And randomly he began to hit those on both his right and his left. I was afraid of what might happen, especially because only a few hours before I had given him [Fr. Titus] a consecrated host which he had put into his glasses case. Such a thing was absolutely forbidden, not only because of what it was, but because no one was allowed to bring anything into the dormitory except a nightshirt, and even that was searched. Had the dean discovered what Fr. Titus was carrying, the consequences would have been inconceivable.
>
> Finally, he came to Fr. Titus, "You sack of shit!" And he hit him so hard that he fell to the floor. The guard's rage was out of control, and he continued to hit and kick the fallen priest. Finally, Titus managed to get up and make his way into the dormitory under a storm of blows and curses.
>
> I supported him and helped him onto his bunk; I asked if that animal had done much harm.
>
> "Brother," he whispered, "I knew who I had with me," and he showed me how he had hidden the glasses case under his arm. Then he added, "Come, Brother, let us pray the *Adoro te* together."
>
> I wanted to kneel, but he wouldn't let me. In a low voice we adored the hidden God, the patient Prisoner in the Most Holy Sacrament, as Fr. Titus called him; and after giving me a blessing with the Sacrament, we went to bed.
>
> In the morning I asked him if he had slept well; he answered, "I have been awake since two o'clock, but I was happy to have been able to keep watch with the Lord."[21]

Another prisoner reported that Titus was praying silently all the time: on the parade ground during roll call, while making his bed, while marching, while working, during the night, on getting up. "With our morning prayer," he told me, "we begin the day on the right foot." He went to confession frequently, with Fr. Keuller among others.

Clandestine Communions

On January 15, 1941, the camp administration issued an unexpected order: a chapel was to be built in the first *Stube* of barracks Nº 26, the one that housed the German priests. It did not take long to do.

The reason for this novelty was that Heinrich Himmler had announced that he was going to make a personal inspection of Dachau.[22] By January 21 the chapel was ready, and the first service was held. The windows had been painted over and access was rigorously prohibited to other prisoners. The camp chaplain, Fr. P. Prabutski, celebrated the first Mass the following day.

As might be expected, the chapel was rudimentary. The only vestments were some brought by the military chaplain from Sachsenhausen in a small suitcase. Until March 1943, only the chaplain was allowed to offer Mass; after that date each of the German priests was allowed to celebrate annually one Mass for each year he had been a prisoner. There was only one door into the chapel, and none of the other prisoners was permitted to enter. At night the door was locked with a key; during the day the priests who were unable to work had to keep it clean. The SS hoped this would prevent any contact between the German priests and the rest of the prisoners; nevertheless, contacts were made during work.

From the start the German priests had to deal with all kinds of difficulties in order to hold religious services decorously. From the SS they received nothing but curses and sarcasm. Sometimes guards would barge into the chapel smoking to interrupt the services, spitting on the floor, stepping on medals and rosaries. One of them once grabbed the Sacred Host out of the hands of the celebrant and threw it to the floor, shouting "If this is your Lord, let Him come to help you."[23]

For fear that the chapel would be closed, the German priests were very strict with regard to the rule that no one else was to enter. This caused a protest by the other prisoners, especially by the other priests who could only look with faith toward the place where the sacred mystery of redemption was being renewed. They yearned to participate personally; since that was not permitted, they did so at least spiritually.

"Fr. Titus and others frequently tried to follow the Mass being celebrated on the other side of the street by a German priest for Germans. But we were always forced to move away," reported Brother Raphael.

Nevertheless, the German priests did their best to minister to their fellow sufferers, whether priests or laymen: they would secretly pass them consecrated hosts for the comfort of the sick as well as for themselves. These they would hide in little pieces of paper or in tobacco packages and give them to other priests when passing by on their way to their work groups. The SS officers and the *Kapos* must have heard rumors of what was going on, or at least had some inkling of it. The prisoners, however, were all too aware of what would happen if any of them was discovered with a sacred host, or if they were found in the chapel. Such an offense would have brought on a punishment too severe to even think about.

Nevertheless, the Eucharist was so incredibly important, especially to the priests, that they were ingenious in finding ways to escape the watchful eyes of their guards. But it was only by maintaining a most careful watch and absolute secrecy that they avoided paying for their brashness with their lives. A Capuchin, Fr. Otmarus Lips, for example, gave Fr. Titus a host he had hidden in the waist of his pants.[24]

Brother Raphael recalls:

> Once Fr. Richard Schneider, a German priest, agreed–under a promise of absolute secrecy–to give me a consecrated host each day to take to our Dutch brethren. I asked Fr. Titus, since I am not a priest, whether I could do that, or whether it would be better to tell Fr. Schneider to give it to one of the priests himself. Titus assured me, "If you can get one, do so, then bring it to me; they are not so likely to search you." We were all aware that from time to time the priests were searched, so I was very happy to take on this privilege.
>
> Every morning then, as we went back and forth in the dark along the main street on our way to our work details, that German priest brought me the Body of Christ wrapped in a scrap of paper. I had taken some stitches out of the waist of my pants underneath my belt, and there I hid the host and returned immediately to our barracks to find Fr. Titus. As soon as we were certain no one was watching, I would give it to him, and he would divide it into two parts, one for the communion of the Dutchmen–there were sometimes ten of us–and returned the other to me for safe-keeping during the rest of the day.
>
> As he returned it to me, he would say, "Brother, remain in adoration all day like St. Tarcisius;[25] and always be aware of who you carry with you."

When we went back to barracks at nightfall, I would return the sacred host to him and he would hide it underneath the lining of his glasses case. Often, he reminded me that St. Teresa had claimed that Holy Communion was not only food for the soul, but that It also provided strength for the body.[26]

Titus' spirit received a boost on July 16, the Feast of Our Lady of Mount Carmel. He had no sooner gotten up than he went hurrying around to the bunks of his Carmelite fellow-prisoners, embracing each warmly and greeting them, "Happy Feast, my brother, it is the Feast of Our Holy Mother!" Then–he had only a few minutes–as they were going to join their work details, he received the profession of a Polish diocesan priest, Tadeusz Zielinski, into the Carmelite Third Order. He had himself prepared Fr. Zielinski during the nine days preceding the Feast, providing him with spiritual encouragement amidst the noise of the beds and the shouts of the *Kapos*. It was dangerous, of course; but for men already condemned to death, a few more beatings had little significance.

"When you are free back in Poland, you should renew your profession publicly and with a proper ceremonial," he told the new Tertiary. "Thank you, Father," he replied; "I don't believe that will ever happen."

Thoughts of Mary the Mother of Jesus were one of the few things that were able to lift the spirits of those doomed to the bitterness of camp life. "Brother," Titus told Brother Raphael, "Mary will help and sustain us. She extends her hands over us. With her help we can better endure whatever happens to us."

And then he added: "Before going to work you ought to repeat that beautiful prayer we said in the priory." As they walked along to their crews they prayed: "Most holy and immaculate Virgin, Light and Splendor of Carmel ..."

"Titus prayed continually: while working and while standing in formation awaiting the commands of the officers. His favorite prayer was the rosary. Fr. Rupieper remarked, "How many times he prayed it, counting on his fingers."

"Let's pray it for them," he would say, referring to the camp guards.

ENDNOTES

1. Only the foundations remain, except for the first two prisoners' barracks.

2. Paul Berben, Dachau: *Historia oficial del campo de concentración nazi 1933-1945*, Madrid, 1975. pp. 321 ff.

3. An International Committee has tried to preserve the camp "in memory of the dead and as a warning to the living" as the inscription on the monument to the prisoners reads. But the tragic atmosphere of the camp is gone. The only building that does not belie the reality is that of the Contemplative Carmelite Nuns, whose Monastery of the Precious Blood was opened in 1964. It is entered through the north watchtower and lies outside the camp. Of the original camp all that is left are: the *Jourhaus*, the Administration Building– now a museum– the crematory, the punishment building, the wall, the watchtowers, and two barracks. The museum attempts to give the visitor a sense of the insane atmosphere of the camp, but is only partially successful.

4. See *Appendix III*.

5. See *Appendix VI*.

6. Fernando Millán Romeral, O. Carm., "Carmelitas en Dachau: La apasionante historia de los carmelitas polacos que vivieron el drama de los campos de concentración," *Escapulario del Carmen* 91 (1994), 120-129. Idem, "Carmelitas en Dachau: Las cartas del P. Urbanski desde el lager, en el 50 aniversario de su liberación," *Carmelus* 42 (1995), 22-43; Martinez Carretero, *Figuras del Carmelo*, pp. 369-376. See too Kilian Healy, O. Carm., *Prophet of Fire* (Rome: Institutum Carmelitanum, 1990), pp. 181-184.

7. On a wall in the Camp museum there is one of the original signs with this schedule.

8. Berben, *Dachau: Historia oficial*, pp. 80-88, 140-141, 190, 196.

9. *Ibid.*, p. 50.

10. *Ibid.*, p. 113.

11. SU 79, p. 389.

12. SU 79, p. 357.

13. SU 79, p. 349.

14. SU 79, p. 355.

15. SU 79, p. 348.

16. See *Appendix VI*.

17. SU 79, p. 157.

18. SU 65, p. 259.

19. Tijhuis, "Dachau Eye-Witness," p. 65; Meijer, p. 653.

20. SU 65, pp. 37 and 249.

21. SU 70, p. 545.

22. Previously the administration had been firmly opposed to any concession being made in favor of the clergy; indeed that situation did not change until September, 1942, when Weis became Commandant.

23. Berben, Dachau: *Historia oficial*, pp. 176-183.

24. SU 79, 374.

25. St. Tarcisius was martyred while carrying the Blessed Sacrament to prisoners during the reign of Valerian (3rd century). He is described in the Roman Martyrology as an acolyte; from the sixth century he has been considered to have been a young boy. Translator's note.

26. Cf Santa Teresa of Jesús, O. Carm., *Obras completes* (Transcripción, introducciones y notas de los padres Efrén de la Madre de Dios, O.C.D., y Otger Steggink, O. Carm.) BAC, Madrid, 1967. *Camino de Perfección* 34, 6.

Chapter XIII

Holocaust

The Final Letter

The last letter Father Titus Brandsma wrote was the only one from Dachau. Despite his suffering, he assured his family he was doing well. The text of this letter, when compared with the earlier ones, confirms that he was maintaining his habitual union with God, his incredible serenity of spirit, and his close relationship with his brothers in Carmel. He wrote:

My dear Brother-in-law and Sister,

Although I have been sending my letters to Fr. Prior in Nijmegen, this time it is better that I write to you. Be sure you send it on to the prior and he will take care of forwarding it, as he has been doing, and of sending me your replies.

Your reply must be brief and written in German. You should use no abbreviations that cannot be easily understood; otherwise it will not be given to me. I was permitted to read the letter Fr. Prior wrote me in Kleve, but I was not allowed to keep it since it was written in Dutch. I want to thank Hendrik, Fr. Prior, and all the others.

I am well. One has to get used to the new situation, and here too I will get along by the grace of God. I have no doubt but that Our Lord will continue to help me.

I am allowed only one letter a month; this is my first. I would very much like to know how many new novices and new priests we have; also, what decisions have been made with regard to Oss and Oldenzaal; likewise about the health of Hubertus and Cyprianus and the other members of the Province.

Please God, Fr. Subprior will soon recover. You can send me forty marks each month; Fr. Prior will be happy to do so.

From Hendrik's letter I see that Father Kaeter has been transferred to Eibergen. Congratulate him for me. Have any of the other pastors I know been transferred? My greetings to the pastor and associates in Bolsward, to Fr. Provincial, and to all my confreres.

Let us remain united under the protection of Jesus, Mary and St. Joseph. Don't worry about me.

In Christ,
Your Anno (Titus)[1]

As can be seen, half of the letter is concerned with instructions about how to answer, significant for our understanding of the meticulous details governing every aspect of camp life, as well as the consequences of failing to observe them. Next is his concern for others. He writes little about himself, only that one has to learn to live under new conditions, that with God's help he will make do. It is here that we find insights into his habitual experience of the presence of God, his union with God and his acceptance of God's will, his great peace of soul.

Considering the inhuman treatment to which he was being subjected, his words indicate something about the "high places" where the spirit of this holy prisoner was walking.

To the Infirmary

Titus did not see well, due both to the weakness of his eyes and to the fact that his glasses had been broken. Sometimes he was unable to see just where he was. One morning, hoping it would help him to work better, he had wrapped his fingers with some scraps of cloth a friend had given him. This, however, violated camp regulations.

Another prisoner saw one of the *Kapos* approaching Brandsma with a gleam in his eyes; the man tried to warn Titus with a gesture, but he was unable to see it. The supervisor then ordered Titus to go to the tool room where one of the guards was waiting for him. As soon as he saw his victim the guard came out and, without a word of explanation, struck him on his back as hard as he could and at the same time kicked out at his legs.

He ordered Titus to kneel. Titus knelt in the mud for four hours with a continual fine rain falling on him.

What would he have been thinking all that time? We can be reasonably sure: when asked his opinion of these brutal tormentors on an earlier occasion, he had replied, "They fill me with so much compassion that I cannot wish any evil to befall them."

Indeed, he prayed for the guards continually. Not content with this, he even felt it his duty as a priest to do what he could to bring them to God. When Brother Raphael remonstrated with him about this, pointing out that it was not only futile but would very likely earn him an extra beating, his reply was "Who knows? Possibly they can still be touched."

To his fellow sufferers he was an example of courage and perseverance; to the wavering, he offered the power of his word and example; to the despairing– some even at the point of suicide– he spoke with the language of the heart, striving to share with them his own inner peace. In the camps it was a constant temptation for prisoners to run deliberately toward the electric fences in order to die, either shot from the watchtowers or electrocuted on the fences.

Titus' health grew worse by the day. Being forced to kneel in the mud for four hours used up the last of his physical strength. Later that same day, standing in formation for roll call– prolonged even more than usual– someone asked him, "Father, can you still make it?" Finally, he admitted, "No, my friend, I have no more to give. Still we have to hope."

The next morning his lungs were totally congested and each cough seemed to bring him closer to death. He craved air, fresh air; he was suffocating. Though he suspected death was near, still he did not want to go to the infirmary.

The following day he was barely able to get out of bed; he felt like he was drowning and left the barracks for air before it was time. It was cold and drizzling. When they realized what he was doing, Brother Raphael and Father Rothkraus ran after him. Unfortunately, a guard had seen them; shouting he began to beat all three.

Not long after, *Stube* Dean Becker, walking down the street next to Fr. Kuyper, noticed Titus; "Brandsma," he remarked, "you ought to go to the hospital." Recalling this incident Fr. Kuyper stated, "That really surprised us; normally Becker was all brutality."[2]

Brother Raphael has described Fr. Titus' final days in the barracks:

> The next day we Hollanders discussed what we should do for him. Not knowing what card to play, I decided to approach Section Chief Georg personally. Once I got to him, I asked if there were any possibility of getting Professor Titus Brandsma admitted to the infirmary.

"Who is this Titus?" he asked.

I explained who he was and the condition of his health.

"You come back tomorrow," he told me, "and bring this Titus with you."

I returned to the barracks and told the others what the chief had said. Everyone agreed that this was the best we could do for him. Then I told him what we had decided.

"If you are all in agreement," he said, "it must be God's will."

The following day he said goodbye to each of us and I went with him to the infirmary. We were all convinced we would never see him again. As we approached. we saw Georg waiting for us. "Here you are," he said. "Your doctor will be with you ..."

We were amazed at this unusual kindness. He began to talk with Fr. Titus while they were treating his wounds. They must have talked for a quarter of an hour.

Finally, a nurse told me, "You can go on back to your barracks. I will see to his bed myself."

I said goodbye to Fr. Titus, and he thanked me warmly for all the help I had given him and asked me to take his best wishes to all his fellow prisoners; then he added, "This will only be for a few days, Brother. By August we will all be home."

This was the expression he used whenever he was trying to encourage someone, even though he himself knew better. Those were the last words I heard from his lips.[3]

It was Saturday, July 18, 1942.

Originally the infirmary had been located in blocks A and B, but in 1940 and again in 1942, it had been expanded. During Titus' time in Dachau it took up seven barracks, one of which was given over to offices, pharmacy, laboratory, and rooms for the experimental departments.

The hospital was independent of the rest of the camp; under the direct jurisdiction of the medical section of the SS, it was supervised by the *Lagerarzt* (camp doctor). Thus, even though it lay within the perimeter of the camp, it was not under the control of the commandant of the camp. "The *Lagerarzt* and his colleagues rarely appeared in the wards, especially in those set aside for patients considered contagious. They were quite careful not to dirty their hands nor to waste their time on cases judged hopeless. With rare exceptions these doctors showed more concern for their appearance– e.g., that their boots were perfectly shined– than for the content of medical charts. Those who retained even a spark of humanity did not last long, and they were delighted to be transferred to other assignments."[4]

The fate of the patients depended almost entirely on the prisoners assigned to the infirmary detail. For years, unfortunately, this infirmary had been under the control of self-serving, unscrupulous people, people who were more interested in improving their own situation than in caring for the sick. Abuses, excesses, criminal actions were common.

Human Guinea Pigs

Why had Fr. Titus Brandsma resisted going to the camp infirmary for so long? All the prisoners feared becoming ill or being accused of malingering. Simply mentioning that one was not well might be taken by the SS as an act of rebellion, an attempt to escape work. It could have very serious consequences.

Titus, however, was not afraid of suffering, still less of death. Rather he was repelled by the prospect of biochemical experiments known to be inflicted on prisoners.

The concentration camps had been set up originally to eliminate the political enemies of the regime; it was not long, however, before the Nazi medical establishment conceived a program to take advantage of those "less than human" victims to "foster progress in German medical science." They had convinced themselves that, in the face of Germany's inevitable victory over Europe and the entire world, these prisoners would never be released and that, consequently, the world would never know about the atrocities they were committing in the name of medical research. Even if it ever should be revealed, no one would believe it.

Consequently, the prisoners were to become something useful: they would serve as laboratory animals, human guinea-pigs, for medical experiments. The Dachau medical staff was involved in several kinds of experimentation, without consideration of the suffering inflicted on their victims. Whether they lived or died was secondary to the progress of "medical" research.

The *Summarium* (the official transcript of the hearings) of the Cause includes several pages of testimony about the medical experiments done at Dachau. Paul Berben's history of the camp describes those experiments in detail and provides a chilling summary of the number of prisoners forced to undergo them.[5]

Dr. Klaus Schilling used insects to infect over 1,100 prisoners, mostly Polish clergy between the ages of 20 and 40, with malaria. Nearly all died.

Dr. Rascher set up a series of experiments dealing with atmospheric pressure and exposure at high altitudes; he wanted to find out what happened when an aircraft's cabin suddenly lost pressure under such conditions. The victims were placed in a pressure chamber simulating an altitude of 20 kilometers (about 12.5 miles), then subjected to a sudden total loss of pressure. Rascher would immediately dissect the bodies of those who died; in several instances the victim's heart was still beating. Dr. Rascher experimented with more than 200 prisoners– Jews, Russians, Poles, Germans; more than eighty died.

This same doctor also experimented with freezing. He was searching for a way to save the lives of German flyers who fell into icy water during the winter. He immersed laboratory patients in water chilled to some –5º to –15º F. Others were simply left outside during the winter covered with nothing but a sheet, while buckets of cold water were thrown on them every hour. In one of his own research summaries Dr. Rascher wrote: "Thanks be to God winter has returned to Dachau. I have been able to leave several individuals in the open at a temperature of –6º. Seventy died."

Dr. Rascher had a variety of interests. He also did experiments with blood, testing the effects of a coagulant that might save the lives of wounded soldiers.

Dr. Wolter, the head *Lagerarzt*, was working on abscesses or artificial tumors. He chose his patients from among the Catholic priests, without regard for nationality. Testing allopathic and biochemical pharmaceuticals, he inoculated his victims with a few cubic centimeters of pus and, once infected, lanced them. More than 40 priests died in atrocious pain from infection and blood poisoning.[6]

According to eye-witnesses– one of them, the nurse in charge of him during his stay in the hospital– Fr. Titus Brandsma was a victim of this latter experimentation by Dr. Wolter. Eyewitnesses have reported that, during his first week in the infirmary, Titus was able to console those close enough for him to reach with extraordinary gentleness and kindness. He possessed an incredible ability to encourage them through his ministry. As for himself, he spent his few remaining days in prayer.

"I still remember our dear brother in Christ in the baths," recalled Pastor Overduin, a Protestant clergyman. "Physically he was finished–all skin and bones, legs swollen by edema–but spiritually he was as strong as ever, loving, happy in the Lord. Hurriedly, being sure no one saw him, he passed me his last package of tobacco, whispering, 'My friend, take this; it may be of some use to you.'"

Even his executioners were impressed with his goodness; Dr. Wolter himself once remarked, "He is a truly comical character. He never objects to what he is asked to do, and he does it."

One can easily believe that, knowing his death was fast approaching, Titus united himself ever more intimately with the suffering Christ. Perhaps he recalled the words he himself had composed for the Twelfth Station of the Cross while in Scheveningen:

> O Jesus, for us it is an incomprehensible mystery how you finally willed to die for us, wished to enter the realm of death as if your whole mission had failed, as if all your life had been useless; an apparent victory for your enemies. O Mary, it must have been terrible for you to witness this end to your divine Son's mission, to see him die before your eyes the most cruel and shameful death, even though your faith told you that precisely thus, he wanted to return life to us.[7]

Among the people Fr. Titus encountered in the hospital was Dr. Fritz Kuhr, a prisoner who had been assigned to serve as secretary for the staff; he was the only Catholic who was able to move within the area freely, though very cautiously. As soon as he met the little Dutch Carmelite, Kuhr was fascinated by his spiritual personality. Dr. Kuhr had a few friends in the German priests' barracks; they were more than happy to entrust him with the Blessed Sacrament which he would then take to the sick and dying who requested it. On two occasions he was able to give Fr. Titus Holy Communion. He also gave him a rosary.

One of the German priests, Fr. van Gestel, S.J., later Assistant

General for Germany, recounted:

> "When Fr. Titus was in the hospital where he was to die, I was not at all well myself and had little contact with anyone; still I was kept informed about Fr. Titus through Fritz Kuhr who became a St. Tarcisius to take him Communion. One day Fritz told me he was very worried, because Titus was very bad, had lost consciousness and was taking no food at all; he asked me for a tiny particle of a Consecrated Host to give him. Fritz held Fr. Titus in great admiration. But all during that summer, it was extremely dangerous to say anything to anyone about such things, so there are probably very few who will remember him."[8]

Dr. Kuhr gave Titus Holy Communion on the final day of his life. With that Holy Viaticum he was prepared to set out on his final journey, one that would lead finally to his encounter with the Lord.

"I Killed a Saint"

At this point let us consider the words of a most unusual witness to what took place during those last days in the life of Titus Brandsma. This witness was an employee of the SS and testified under oath during the process of beatification about what she personally witnessed and did. It was she who gave Fr. Titus the injection that, within a few moments, ended his life.

Her testimony was given on May 28, 1956, in Kamp-Linfort, the Federal Republic of Germany.

She had come forward voluntarily even though, had she been publicly identified, she would have been arrested and tried as a war criminal. Consequently, her sworn statement was given under conditions of strict secrecy: in the official acts she is identified by the assumed name of 'Tizia.' Her testimony is indispensable to our knowledge of Titus' final moments, which would otherwise be forever lost. She is Dutch and Catholic.[9]

In her testimony Tizia declared: "I have killed a holy man."

In her statement she affirmed, "I was brought back to the right way through the intercession of Fr. Titus. Personally I consider him a martyr because National-Socialism was a kind of anti-Christ."[10]

Fr. Titus dressed in the attire of a Dachau prisoner: a striped suit, the number and the triangle in red. This is a drawing of Br. Raphael Tijhuis, O. Carm., a fellow Dutch Carmelite and prisoner with Fr. Titus at Dachau. Br. Raphael created several drawings of camp life which are in the Archives of the German Province of the Carmelites. He survived and wrote of his own journey through the camps which was published in English as *Nothing Can Keep God From Us*.

"I was 16 when I went to Berlin as a Red Cross nurse," she declared. "I was required to take an oath that I considered Hitler as my god and that I would never again set foot in any religious place. The Church and all such things were frauds; the Jews were to be exterminated, etc. This was the beginning of our education. I was too young to understand the consequences of such an oath."[11]

With regard to Fr. Titus Brandsma she testified:

> In Dachau one had to work hard but was not given much food; 30 or 40 people would die each day, from typhus, mistreatment, exhaustion. The people in charge told us that the prisoners were part of the resistance and that they were criminals who ought to disappear from society.
>
> Some prisoners who came to the infirmary ended up receiving the "injection of grace." Often they were beaten to death, or died after mistreatment.
>
> They were used for experiments such as their resistance to heat and cold, to infections, etc.
>
> Members of the staff who refused to take part in the mistreatment of the sick were caught in a dilemma: we could commit suicide or be shot. That is why we did not dare disobey the orders of the Lagerarzt.
>
> Even had Titus arrived at the camp in perfect health, he would not have lived, because they hated prominent clergymen. When he came to the infirmary he was already destined for death. This I know because the doctor pointed him out as one of the ones who, after a time, was to receive the "injection of grace." I hardly ever saw any patient recover after our care.
>
> When Titus came to the infirmary his feet were terribly swollen with edema, and he had a severe case of dysentery as well. No one ever told him what to expect, but as soon as he arrived, he was on the list of those to die soon.
>
> The cause of death of the patients, apart from our ill-treatment, was invariably the same: cardiac embolism.
>
> Fr. Titus treated me with great compassion. He asked me how I had come to be there. I told him what had happened. He did not show any disdain. Once he took my hand and said, "Poor girl, I will pray a great deal for you."
>
> He even gave me a rosary[12] so that I would pray it. I told him I was unable to pray, and therefore it was of no use to me. He replied, "Even if you don't know how to pray, you could say on each bead, 'Pray for us, sinners.'"

I began to laugh. But he assured me that if I would pray it, I would not be lost.

Normally I felt only disgust for the patients, even the priests made no impression on me. The only one I found to my liking was Fr. Titus, and I liked him a lot because he was very kind and patient. One day I told him I felt a real dislike for priests, and he said, "The best priests are not always those who go into the pulpit to preach beautiful sermons, but those who suffer a great deal and who offer their suffering for sinners. I am happy I can suffer...."

Father Titus Brandsma, in spite of his physical conditions, also had to submit to a despicable medical experiment. I recall that, nearly dead, he said, "Let your will, not mine, be done, O Lord."

Those were words that made a deep impression on me.

Everyone who watched him got the impression that there was something supernatural about him. Usually there was a group of patients around his bed. He knew how to encourage them. Once I was present when a man standing next to his bed in tears told him about his entire life; and I heard how Fr. Titus told him, "Friend, that is nothing serious. You'll see, it will all pass."

Ordinarily the patients were concerned only with themselves, but Fr. Titus was always in good humor and was able to give his support to others, especially to me. I have no doubt he was a saint; otherwise he could never have acted the way he did. I am convinced that there was something supernatural about him.

The last two days of his life he was in a coma. On the first he was delirious. [On the second] the doctor told me I should prepare to give him the "injection of grace" [carbolic acid]. He gave me the order at 1:30 in the afternoon. Dr. Wolter himself prepared the injection, something he always did personally. Then I injected it into Fr. Titus' vein.

The other patients were completely aware of what that injection meant, and they hated us for it with all their hearts.

It was about ten minutes before two when I administered the injection. This was on July 26, 1942. I felt bad the rest of the day. Even though on other occasions I gave these injections as a matter of routine, that time it made a deep impression on me.

He died at two o'clock in the afternoon. I was present, as was the doctor with a stethoscope, to cover appearances. As soon as his heart stopped beating, the doctor told me, "This son of a bitch is already dead."

We left immediately. After the cadavers were stripped of their clothing, some were thrown into the common grave with quicklime, others doused with gasoline and burned, others sent to the crematorium. I do not know what was done with Fr. Titus' body.

The doctor left when I did, as I said, and he filled out the death certificate with the cause of death."[13]

At the time of his death, Fr. Titus Brandsma was 61 years, 5 months and 3 days old.

Well-Contained Emotion throughout the Camp

A squeaking cart bore the remains of Fr. Titus Brandsma to the old crematory where two ovens burned day and night. The new crematory had not yet been completed.

Three days later his body was thrown into one of those ovens and reduced to a few puffs of smoke, a handful of ashes, and a little mound of carbonized bones that would be used to fill potholes in some road or perhaps thrown into a pit behind the crematory. Incineration took several hours.

Paul Berben, in his history of Dachau, states:

> In theory, the ashes were to be collected and placed in urns. The families of the deceased could request that the urns be sent to them, at their own expense. Of course, such a privilege was only for citizens of the Reich, whose families were notified of the death; however, only about one out of a hundred made use of this privilege. In any case the urns held ashes taken at random, because several bodies were cremated at one time. It wasn't long before the use of urns was abandoned, and the ashes were simply buried in the ground surrounding the crematory.[14]

Brother Raphael recounts,

> "That day, July 26, was a Sunday. After eating I was walking past the dean of the barracks; laughing, he showed me a paper on which was written that Titus had died. I read:
>
> > Anno Sjoerd Brandsma
> > Born: February 23, 1881
> > Barracks: 28-3
> > Released through death
> > Death: July 26, 1942, 14:00 hours
> > Concentration Camp of Dachau 3-K
> > W. G. (Revier: Registration Office)

Clowning around, the dean grabbed the paper back out of my hands, laughing and uttering a series of insults against the priestly state."¹⁵

That night, when the doctor announced, "In my ward, only Brandsma died today," a quiet sadness reigned in the infirmary. To the executioners it meant nothing: one more useless being had achieved the goal for which he had been brought here–death. But to the remaining patients, listening silently and in their own way mourning, came the conviction that one of their own was now in the presence of God, rejoicing, free of the miseries of the camp. They were sure that he was a saint.

"On hearing the news," insisted Brother Raphael, "we all said he was in heaven."¹⁶

A few days later an impersonal notice was sent from Dachau to the family farm at Oegeklooster in Frisland. His sister Gatske, wife of M. J. de Boer, received the curt message announcing the death of her brother:

> Concentration Camp of Dachau. Dachau 3-K
> Comandos Rep II. August 5, 1942
> To Mr. M. J. de Boer
> Oegeklooster, Off. Post. Bolsward (District Frisia)
> Your brother-in-law Anno Brandsma, born February 23, 1881, died on July 26, 1942 in the camp hospital as a result of a intestinal infection.
> The body was incinerated on July 29, 1942, in the ovens of the state crematory. The certificate of death has been sent.
> The Commandant of the Concentration Camp of Dachau [illegible signature]
> SS Obersturbannführer (Captain of the Special Police)¹⁷

In 1942 alone some 800 clergy died in Dachau.

Dachau continued operating until April 29, 1945, when it was liberated by the armies of the allies. At that time there were 32,000 prisoners, living skeletons all, and 50 boxcars containing 2,130 bodies of those who had died while being transported during a month-long trip. These are but a few of the chilling statistics gathered from the records of General of the Armies Dwight D. Eisenhower.¹⁸

ENDNOTES

1. SU 79, pp. 537-539.
2. SU 79, p. 384.

3. SU 79, p. 361.
4. Berben, *Dachau: Historia oficial*, pp. 131-132.
5. SU 79, pp. 540 ff., and Berben, *Dachau: Historia oficial*, pp. 151-166.
6. SU 79, pp. 540 ff.
7. Valabek, p. 123.
8. SU 79, pp. 395-396.
9. Redemptus Maria Valabek, O. Carm., "Mary and Ourselves: God-Bearers," p. 184.
10. *Silloges probationum judicialium de fama martyrii nec non de martyrio servi Dei Titi Brandsma*, Roma, 1973, p. 13.
11. *Idem.*
12. See *Appendix IV*.
13. INF 69, p. 87.
14. Berben, *Dachau: Historia oficial*, p. 25.
15. SU 79, p. 361.
16. SU 79, 365.
17. SU 79, pp. 548-549.
18. Hans Reiner, *Los horrores nazis* (Barcelona: n.p., 1977), pp. 100 ff.

Chapter XIV

Saint and Hero

Reactions of Church and Nation

Back in the Netherlands the Dutch Bishops were promulgating a new pastoral letter to be read at every Mass on the very Sunday when Titus was dying. It began with the observation, "These are times of great afflictions, two of the most unjust being the oppression of the Jews and the sentences to forced labor in concentration camps ..."

It concluded,

> Let us pray to God, beloved brothers and sisters, through the intercession of the Mother of Mercy, that He be a refuge for those men and women who, torn from their beloved families, are condemned to forced labor. ... May He protect them body and soul, preserve them from despair and discouragement, and keep them true to their faith. May the Lord also grant strength to their families who were forced to watch as they were taken away. May He aid the afflicted and oppressed, the imprisoned and the flogged, all those who see themselves under the threatening cloud of danger ....

How mysterious the ways of the Lord! At the very time when Titus was passing from this world to the Father in Heaven, the entire Dutch Church was praying for him. The pastoral letter of the Dutch hierarchy had great impact on the entire country. It had also made an equal, though contrary, impact on the Nazi forces of occupation. Reprisals were not long in coming. The commissar of the Third Reich made his response with actions: on August 2 all Catholics in the Netherlands who had Jewish ancestors were arrested and sent to concentration camps. The commissar stated publicly: "All this is in retaliation for the pastoral letter of the bishops."[1]

As soon as the details of Father Titus Brandsma's holy death–along with his writings from prison–became known, he was hailed on all sides as a saint and a national hero. Both the members of his family and his brother Carmelites began receiving a curious mixture of correspondence: letters of condolence on the loss of their dear brother and confrere, and letters of congratulations on the death of one who had given his life for the Christian faith as a true martyr.

Among the first of these letters to be received was that of Archbishop De Jong of Utrecht. On August 6 he wrote to the prior of Nijmegen:

> Permit me to express to you and to your Order my profound regrets for the tragic death of your confrere Fr. Brandsma.
>
> He was a holy religious and priest as well as a man of great merit in so many fields. He was ever ready to assist me in any task, and for this I am forever in his debt.
>
> He gave his life for the Church. God will not deny him his eternal reward.

A few days later, August 11, Titus' dear friend Fr. Hubertus Driessen wrote to the soon-to-be-famous Carmelite theologian, Fr. Bartolomé Xiberta, in Rome, a letter that expressed the feelings of the Carmelites.[2] Among other things, he wrote:

> What great sadness the death of Fr. Titus has caused. May God's will be done. ... We have no details of his death, and perhaps we never shall. They gave us permission to hold a funeral service, but without solemnity and without publicity–a simple sung Mass with a few invited guests. Everything else was forbidden. There was a service in Nijmegen as well, and also in his birthplace.
>
> Everyone is talking of Titus as a saint; indeed, it was the Protestants who were the first to bestow this title on him. Already a biography is being written and there is talk of opening a museum with all his memorabilia. ... Hopefully we will be able to do something worthy of Titus. Without any doubt he was the first among us, the greatest Carmelite of our province. We always considered him as an example, a truly holy man. He was second to none in his love for the Order and for Our Lady. Every one of his sermons, articles and other publications ends with a few words to the praise and honor of Mary. Only a year ago he preached the retreat for the community in Oss and he spoke only of Our Lady. No wonder we always looked at him as an example, a true saint. We all want to see him beatified soon. ...
>
> It was this very morning that we celebrated the solemn funeral rites for that holy, blessed soul, to whom from now on we will always

go with full confidence that he will hear us. He never failed to help when he was with us; all the more will he do so now."³

When the war was over and Queen Wilhelmina of the Netherlands had returned from exile, she publicly expressed her admiration of Fr. Titus to his sister, Gatske de Boer-Brandsma. In a letter dated November 4, 1946, she wrote:

> I feel an obligation to tell you, the elder sister of the deceased Professor Doctor Anno Sjoerd Brandsma, and your two sisters and your brother, of my heartfelt sympathy for the loss of this great and sincere patriot.
>
> As a Catholic priest and professor of the Catholic University of Nijmegen he did not hesitate for a moment to set out clearly the religious and patriotic principles for all those who sought his advice. Even from prison, he was unafraid to express his evaluation of National-Socialism. Similarly, in his diary, he allowed us an insight into his own inner spiritual strength, a witness that today as then has a great value for all.
>
> Through his death in the concentration camp of Dachau we have lost a great patriot and you a most dear member of your family. May his courageous example of fidelity remain for all of us a continuous comfort for our lives

Testimony of His Fellow Prisoners

It is to the survivors, Protestant as well as Catholic, to his fellow-prisoners in Scheveningen, Amersfoort, Kleve and Dachau, to those who personally witnessed his imprisonment and his death, that we turn for the most significant personal impressions of his selfless ministry to his companions and finally of his martyrdom. The following are but a few selected examples of their testimonies:

Fr. van Genuchten, O.F.M.:

> I thank God for the privilege of knowing this man who was full of light. When Fr. Brandsma arrived, Dachau was even more of a hell than it had been previously. In spite of this, he was always smiling and seemed filled with joy. He was an example for all of us. I shall never forget Fr. Titus and I hope he will not forget us.

Th. van Mierlo:

> Professor Brandsma was very weak physically, but spiritually he was the strongest of us all. He rose above his suffering. I never saw him discouraged. Everyone loved him for his natural, kind manner. He didn't know the meaning of hate, impatience, callousness. I never

saw any defect in him.

Fr. H. J. Kuyper, formerly a military chaplain, later dean of his Diocese:

> The eminent Professor Titus Brandsma was a man with a heart of gold and an excellent character. He was not naïve. He maintained perfect control over himself. The fact that he never lost his peace when mistreated in the camp was due to his uncommon moral strength. He was good-natured and self-effacing. He was totally humble and candid, and never did anything to call attention to himself.[5]

Mr. A. Blaisse: "He was holiness in flesh and bone. ... It was difficult to find anyone like him."

Fr. Verhulst:

> He did not know the meaning of hate; rather he was full of kindness for everyone. When we had some problem or other, we would go the priests, especially to him. When I went home a free man, I told my mother Titus was a saint. I think that sooner or later they will canonize him.

Dr. Joseph Kentenich: "His presence and his words produced such peace, such resignation, such hope that no one could forget him."

Fr. Othmarus Lips, O.F.M.Cap.:

> To be a saint in Dachau was easy and difficult at the same time. Easy, because living on the edge of life and face to face with death, one felt totally dependent on the will of God. But it was also difficult, because one was living side by side with fellow prisoners who had their eyes on you every single moment of the day. There was never any privacy. Titus was always living in the presence of God; so he was able to live in the midst of 1,200 clergymen simply and without any self-consciousness, always with a smile and with a mystical patience born from within himself. He paid back offenses just as Jesus did: "Lord, forgive them for they know not what they are doing." No one had anything against him. He was a saint.

Fr. L. de Coninck, S.J.: "He died happy, truly happy, because he had been dealt with and scourged as was Christ."

Chaplain Kees Höppener:

> The most impressive quality in him was his peace, his confidence in God. Psychologically Fr. Titus was strong, youthful, optimistic with a kind of supernatural optimism. For him, suffering for Christ was an opportunity, a joy. There was no thought of revenge. We

Catholics used to say, would to God we were all like him! The others would say, would to God all Catholics were like him!

N. Bogaarts: "All of us prisoners had an extraordinary respect for him. Some kind of beneficent power seemed to flow from him. No other priest or minister was as kind as he. How much happiness we found in him!"

R. J. de Groot: "He was always in good spirits, happy, content, totally resigned, so much so that I often thought, if that man is not a saint, no one is."[6]

Bro. Raphael Tijhuis, O. Carm.:
> We all considered him a saint. After his death we said, "This man is already in heaven." Without any hesitation I can assure you that we all thought of him as a martyr. As for myself, I invoked him as soon as I heard of his death.

Fr. P. van Gestel, S.J.: "Everyone who shared his life in Dachau considered him a saint because of his great virtues. This reputation for holiness continued after his death."

Chaplain J. M. E. Lemmens: "We all considered him a saint. After his death I myself, along with the other clergymen, considered him a martyr, a martyr for the faith."

Nor was it only Catholics who admired him, but the members of other churches as well, and even those who had no religion:

The Calvinist minister J. Overduin:
> I shall always remember our dear professor as a fiery brother in Christ. I remember his limbs all swollen with edema and his fleshless body. ... In his heart he had already found heaven before he found himself in the hell of the camp. Titus Brandsma was a child of God by the grace of Jesus Christ.

Dr. P. H. Ronge:
> Although I am Lutheran, I have to say that in all my life I have rarely met anyone who made such an impression on me as that Catholic priest. In Amersfoort he was the most friendly of us all, he helped everyone even the non-Catholics, and not excluding even the communists. From the moment I met him I knew him to be a man well above average.

Dr. C. P. Gunning: "This deeply spiritual and quiet man introduced us to Catholic mysticism. We considered him an authentic Catholic and his example was a blessing."

P. A. van Coorst: "Father Titus was warm and cultured. A splendid and attractive figure of a man. His presence was most welcome to all of us, whatever creed we held."

The Rescue of Key Documents

The transcripts of the interrogations and the condemnation of Titus Brandsma demonstrate both the Nazis' persecution of religion and Titus Brandsma's sanctity and martyrdom. Titus is the first victim of Nazism to be beatified as a martyr.

The very survival of those documents amidst the ups and downs of World War II was itself providential; indeed, it was a unique event in the history of Nazism. From September 1944, the Gestapo attempted systematically to destroy such records to keep them from the hands of the allies. Thanks to the research of Fr. Adrianus Staring, O. Carm., we have learned how the Brandsma documentation came to be saved.[7]

Three series of Brandsma documents were rescued: 1) his interrogations and condemnation by the Gestapo; 2) his writings while in Scheveningen prison; 3) several of his unpublished works from various periods of his life.

The interrogations to which Fr. Titus was submitted and his subsequent condemnation are a unique source for a realistic judgment of Nazism. Of all the cases initiated by the Gestapo, the transcripts pertaining to the Brandsma case are the only ones known to have survived. During the winter of 1944-1945 the Gestapo built an incinerator in Glanesburg, near the German frontier, for the destruction of documents originating in The Hague. To salvage as much as possible, Dutch partisans asked the British to bomb the building housing the Gestapo offices in Amsterdam; then, pretending to be firemen, they "rescued" the documents. Cardinal de Jong has testified that the Brandsma documents were sent to him by Fr. Brocard Meijer, O. Carm. The originals are currently in the Carmelite archives in Rome.

The account of the rescue of Fr. Titus' writings from prison is truly moving.

After Titus' death, Titus' relative, Asuerus Brandsma the lawyer, wrote to Dachau to claim his personal effects; these were sent shortly before the bombing of the SS quarters there on October 5, 1942, which resulted in the burning of the storage area for the personal effects of some 30,000 prisoners. Brandsma had died but two months earlier.

Asuerus turned them over to the prior of Nijmegen, Fr. Christopher Verhallen, who kept them in his own cell. On July 13, 1944, the Gestapo confiscated them and were about to arrest the prior.

On May 5, 1945, after the surrender of the German forces in the Netherlands, the prior– having learned that Fr. Titus' effects had come into the possession of a well-known lawyer, van Velzen by name– went personally to the lawyer's house. The lawyer, greatly moved, related how they had come into his possession:

At the request of the Diocese of Roermond, he had been trying to help some imprisoned clergymen. To this end, in September 1944, he had spoken with a Professor Nelis, the official who in July 1942, had replaced Hardegen, the magistrate who had presided over the interrogations of Fr. Brandsma.

While they were talking, Nelis had been called to the telephone. He returned, pale, and said, "We must go; I have strict orders to burn everything before leaving."

Nelis then took an entire stack of files and said, "These I have no problem burning because they are worthless; but there is one file that is important. It contains documents that refer to a very spiritual person, a pious person, a man so holy that I cannot bring myself to burn it, because it may serve for a canonization. I don't know what to do. I am not allowed to spare it, but I don't want to destroy it."

Van Velzen suggested that he would take it when he left. After considering the dangers to them both, Nelis turned that file over to van Velzen. The latter took it to his own home and hid it under a carpet until, after the war, he could turn it over to the prior of Nijmegen. Professor Nelis, the man so concerned about those invaluable documents, was a laicized priest, an instructor at the University of Frankfurt.

The rescue of Fr. Titus' unpublished writings is important for understanding him as a human being, as an intellectual, and as a mystic. When Titus was arrested by the Gestapo on

January 19, 1942, 137 files had been left in his room under seal until the Gestapo's search on July 13, 1944. Afraid that the Gestapo would return once again to remove them; the friars broke the seals on the door and transferred them all to Boxmeer for safe keeping. There the owner of a factory hid them in refrigerators inside his plant.

Chapel and Museum

Shortly after Titus' death, some of his friends gathered what they could of the things that had belonged to him. These they began to exhibit in places that might be frequented by the public. In 1960 a small chapel-museum was erected according to plans drawn up by Pieter Dijkema. Constructed of earth-toned brick reminiscent of the bunkers of the concentration camp, the rectangular, windowless structure is located in a small square off Doddendaal Street, Nijmegen, adjacent to the priory Titus had founded. The only external adornment is a small mosaic of the Virgin Mary above the door and, in the door itself, a window depicting Titus. Across the facade, in bronze letters, the name Titus Brandsma.

Inside there is a hall whose walls contain several tablets of white stone with inscriptions relative to the martyrdom of Fr. Brandsma, and a few frames with photographs, manuscripts, and other objects that belonged to the Carmelite martyr.

To the left of the corridor there is a bronze bust of Titus, the work of Peter Roovers; beneath it a dark red clay amphora containing ashes from the common grave in Dachau. On the right is a book where visitors can write their petitions.

Three openings without doors open into the chapel in the center of the building, which can accommodate about thirty people.

A skylight above the altar provides the chief source for natural light.

Over the altar there is a modern painting of the Pantocrator; on the left as one faces the altar is a portrait of Titus, dressed in his prison uniform, after the drawing done in the concentration camp of Amersfoort by John Dons. Beneath it there are always fresh flowers. On the right is a bas-relief of Our Lady of Mount Carmel, where vigil lights burn.

Continuing the image of a concentration camp, in one corner of the little square is a column made of four metal beams, joined at the top with a bronze sculpture and resembling a watch tower in the death camp.

The chapel is very secluded, devotional; there is always at least one of the faithful in prayer. Mass is celebrated daily.

A Bell Sounds in the Camp

Prayer continues in Dachau.

During my pilgrimage to the concentration camp of Dachau as I was walking from place to place and visiting the various areas of the camp, trying to assimilate all I was experiencing, suddenly there was the deep, solemn tolling of a great bell. It was coming from the Chapel of the Agony of Christ located at the end of the camp's main street. We visitors looked at one another, wondering what it was all about.

Instinctively I looked at my watch: it was three o'clock in the afternoon, the hour when Jesus had died on the cross. I was overwhelmed by the significance of that thought– the death of Jesus, the death of the martyrs– being proclaimed by the voice of that mournful toll.

Someone quietly confirmed my intuition: "At this time every day," he said, "the bell tolls in memory of the death of Jesus and that of the thousands of innocent victims in this place."

As the tolling of the bell came to an end, another, smaller bell began ringing, the bell of the Carmelite Monastery of the Most Precious Blood, located outside the camp behind the Chapel of the Agony of Christ.

All of us, tourists and pilgrims alike, were drawn toward Carmel; there a group of contemplative nuns was beginning to chant the Hour of None, the hour when Jesus gave up his spirit to the Father. The voices of the religious and of the visitors fused into a single prayer uniting praise of God and communion with those who had died here for love, for liberty, for truth.

I felt Titus Brandsma was present with me.

The Process of Canonization

For some thirty years Titus Brandsma was once again on trial; this time it was not for the crime of sabotage but for the evaluation of his courage and virtue. The process of canonization put its seal on his spiritual victory, much as the Nazi process had placed its seal, albeit unintentionally, on his moral victory through death in the camp.

The diocesan process began on January 11, 1955, in Nijmegen, the Diocese of Den Bosch.

The investigation was based on the sworn testimony of some fifty eye-witnesses to his life and martyrdom: a cardinal, two bishops, four professors from the Catholic University, and most especially inmates from the prisons and concentration camps where he had been held. Among these latter were four non-Catholics and a few agnostics.

From his family there was the testimony of his brother, Fr. Hendrik, a Franciscan priest; his sister, Gatske; and the lawyer, Asuerus Brandsma.

Most important of all was the testimony of the SS nurse, known to us only as Tizia, from the extermination camp of Dachau. Her deposition was taken in 1956. The impact of her confession extended even beyond the canonical procedure: its importance is unparalleled for any honest judgment of the nature of Nazism.

During the process it was necessary to review the contents of the 137 files taken from Titus' room and providentially preserved from incineration; thirty of them contained more than 750 articles published in newspapers. This may well be the first time that a process of canonization has made extensive use of the writings of a journalist– all too frequently produced on the spur of the moment and under the pressure of deadlines, and frequently without the luxury of time for either thorough research or consideration of the impact on readers.

As with any canonical processes for canonization, this one included letters from bishops from around the world petitioning that its Acts be forwarded to the Congregation for the Causes of Saints. Such letters are not a mere formality. On the contrary, each one expresses the judgement of an individual bishop about the

Plaque at Dachau commemorating two Carmelites who died in the camp. Left is Fr. Hilary Januszewski, the prior in Krakow, Poland who died in Dachau on March 25, 1945, a short time before the camp was liberated by American troops. He volunteered to help with the prisoners suffering from typhus 21 days before. He was beatified on June 13, 1999 by Pope John Paul II. To the right is Fr. Titus Brandsma who died at Dachau on July 26, 1942. The plaque was unveiled and blessed by the prior general of the Carmelite Order, Fr. Fernando Millán Romeral, during a 2018 Carmelite formation program which included a pilgrimage to the Dachau concentration camp. Fr. Titus was canonized by Pope Francis on May 15, 2022, during a Mass in St. Peter's Square.

justification for the introduction of the cause, about its timeliness, and about its benefit for the People of God. What is involved is not simply the sum of the bishops' personal judgments, but rather a concert of coinciding opinions, the voice of the one College of Bishops as described in *Lumen gentium*, N° 23.

These are letters that reveal clearly the mind of the bishops about National-Socialism and its relationship with the Church: their opinion of totalitarian states in general, especially when they suppress the rights of the Church and the demands of freedom of conscience; their condemnation of the horrors of the concentration/extermination camps, and of the holocaust itself which involved thousands upon thousands of innocent victims.

On December 20, 1957, the completed diocesan process was sent to Rome. Additional sworn testimonies were gathered and studied in depth; only then did the members of the Congregation for the Cause of Saints declare that they were considering an outstanding candidate, one worthy of public veneration.

The process was twofold: Titus Brandsma was being proposed both as a confessor and as a martyr. The former would indeed have been less difficult, for the Church does not easily bestow the title "martyr." Moreover, this cause was precedent setting, a groundbreaking, "pilot" process that might open the doors to others of a similar nature. It went beyond the traditional concept of martyrdom into an area that would include new realities: death for the Faith within situations that we call "war." Here the Church must discern whether an individual died for his Faith or in defense of his country. The Nazi executioners had made every effort to hide their true intentions in the hope of escaping the condemnation of history.

On December 10, 1973, the cause was accepted by the Congregation as truly involving martyrdom. On December 9, 1984, Pope John Paul II signed the decree recognizing Titus Brandsma as a martyr and set the date for his solemn beatification in the Basilica of St. Peter in Rome. Some years earlier, when he had been informed about the cause of Titus Brandsma, Pope Pius XII had exclaimed: "This man was a true martyr."

During the early sessions of Vatican II, when the position of the Church in relation to the media was being discussed, Pope John

XXIII had spoken with great enthusiasm about the example of Fr. Titus. During these discussions each of the Council Fathers was given a brief summary of Fr. Titus' life.

A few months earlier an Italian biography had been published by the Director of the Press Office of the Council, the future Bishop of Alba, Monsignor Fausto Vallainc. When Monsignor Vallainc welcomed the journalists assigned to the Council from around the world, he pointed out that theirs was a delicate, responsible mission, one that he entrusted to the spiritual protection of the Servant of God, Fr. Titus Brandsma.

A copy of this biography was presented to the Holy Father. A few days later Pope John told the author, in the presence of several others, that he had found it so fascinating that he had not been able to put it down until he had finished, and so had lost a night's sleep. He promised to speak about it publicly.

True to his word, in an audience for foreign journalists on October 25, 1961, he shared with them his impressions of Fr. Titus, a man he described as an intrepid yet popular Dutch Carmelite journalist. "His was a beautiful life, one that has become a glory for his country; there he was very well known, and his writing read and admired."

He went on to mention Titus' position as Ecclesiastical Consultant to the Dutch Catholic Press, and his subsequent arrest, imprisonment and death in Dachau, a victim of his love for and defense of truth. In the face of extraordinary trials, he had never ceased to love both his brethren and his persecutors. Over and above the reality of human suffering, the Holy Father continued, here was a man who witnessed with his life to the presence of Christ in the world.[8]

Celebrating His Memory

Both the media–press, television, movies–and the academic world celebrated the beatification of Titus Brandsma.[9]

In the Netherlands a national monument was dedicated to Titus. On the campus of the Catholic University of Nijmegen a sculpture, the work of G. Mathot, was dedicated. In the front gardens of the Lyceum Titus Brandsma in Oss, founded by Fr. Titus, and near the city library, also founded by him, a bronze statue was erected.

The Carmelites of Nijmegen opened a spiritual center in honor of the new Blessed. Many streets, schools, associations and parishes– and not only in the Netherlands– bear his name, and biographies have appeared in almost all European languages.

In the United States Sheldon Cohen, a well-known composer, produced a Mass in his honor. In Italy "Le due croci (The Two Crosses)," the story of Titus' life, produced by Silvio Maestranzi and staring the German actor Heinz Benet, was seen in the theaters.

In 1988 the World Congress of the International Union of Catholic Journalists established the Titus Brandsma Prize, bestowed every three years on practicing journalists and formers of public opinion distinguished for their publications and initiatives.

Spanish Carmel established the Titus Brandsma Chair in the Pontifical University of Salamanca for studies about issues of human rights and freedom of expression as related to journalism.

Domingo Cols, a musician of Barcelona, has provided a setting in three voices for Titus' poem, "Before Jesus."

By the end of the twentieth century a museum devoted to the multifaceted, remarkable life Titus Brandsma– recently named Dutch "Catholic of the Century"– was opened in Bolsward. The Catholic Friesland Foundation has acquired a three-story building on the canal side of the Hanseatic city and will display documents and artifacts that belonged to the Brandsma-Hettinga family as well as items provided by the Dutch Carmelite Province. The museum will provide both permanent and temporary exhibits on the first two floors, with offices and work rooms above. A room for meditation, reminiscent of the prison camp atmosphere will also be created.[10]

On various occasions Pope John Paul II has questioned the Carmelites about the progress being made with Blessed Titus' cause. During an audience granted to the members of the General Chapter of the Order, September 23, 1995, he indicated his interest in declaring him a saint.

Before that can happen, of course, one of the healings under study by the Congregation must be recognized as miraculous. We pray that the desire of the Holy Father, and of Christians around the world, may soon be realized. During his trial by the Nazis

Titus Brandsma affirmed, "God always has the last word." God has indeed spoken, through the Church, by raising Titus Brandsma to the honors of the altar.

ENDNOTES

1. Among the religious arrested was the German-Jewish philosopher Edith Stein, in religion Sister Teresa Benedicta of the Cross, a cloistered nun living in the Carmel of Echt, where she had been sent in the hope she might escape the Nazi persecution in her own Carmel of Cologne. She was deported to the extermination camp at Auschwitz, Poland, where, on August 9, 1942, she was killed in the gas chamber. She was canonized as a martyr by Pope John Paul II on October 11, 1998.

2. Cf. Fernando Millán Romeral, O. Carm., "Un testimonio de primera mano sobre la muerte del P. Tito," *Analecta Ordinis Carmelitarum* 44:1 (1993), 34-39. This letter was found among the papers of the late Fr. Bartolomé Xiberta, O. Carm., in the Carmelite priory of Barcelona.

3. Millán Romeral, "Un testimonio de primera mano," pp. 34-39.

4. SU 79, p. 554.

5. SU 79, p. 393.

6. SU 79, 344.

7. Adrianus Staring, O. Carm., Boletín del "Comitato Italiano Tito Brandsma",1984-1985. Cf. *Servicio Informativo de los Carmelitas de la Bética*, N° 21 (Julio-Agosto, 1985), 11-17.

8. Cf. *L'Osservatore Romano*, October 26, 1961.

9. For an account of the Beatification ceremonies, see *Appendix VII.*

10. "Titus Brandsma Will Have a Museum in His Native Town." *CITOC*, May-June 2000, pp. 53-54.

Carmelites from around the world came to Dachau in 2018 as part of the multi-week program studying on the life and spirituality of St. Titus. Here they are entering the Dachau concentration camp through a former guard tower after having celebrated Mass at the enclosed Discalced Carmelite monastery of *Heilig Blut* (Precious Blood Monastery).

Appendix I

North American Lecture Tour[1]

At the invitation of Fr. Malachy Lynch,[2] then novice master of the Irish Province, Titus spent three weeks in Ireland to practice English (see Appendix II). During an earlier visit in the Netherlands Fr. Malachy had helped translate Titus' lectures into English.

On July 19, 1935, Professor Titus Brandsma sailed from Cobh, a seaport in County Cork, Ireland, for New York. Preparations had been made for his tour by Fr. Lawrence Diether, prior provincial of the Province of the Most Pure Heart of Mary. On arriving in New York, Titus immediately boarded a train for Washington, D. C., where, at the invitation of Bishop James Ryan, rector of the Catholic University of America, he gave his first lecture in the auditorium of McMahon Hall.

Understandably, he was somewhat apprehensive, as he confessed in a letter to his brother. In this first of his talks in North America he gave an outline of Carmelite spirituality from its origins to the doctrine of spiritual childhood proposed by the recently canonized St. Therese of Lisieux. Titus must have been pleased that not only was his presentation well received, but that–as he was later informed–it was the best attended lecture of the entire summer session.

During his brief stay in Washington he lived at St. Therese Priory with the Carmelite students studying at the Catholic University. He reported it "well situated, not far from the university," and hoped that it would be enlarged. He was no doubt delighted to hear only five years later about the dedication of the new residence, Whitefriars Hall.

From Washington Titus went to Pittsburgh where he spent time with the Carmelites of Holy Trinity priory before continuing his journey to Chicago; there he headquartered at St. Cyril priory. He was particularly impressed with the community's principal apostolate, Mount Carmel High School.

Following their novitiate, the newly professed Carmelites, in addition to their college courses, did double duty teaching in the high school, and also attended summer school at one of the local universities. Consequently, they had only a few weeks for relaxation between the end of summer school and the beginning of the new academic year. Their vacation was spent at Camp Carmel on Hudson Lake in Indiana.

For the benefit of the members of Chicago's St Cyril Community and Joliet's St Elias Community he also took his presentations to them.

Recalling the experience, one of the students would later write that the *fratres* were less than enthusiastic at the prospect of spending three hot August days of their precious recreation time sitting in their habits while listening to spiritual talks by a foreigner. He described the encounter:

> ... after Office, Mass, and breakfast, we all assembled in full habit in the combination dining room, hall and chapel awaiting his [Fr. Titus'] arrival. He astounded us, walking up the aisle in a pleated white cloak. ... Then to our amazement and delight said, "You young men would look more comfortable without the habits." ... Immediately he won us over and all feelings of animosity melted away. He, himself, continued to wear his habit and white cloak for the talks.
>
> Then he became one of us–went swimming and boating–just one of the group. ... He was one of and with us "kids." There were no formalities; he fit right in with us."[3]

During his stay in Chicago Titus was also able to visit the two Carmelite communities in Joliet: St. Mary Carmelite priory and parish, and Joliet Catholic High School served by the St. Elias priory. It was also during this period that Fr. Lawrence Diether asked permission to publish Titus' lectures.[4] Fr. Titus accompanied Fr. Lawrence by train to Niagara Falls, Ontario. There he assisted at the reception of seventeen novices and the first profession of twenty-five *fratres* at Mount Carmel College. His lectures were spread over five days, and once again he won the students' admiration with his opening statement: "As a visitor I must wear my habit, but it's so hot, why don't you take your habits off?"[5]

When not occupied with lectures Titus was given the "grand tour" of the area. He visited the Carmelite parish of St. Patrick as well as many of the sights for which the Niagara Falls area is justly famous. He recorded his own impressions of the Falls:

> ... I listen to the roaring and rushing of Niagara Falls. This cataract demonstrates beautifully how water, subject to the laws of gravity flows down to the lowest parts on the earth.
>
> ... Someone, who is metaphysically minded, will probably get lost in contemplation of the wonderful potentiality of water, being attracted through the so much greater mass of the earth. Suppose what had not this potentiality, this urge towards the centre of gravity of the earth, then there would not be a cataract. Suppose the water was not fluid, then it would not break into millions of drops, which make it look like an avalanche of snow. Had not its particles the faculty of absorbing and reflecting light, the masses of water would not glitter like crystal, and the rainbow would not be there at our feet. Had the water not that power of resistance, it would not thunder in our ears when we venture in its proximity.
>
> ... The water of the Falls is an image of our human nature. ... I, personally, meditate rather about what lies behind this beautiful phenomenon; not only eye and ear are here fascinated but much more my intellect, which ponders over all God has hidden in the water.
>
> I see not only the beauty of nature, the immeasurable potentialities of the water, but I see God at work in His creation, in His revelation of love. Nevertheless my eyes and ears are also captivated and time after time I return to see and hear.[6]

From Niagara Falls Titus returned to New York City where he visited several communities of the Province of St. Elias: Our Lady of the Scapular priory in Manhattan, St. Simon Stock priory in the Bronx, Transfiguration priory in Tarrytown, and St. Albert's priory in Middletown, the location of the novitiate and formation house. In each he was able to deliver one or more presentations.

While in Middletown he also addressed the Corpus Christi Carmelite Sisters living in a house known as the "Thistles"; it was also around this time that he paid a visit to the cloistered Carmelite nuns in Allentown, Pennsylvania. Sister Elizabeth Lanshe, a junior nun at the time, wrote:

> ... the nuns crowded about the grille so as not to miss a word. I would say that his message was all about Carmel, the Carmelite vocation and Mary. ... Of course, it was only one conference.
>
> ... To me he seemed to have the same spiritual-religious caliber of a Father Xiberta[7] and a Father John Brenninger,[8] and the genuineness, etc. of a Father Hilary Doswald.[9] These, to me, were great men of God. ...[10]

From Middletown Titus was driven to St. Cecilia priory in Englewood, New Jersey. From there, he embarked on the S.S. Washington en route to Ireland and then back to Nijmegen.

FOOTNOTES

1. With special thanks to Leander Troy, O. Carm., "Blessed Titus Brandsma's Trip to the United States and Canada in 1935." *The Sword* 52 (1992), 25-35.

2. Fr. Malachy Lynch, O. Carm., is best remembered as the first Prior of Aylesford after the persecution of Catholics begun in the 16th century under King Henry VIII.

3. From a letter of Francis Blum, O. Carm., to Leander Troy, O. Carm., July 9, 1986.

4. The original publication, *Carmelite Mysticism: Historical Sketches*, appeared in 1936. A 50th Anniversary Edition was published in 1986 (Darien, Illinois: The Carmelite Press).

5. Norman Werling, O. Carm., "Journey to Dachau," Introduction, p. 2

6. The Beauty of Carmel, in Troy, "Blessed Titus Brandsma's Trip, " p. 33.

7. Fr. Bartholomew Fanti Xiberta, O. Carm., a renowned theologian, peritus at Vatican II; his cause has been opened in his native Catalonia.

8. Fr. John of the Cross Brenninger O. Carm., prior of the Collegio Internazionale di Sant'Alberto in Rome, compiler of *Vita Camelitana* and author of a manual of formation of novices, *The Carmelite Directory of the Spiritual Life*.

9. Fr. Hilary Doswald, O. Carm., Prior General of the Order (1931-1947).

10. From a letter to Leander Troy, O. Carm., July 27, 1987.

Appendix II

Trips to Ireland in 1935

Writing to the prior provincial of the Province of the Most Pure Heart of Mary (PCM), Fr Lawrence Diether, O. Carm., the Prior General of the Carmelite Order, Hilary Doswald, O. Carm., suggested an invitation could be extended to Titus for the summer of either 1934 or 1935 "to give lectures on Carmelite Mysticism at Niagara Falls and possibly at the Catholic University of Washington." Fr. Doswald expressed his view that a visit by Titus, as former rector magnificus of the Catholic University of Nijmegen, would help to raise the profile of both the Order and the Province in the United States.

Titus' visit to the United States was eventually fixed for the summer of 1935 (see Appendix I). In preparation for his trip, Titus came to Ireland in January of the same year with the intention of combining a vacation with the opportunity to work on his knowledge of the English language. He stayed with the Carmelite communities at Kinsale, in County Cork, and at Whitefriar Street in the center of Dublin City. Titus sent several postcards to his family during his stay in Ireland.

Titus was particularly taken with the beauty of Kinsale, located as it is on a hill by the sea. For some time afterwards locals recalled Titus celebrating Mass with a discernibly "foreign" accent. The Kinsale friary was at the time of Titus' visit the location of the novitiate of the Irish Province of Carmelites. A novice at the time, Patrick 'Patsy' Keenan, O. Carm., recalled how personable Titus was and how keen he was to practice his English by engaging with him in conversation. Titus even asked his advice on how best to translate sections of the Carmelite Rule; Titus was obviously working on the text of the talks on Carmelite mysticism he would deliver in the United States that summer.

In correspondence Titus several times expressed his liking for Dublin. He found the community at Whitefriar Street particularly welcoming. In fact, so attentive were they that he told his family he hardly had time to write. Titus was impressed by the church at Whitefriar Street, especially by the number of people who attended Mass there. He was particularly struck by the Calvary scene in the entrance hall and sent a postcard of it to his family in the Netherlands. Shortly before leaving Dublin to return to the Netherlands, Titus paid a visit to the leading Irish politician and statesman, Mr Éamon De Valera. De Valera was president of the Executive Council of the Irish Free State as well as Minister for External Affairs.

The purpose of his meeting with the De Valera is not entirely clear. Historically De Valera enjoyed good relations with a number of Carmelites in Ireland and the United States. In 1958, on a visit to Rome, he was made an honorary member of the Order–the highest honor the Order can bestow–and was buried in the full Carmelite habit on his death in 1975. It is possible that Titus–given his interest in the cause of Frisian cultural and linguistic emancipation—was keen to meet a leader of the Irish emancipation movement but it is also likely that Titus wanted to meet with De Valera on account of the high level of influence the Irish man had achieved in the League of Nations in the mid-1930's.

Titus paid a return visit to Ireland in July 1935, stopping over on his way to the United States for one night at Whitefriar Street (he mentions in correspondence that the provincial of the Irish Province resided there) and for several nights at Kinsale.

Later, on his return journey to the Netherlands, in September 1935, Titus stopped over one more time at Kinsale, once again expressing his immense affection for the place. He left Ireland on 4th September for England from where he would return to the Netherlands.

Appendix III

Brother Raphael Tijhuis, O. Carm.

Brother Raphael Tijhuis[1] plays a most important role in the final days of St. Titus Brandsma, both as a witness and, perhaps even more importantly, as a companion, a protector, a friend, and a brother in Carmel.

Bernardus Antonius Tijhuis was born in Rijssen on October 10, 1913. He was professed as a Carmelite brother in 1933, taking the name "Brother Raphael."[2] He had then been assigned to the Carmelite community in Mainz.

One of his letters home had been opened by the German censors; in it he had complained of food shortages, how difficult it was to find butter. To the Nazis this was a punishable offense, particularly since only a short time before Hermann Göring had been bragging that Germany had all the food it needed.

Brother Raphael was arrested and condemned to eighteen months in prison. He spent time in five different prisons before–on March 13, 1942–being sent to Dachau.[3] There he was when Fr. Titus Brandsma arrived on June 19, 1942.

Although he underwent the beatings, hunger, and medical experimentation–he was infected with malaria–he assisted and even tried to protect his sick and elderly confrere as much as possible. Titus, in his turn, did all he could to maintain the spiritual well-being of Raphael.

Brother Raphael was liberated by the allied forces on April 28, 1945, although he never completely recovered from the psychological and physical tortures to which he had been submitted. After liberation he spent some time in Aalsmeer and in Nijmegen, and then in May 1947, he was called to Rome where he joined the community of the Collegio di Sant'Alberto (now called CISA).

While in Rome he took training in library science in the Vatican and helped in the formation of what has become the *Biblioteca Carmelitana* of the Centro Internazionale di Sant'Alberto. He also served both as sacristan and porter.

He was an avid stamp-collector and a capable artist; he did a portrait of Fr. Titus in his camp uniform, now preserved in Boxmeer (see page 239). He developed a heart problem and went to Almelo for treatment. After spending 30 years in Rome he was assigned once again to Mainz. There he was provided with a pacemaker. He would return to live in Rome once more for a short period of time in 1979-1980. He died on June 5, 1981 and is buried in Zenderen.

FOOTNOTES

1. See Adrianus Staring, O. Carm. "Chronicon Provinciae Neerlandicae," *Vinculum Ordinis Carmelitarum I* (1948), 61-68.

2. *Analecta Ordinis Carmelitarum* 35:3 (1981), 150-152.

3, Upon his return to the Netherlands after the war, Brother Raphael wrote about his arrest and subsequent life in the various prisons and concentration camps. Part of his incredible account was published by Edizioni Carmelitane under the title *Nothing Can Keep God from Reaching Us: A Dachau Diary by a Survivor* (2007).

Appendix IV

St. Titus' Rosaries

One of the rosaries purportedly made for Titus Brandsma. One was made by fellow prisoner Piet Hoefsloot in Amersfoort. Hoefsloot was executed by a Nazi firing squad for being a resistance fighter.

When Titus was *Rector Magnificus* of the Catholic University of Nijmegen, he received a rosary from Pope Pius XI. This rosary is now in the possession of the Brandsma family.

During his imprisonment St. Titus used several rosaries. He regretted that he had forgotten to bring his rosary with him when arrested and was forced to count the prayers on his fingers.

In Amersfoort a rosary was made for him by Piet Hoefsloot, a fellow prisoner and resistance fighter from Arnhem; this man, the father of a large family, was among those who was to be executed by firing squad. This rosary Titus gave to Pastor Leo Siegmund when he was released on April 20, 1942. Pastor Siegmund testified during the process leading to the beatification of Fr. Titus. According to his son, Theo, the pastor kept the rosary as a precious keepsake and hung it on the wall in his home in Oldenzaalse Straat in En-

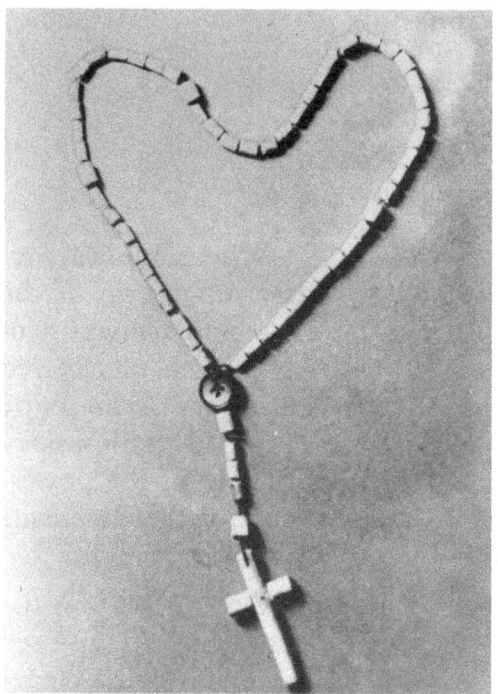

The rosary believed to be the one that Titus Brandsma gave to the nurse who eventually ended his life with a fatal injection of carbolic acid. This rosary is now in the Titus Brandsma Parish in Colmschate, Netherlands.

schede. On his father's death, Theo kept the rosary in a cash box.

Apparently Pastor Siegmund was under the impression that this rosary had been made by Professor Brandsma himself. Manual dexterity, however, was not among St. Titus' many talents. In the words of Fr. Gijsbertus Megens, O. Carm, "he was much too clumsy for that."

The prison chaplain in Amersfoort is also known to have given Titus a rosary.[1]

The most famous of the rosaries, of course, is the one St. Titus gave the nurse shortly before she ended his life with a fatal injection of carbolic acid.[2] She later gave this rosary to Fr. Gemmeke, O. Carm., who in turn presented it to Fr. Gijsbertus Megens for the Titus Brandsma Parish in Colmschate.

FOOTNOTES
1. Aukes, p. 254.
2. Aukes, p. 296.

Chapel of the Agony of Christ, the Catholic memorial on the Dachau camp grounds, was initiated by Dachau survivor Bishop Johannes Neuhäusler. It was consecrated on August 5, 1960 during the Eucharistic World Congress. The open cylindrical structure faces the central axis of the former camp. Above the entrance is a crown of thorns made of copper. Symbolically, the structure stands for the liberation from captivity through Christ. The memorial bell rings out once a day shortly before 3 p.m., the hour of Jesus's death as told in the Gospels.

Appendix V

"Before a Picture of Jesus in My Cell"

Fr. Joachim Smet's translation[1] of St. Titus' best known poem is perhaps the most literal of the three which are included in this book:

O Jesus, when I look on you,
My love for you starts up anew,
And tells me that your heart loves me,
And you my special friend would be.

More courage I will need for sure,
But any pain will I endure,
Because it makes me like to you
And lends unto your kingdom too.

In sorrow do I find my bliss,
For sorrow now no more is this
Rather the path that must be trod,
That makes me one with you, my God.

Oh, leave me here alone and still,
And all round, the cold and chill.
To enter here I will have none;
I weary not when I'm alone,

For, Jesus, you are at my side;
Never so close did we abide.
Stay with me, Jesus, my delight,
Your presence near makes all things right.

The translation by Fr. Albert Groeneveld, O. Carm.,[2] is probably the earliest into English and may be still the best known:

Dear Lord, when looking up to Thee
I see Thy loving eyes on me;
Love overflows my humble heart,
Knowing what faithful friend Thou art.

A cup of sorrow I foresee,
Which I accept for love of Thee.
Thy painful way I wish to go;
The only way to God I know.

My soul is full of peace and light:
Although in pain, this light shines bright.
For here Thou keepest to Thy breast.
My longing heart, to find there rest.

Leave me here freely all alone,
In cell where never sunlight shone.
Should no one ever speak to me,
This golden silence makes me free!

For though alone, I have no fear;
Never wert Thou, O Lord, so near.
Sweet Jesus, please, abide with me;
My deepest peace I find in Thee.

ENDNOTES

1. Smet, *The Carmelites*. IV: 237-238.

2. This version is taken from *Proper of the Liturgy of the Hours of the Order of the Brothers of the Blessed Virgin Mary of Mount Carmel and of the Order of Discalced Carmelites* (Rome: Institutum Carmelitanum, 1993), pp. 435-436.

Appendix VI

The "Carmelite Priory" in Dachau

In addition to Brother Raphael Tijhuis,[1] a Dutch Carmelite who figures so prominently in the final days of Fr. Titus' life, there were several Polish Carmelites in Dachau. Fr Titus and Bro Raphael lived in the same barracks, but the Polish friars were in a different one.

The Nazis had a special hatred for Polish academics and clergy. Smet states that not only were churches, seminaries, and religious houses closed, but half of the country's 7,000 priests were killed. Of the 2,800 priests sent to Dachau, only 816 survived.[2]

The Polish Carmelite province was especially hard hit. When the German army invaded Poland, the Polish Carmelites were just recovering from suppressions suffered during the 19th century and the rise of Communism in Eastern Europe in the early 20th century.

Among the Carmelites arrested by the Gestapo and sent first to Auschwitz and then to Dachau, most were from the priory of Krakow.[3] On September 18, 1940, several Carmelites were arrested without charges and sent first to Auschwitz and then, a few months later, to Dachau.

They were:

+ Fr. Leo Michail Koza, subprior, who died in Dachau on the Vigil of the Ascension, May 13, 1942.[4]

+ Fr. Albertus Urbanski, master of students, who survived five years in Dachau.[5]

+ Fr. Marianus Nowakoski,[6] a newly ordained priest.

+ Fr. Elizeusz Wszelaki,[7] also newly ordained.

+ Br. Brocardus Majcher,[8] a cleric and student used for medical experimentation. Although he survived, he suffered their effects for the rest of his life.

+ Bro. Gerardus Kowalski, a brother, who died in Auschwitz on November 25, 1940, shortly before the transfer to Dachau.[9]

The Gestapo returned to the Krakow priory on December 4, 1940, to arrest a sick, elderly priest; the prior of the community, Fr. Hilarius Januszewski,[10] offered himself as a substitute. Shortly before the liberation of the camp in 1945, fully aware he was not likely to survive, he volunteered to care for Russian prisoners suffering from typhus.[11] He was beatified as a Martyr of Charity by Pope John Paul II, on June 13, 1999.

Other Polish Carmelites who died in Dachau were:

+ Fr. Szymon Buszla, prior of Obory, who died on June 30, 1942;[12]

+ Fr. Bruno Makowski, on August 3, 1942.[13]

ENDNOTES

1. See *Appendix III*.

2. Smet, *The Carmelites*, IV: 241.

3. Cf. Ismael Martinez Carretro, O. Carm., *Figuras del Carmelo* (Madrid: Biblioteca de Autores Cristianos, 1886), pp. 369-376.

4. *Analecta Ordinis Carmelitarum* 11 (1942), 219. Fr. Leo Michail Koza was 32 years of age, 15 years professed, nine years ordained.

5. *Analecta Ordinis Carmelitarum* 37 (1985), 217-218. Fr. Albertus Urbanski died in Krakow on March 1, 1985. At the time of his death he was 73 years of age, 52 years of profession, 46 years of ordination. After his release from Dachau in 1945, he earned a degree in Theology, specializing in Mariology and Josephology. He was a sought after preacher and confessor. He was elected to the provincial council and also served as prior provincial. His letters, following the liberation, are a major source of information about the life and death of Blessed Hilarius Januszewski.

6. Pawlak, Leszek, *Email to translator* dated January 22, 2003. This email, from the prior provincial of the Polish province, provided information on Fr. Marianus Nowakoski, Fr. Elizeusz Wszelaki, and Br. Brocardus Majche who later was ordained priest. Following the liberation of Dachau, Fr. Marianus remained in an American camp in Germany for a short time and then worked with the Carmelites of the St. Elias Province in the USA. In 1976 he was incardinated into the Diocese of Albany, New York where he served as a chaplain at St. Clare's Hospital in Schenectady, New York. He died on October 2, 2000.

7. Pawlak, *idem*. Like Fr Nowakowski, Fr Wszelaki too spent a brief period in an American camp in Germany before going to New York where he ministered with the Carmelites of the St. Elias Province. After a short time he requested incardination into the Diocese of Toledo where he served at St. Adalbert Church. While in America he helped the Polish province build up its provincial library. After retirement he returned to Lipno, Poland, where his family comes from; there he died a diocesan priest on January 8, 1990. He is buried in the Carmelite cemetery in Obory.

8. Pawlak, *idem*. Brocardus Majcher returned to the seminary where he made his final vows in the Order and was ordained, but in 1950 he joined the Diocese of Warmia in northern Poland where he served a parish in Dywity and was confessor of students in the diocesan seminary of Otsztyn. He was a witness in the process for the beatification of Blessed Hilarius Januszewski. He maintained a good relationship with the Carmelites in Danzig but suffered a stroke in 1999 and has since died.

9. *Analecta Ordinis Carmelitarum*. 11 (1942), 125, and 12 (1945), 231. Bro. Gerardus Kowalski was 39 years of age, and had been professed 18 years.

10. Fernando Millán Romeral, O. Carm. "Carmelitas en Dachau: Las Cartas del P. Albert Urbanski desde el lager en el 50 aniversario de la liberación." *Carmelus* 42 (1995), 22-43.
11. Cf. Kilian Healy, O. Carm., *Prophet of Fire*, pp. 181-184.
12. *Analecta Ordinis Carmelitarum* 12 (1945), 230. Fr. Szymon Buszla was 34 years of age at the time of his death and had been a Carmelite for 13 years, a priest for seven years.
13. *Analecta Ordinis Carmelitarum* 11 (1942), 256, and 12 (1945), 230. At the time of his death Fr. Bruno Makowski was 52 years old and had been professed for 35 years, ordained for 26 years.

Appendix VII

The 1985 Beatification

It was ten o'clock on the morning of Sunday, November 3, 1985, when Pope John Paul II proclaimed the words of beatification: "We, by our apostolic authority, declare that the Venerable Servant of God, Titus Brandsma, may from now on be called Blessed, and that his feast may be celebrated ...." Amen. Amen. Amen.[1]

For several days, pilgrims had been arriving from around the world. As was fitting, given the broad spectrum of people who had been served by the many-faceted Carmelite who was about to be raised to honors of the altar, there were members of his family and people from the parish where he had been baptized and confirmed in his native Frisland; there were citizens of the cities and towns where he had labored as a young priest; there were academics from the Catholic University of Nijmegen as well as students from schools he had helped to found; there were journalists who for once had come to participate as well as to report; there were his fellow Carmelites, both friars and sisters, from around the world; and there were survivors of the death camps of the Third Reich.

At a national youth conference, a group of some 400 young Italians who lent their exuberance to many of the events related to the beatification, was held outside of Rome.

On November 2 there had been a special program presented in the Great Hall of the Pontifical University of Propaganda Fidei; brief talks were given by those who had known Fr. Titus or who had themselves suffered in the concentration camps, by Carmelite bishops who had lived through difficult times in Zimbabwe, Brazil, and elsewhere–at least one of them, Bishop Donal Lamont, O. Carm.–had been imprisoned himself in defense of the rights of his people.

A musical setting was provided by the Little Singers of the Carmelite parish of Torrespaccata; in addition to more traditional hymns they performed several pieces composed for the occasion by their talented pastor.

That same evening there was a gathering of journalists assembled by the efforts of Bishop Fausto Vallainc, a Vatican Press officer under Pope John XXIII and the author of one of the first biographies of Titus. One of the speakers was Raimondo Manzini, a former editor of *L'Osservatore Romano*, as well as Giorgio Liverani, vice-director of the Roman daily *Avvenire*. Other journalists included the International Secretary of the Association of European Journalists, the former president of the International Catholic Press Union, the president of the Italian Catholic Journalists. All held up the example of Titus Brandsma as "a defender of the most genuine Christian tradition" and challenged all journalists to follow in his footsteps in an untiring proclamation of truth.

Among the most significant witnesses of these days was the coming together of Dutch and German pilgrims in what can only be described as authentic reconciliation. The impressive pilgrimage of 1,300 Germans and Dutchmen, led by the priors provincial of the Upper German and Dutch provinces, had met in Dachau on All Saints Day where they had paid homage to the victims of this infamous camp. Following a simple, silent ceremony the two provincials had placed wreaths on the symbolic memorial and grave of thousands unknown.

From Dachau it was on to Rome where the bus caravan arrived at the Carmelite Church of Santa Maria in Transpontina, located appropriately on the Via della Conciliazione (the Street of Reconciliation), where they celebrated Mass.

Immediately after Mass there was a torch-light procession up the broad avenue to St. Peter's Basilica, into the Courtyard of St. Damasus where the Holy Father led them in praying the rosary.

A young German pilgrim confessed: "For us Germans it is painful to ... take part in these festivities. It is as if history persecutes us. On the other hand, the reconciliation we desire cannot be separated from penance. I think that for us Germans this is the meaning of this grand encounter of reconciliation in honor of Fr. Titus Brandsma."

A few moments later his thoughts were echoed by the pope: "I cordially greet the Dutch youth who have come to Rome for the beatification of Titus Brandsma. May his example of love until the end inspire you to a life in the spirit of love and reconciliation." He added; "Heartfelt greetings to the young people from Germany. ... The new Blessed be for you an example and intercessor."

The great day arrived. The Vatican Basilica was filled with faithful from the early hours of the morning; some 1,500 men and women from every continent, including over 500 Carmelites. The altar was adorned with thousands of flowers sent directly from the Netherlands as a gift of the Dutch gardeners. Although the Mass itself did not begin until 9:30, a prayerful spirit was provided by the Little Singers of Torrespaccata, the Titus Brandsma Orchestra and Choir of Nijmegen, and of course the Sistine Choir.

The papal procession entered the basilica and mass began, presided over by the Holy Father and concelebrated by numerous cardinals–the Dutch Cardinals Willebrands and Simonis, among them– the Carmelite Prior General, Fr. John Malley, the chaplain of the camp of Dachau, as well as the pastor of Bolsward.

Following the singing of the Kyrie, the Bishop of 's-Hertogenbosch, accompanied by Fr. Redemptus Valabek, Postulator General of the Order, formally requested the Holy Father to beatify the Venerable Servant of God Titus Brandsma.

Standing, the Pope made the formal declaration: "We, by our apostolic authority, declare that the Venerable Servant of God, Titus Brandsma, may from now on be called Blessed, and that his feast may be celebrated .... In the Name of the Father and of the Son and of the Holy Spirit."

The proclamation was received with an outpouring of joy and the applause of those present and the ritual three-fold "Amen."

All eyes were looking upward toward Bernini's magnificent Gloria over the Altar of the Chair, where a painting of the newly Beatified was unrolled, the work of Franciscan artist Andrea Martini.

The Holy Father then intoned the "Gloria" of the Mass. For the first time the newly Beatified was named in the prayer of the liturgy.

The first reading was proclaimed by a grand niece of the new Blessed. Thirty-seven of Titus' relatives were present.

In his homily John Paul stated: "Today a man who underwent the tortures of the concentration camp at Dachau– an infamous blot on our century– one whom God has found worthy of Himself; a man who was victorious over his trials because, in a world filled with hatred, he was able to love everyone, his executioners not excluded; today this man, Titus Brandsma, has been raised to the honors of the altar."[2]

The prayers of the faithful and the offertory procession reminded all present of just why this diminutive, dangerous little friar had been raised to the honors of the altar: his multiple apostolates, his fidelity to the Church, his defense of human rights, his support of Catholic education, his ministry to those vowed to a life in Christian community, his guidance of those who work in the media, and his example to his companions in suffering, both the living and the dead.

As the Eucharistic action continued one could scarcely forget how precious it had been to St. Titus, how much it had pained him not to be able to celebrate daily, how overjoyed he had been to receive Holy Communion during those long, dark days of imprisonment.

The solemn ceremony concluded with the singing of the *Salve Regina* to Our Lady of Mount Carmel whom St. Titus loved so dearly.

Following the beatification, the Holy Father received the superiors of the Order and the members of the various commissions that had been promoting the cause, including the author who gave him a copy of this book, bound in white leather. Then, at noon he prayed the Angelus from his window overlooking St. Peter's Square.

It was raining hard. The Dutch have a saying: "A Dutch saint is no true saint if he does not provide rain on the day of his glorification!" It is clear that Titus is a true saint!

Once again, the pope spoke of "this illustrious son of the Dutch nation– and of the religious family of Carmel– who bore an unconquerable witness to the Faith to a heroic degree."

In the evening the Dutch Ambassador to the Holy See offered a reception in his residence on the ancient Via Appia, so closely associated with the martyrs of the early Christian centuries. The young people gathered in the Church of San Lorenzo, only a block or so from the Vatican, with songs and prayers and witnessing: yet one more proof that the message of Titus Brandsma is sowing seeds in the fertile grounds of the young.

Again, on the following day, the feast of St. Charles Borromeo and the pope's name-day, the pilgrims gathered in the Paul VI Audience Hall. In contrast to the more dignified ceremony of beatification the previous day, this day's gathering was exuberant, even jolly. Both the Nijmegen orchestra and choir and the Little Singers of Torrespaccata provided musical preludes– the latter including several compositions specifically honoring the Holy Father's name-day.

Once arrived at the front of the Hall, the pope was greeted by Cardinal Simonis of Utrecht and several Dutch and Carmelite bishops, along with the Carmelite General Council. In his remarks Pope John Paul emphasized that Titus Brandsma was "a concrete example of the love of God which has manifested itself through the love of a human being for his fellow-man." It was his moral strength– nourished by his theological acumen and his deep personal spirituality, and matured through his academic activities and his function as spiritual guide and director of Catholic journalists–and through it all his unfailing dedication to his beloved Carmel that sustained him in his way of the cross and death."

Indeed, St. Titus lived to the full what he taught his students: "To win the world for Christ one must have the courage to come into conflict with it."

Before bestowing his blessing on the assembly the Holy Father admired an oil painting that had been set up on the stage, the work of the American artist Stephen Andrew Titra; the pope encouraged the young artist and blessed the portrait.[3]

Many pilgrims remained in Rome for the traditional three days of Thanksgiving following a beatification.

The first of these Masses of Thanksgiving took place in the majestic Basilica of St. Mary Major, with Cardinals Simonis and Willebrands as the main concelebrants. Cardinal Willebrands preached the homily, stressing Titus' being "the sign and foundation of reconciliation in the midst of the mystery of evil" through his total abandonment to God's will along with his constant prayer not only for his fellow-prisoners, but even for his persecutors.

The second Mass of the Triduum was celebrated in the Carmelite Church of Santa Maria in Transpontina, only a few blocks in front of St. Peter's Basilica on the Via della Conciliazione. The principal concelebrant was the Carmelite Order's prior general, Fr. John Malley. In his homily Fr. John compared Titus to the great English martyr St. Thomas More, as found in "A Man for All Seasons." In the midst of all his apostolates, St. Titus remained a true contemplative, one who not only "gazed on truth" as St. Thomas Aquinas would have it but did so "under the influence of love" according to the great school of theology in Salamanca.

In the practical order Titus was "truly committed to the life of community and fraternity in Carmel [for] the very basis of our life is that we are brothers and sisters of the Blessed Virgin Mary of Mount Carmel, united with one another in compassion, respect and care. And Titus brought this love from his own Carmelite community to each one whom he encountered."

The third and final day of thanksgiving was celebrated in the Carmelite Basilica of San Martino ai Monti, an inner-city parish served by the Carmelites since 1299 AD. As was fitting, the liturgy was presided over by Cardinal Pietro Palazzini, Prefect of the Congregation for the Causes of Saints.

The offertory procession was noteworthy: various members of the international Lay Carmelite group known as *Donum Dei* carried gifts representing the gift St. Titus had made of himself during his apostolic life and imprisonment.

In his homily the cardinal pointed out that Titus Brandsma was a member of the Ancient Order of Carmel. It was his formation as a novice, his exemplary observance of religious life, his zeal in undertaking a series of activities for the building up of the Body of Christ, that prepared him for what was to come: his was a "harmonious fusion between a life of prayer and apostolic activity."

His entire life embodied Gospel values, values diametrically opposed to the ambition, the egotism, the thirst for power that have been so powerful a force in human history. Even under the oppression of the Nazis, St. Titus knew the Church would survive to proclaim the message of truth and life. And so the Nazis were afraid of "that defenseless friar." His protest "was based not only on the fact that human dignity was particularly threatened ..., but also on the evidence that it was trampled on for precise ideological principles: racist hatred, religious hatred, ideologies of race superiority. ... Our Blessed Titus knew very well that there is no human law which can guarantee the personal dignity and freedom of man as much as the Gospel of Christ."

"Good Carmelite that he was," the cardinal continued, "Blessed Titus retained Our Lady as his light, as his comfort. He constantly called on her when in prison and in the concentration camp. ... He loved Our Lady to the bitter end; he was her fearless knight, strenuous, tireless. Surrounded by suffering he found nothing more pleasing than the love of Our Lady."

Again, "His greatest secret was the life of prayer. ... Blessed Titus never ceased, even in his spiritual and external sufferings, to live the life of prayer! ..." With sincere emotion he concluded:

> Be praised, O my Lord, for Blessed Titus Brandsma, who like our brother fire has brightened the night: and he is pleasing and robust and strong.
>
> Be praised, O my Lord, for the heroism of this heroic life, because yours are the praises, the glory, the honor, O Most High, Omnipotent, O Good Lord!

ENDNOTES

1. For a complete account of the Beatification, of the various celebrations connected with it, and the texts of the major homilies and lectures, see *The Beatification of Father Titus Brandsma, Carmelite (1881-1942): Martyr in Dachau* (Rome: Institutum Carmelitanum, 1986).

2. *L'Osservatore Romano*, November 4-5, 1985.

3. This portrait now hangs in the National Shrine of Saint Therese (of Lisieux) in Darien, Illinois.

Appendix VIII

Reflections on Titus Brandsma

Homily at the Beatification of Fr. Titus Brandsma, O. Carm.
Pope John Paul II - November 3, 1985
Basilica of St. Peter (Vatican)

1. "The souls of the just are in the hand of God" (Wis 3:1) The Church listens to the Word of God today, November 3rd, the Sunday following the solemnity of All Saints and the day after commemorating all the faithful departed.

The Church listens to this word on the day that she raises to the glories of the altar Titus Brandsma, son of the Netherlands and a religious of the Carmelite Order.

Once again, a man who passed through the torments of a concentration camp, in this case, Dachau, is raised to the glories of the altar. A man who "was tested," in the words of today's liturgy (Wis 3:4).

And precisely in the midst of this "test," in the midst of a concentration camp, which remains the shameful blot upon this century, God found Titus Brandsma worthy of himself (cf. Wis 3:5).

Today the Church rereads the signs of this divine approval and proclaims the glory of the Holy Trinity, professing with the author of the Book of Wisdom:

"The souls of the just are in the hand of God, and no torment will ever touch them."

2. And yet, Titus Brandsma suffered torments: in the sight of humanity he was punished.

Yes, God tested him. The former prisoners of the concentration camps know very well what a human Calvary those places of affliction were.

Places of great trial for men and women.

The trial of physical force, mercilessly pushed to the extreme of complete annihilation.

The trial of moral force ...

In this regard, perhaps we are best spoken to by today's Gospel, which recalls the commandment to love our enemies. The concentration camps were organized according to the program of disdain for humanity, according to the program of hate.

Through what trials of conscience, of character, of heart must have passed a disciple of Christ who recalled his words concerning the love of one's enemies!

Not to answer hate with hate, but with love. This is perhaps one of the greatest trials of man's moral strength.

Mystery of Grace

3. From this trial Titus Brandsma emerged victorious. In the midst of the onslaughts of hatred, he was able to love everybody, including his tormentors: "They too are children of the good God," he said, "and who knows whether something remains in them ..."

Of course, such heroism is not something that can be improvised. Father Titus spent his whole life bringing it to maturity, from the earliest experiences as an infant, he lived in a deeply Christian family, in his beloved Friesland. From the words and example of his parents, from the teachings he heard in the village church, from the charitable activities which he experienced in the parish community, he learned to know and to practice the fundamental commandment of Christ on love towards all, and not excluding one's enemies.

This was an experience that marked him deeply, in such a way as to give direction to his whole life. Father Brandsma's activities during his life were surprisingly many and varied. If you wished to look for its inspirational motivation and its driving force, it would be found here: in the commandment to love taken to its extreme consequences.

4. Father Brandsma was principally a professor of philosophy and of the history of mysticism at the Catholic University of Nijmegen. In this ministry, he expended the best of his human and professional energies, providing for the intellectual training of a vast number of students. But he did not stop at passing onto

them abstract notions, detached from their concrete life problems. Father Titus loved his students, and for this reason he felt impelled to share with them the values that inspired and sustained his own life. Thus a dialogue was born between teacher and pupils, one which expanded to embrace not only the perennial great questions but also the questions posed by the events of an era over which the Nazi ideology was casting ever darker shadows.

The students, however, were only a small part of the much larger national scene. Father Titus' heart could not remain indifferent in the face of the many who were outside the academic institutions, and who could also desire an enlightening word. For their sake he became a journalist. For many years he collaborated on newspapers and periodicals, lavishing the riches of his mind and sensitivity in hundreds of writings. And even here his collaboration was not only professional; many colleagues had in him the discreet confident, the enlightened advisor, the sincere friend, always ready to share pains and to instill hope.

5. There was no barrier that could stop the impulse of charity which inspired the great Carmelite. Again, it is love that explains the commitment with which he promoted the ecumenical movement, maintaining an attitude of constant fidelity towards the Church, and one of complete fairness towards those belonging to other confessions. Struck by such a luminous witness of evangelical consistency, a Protestant pastor said of him: "Our dear brother in Christ, Titus Brandsma, is truly a *mysterium gratiae!*"

A singularly penetrating judgment this! In the life of Father Brandsma what above all kindles our admiration is precisely this unfolding, in an ever more manifest way, of the grace of Christ. Here lies the secret of the vast radiation of his activity and the source of the ever fresh wave of his charity. For that matter, Father Titus was himself fully aware of the fact that he owed everything to grace, that is, to the divine life that was working in him, flowing into his soul from the inexhaustible wellspring of the Savior. The words of Christ: "Apart from me you can do nothing" (Jn 15:5) constituted for him the directing principle of his daily choices.

For this reason he prayed intensely. "Prayer is life, not an oasis in the desert of life," he said. A professor of the history of mysticism, he strove to live the discipline that he taught, every moment of his life. "We must not place in our hearts a division between God and the world, but we must rather look at the world while always having God in the background," he said.

From this profound union with God there arose in the soul of Father Brandsma a constant mood of optimism, which endeared him to those who had the good fortune to know him, and which never left him: it even accompanied him into the hell of the Nazi camp. Until the very end he remained a source of support and hope for the other prisoners: for everyone he had a smile, an understanding word, a kind gesture. The very nurse who, on July 26, 1942, injected him with deadly poison, later testified that she always retained the vivid memory of the face of that priest who "had compassion for me."

And today we too see the face of Father Titus Brandsma before us and we contemplate his luminous smile in the glory of God. He speaks to the faithful of his land, the Netherlands, and to all the faithful of the world, reaffirming his lifelong conviction: "Although neo-paganism no longer desires love, love will win back to us the hearts of the pagans. The practise of life will always make it a victorious force which will conquer and hold fast men's hearts."

Endured Everything for Christ

6. When we listen to the biography of Titus Brandsma, when we fix our minds upon the apostolic zeal of this servant of God, and then upon his martyr's death, the words of today's liturgy acquire a particular eloquence: God tested him...

Like gold in the furnace he tried him, and like a sacrificial burnt offering he accepted him (cf. Wis 3:5-6).

Therefore: no torment touched him, because the punishment became a sacrifice patterned after the Cross of Christ. And the sacrifice passed through the torment, overcame it and won. In it is contained that hope which is full of immortality (cf. Wis 3:5).

Thus did the Cross of Christ speak to Titus Brandsma. Thus does it speak to each of us:

"Take your share of suffering" (2 Tim 2:3).

"Remember Jesus Christ, risen from the dead" (2 Tim 2:8). Behold: "the gospel for which I am suffering and wearing fetters like a criminal" (2 Tim 2:9).

7. All of this Titus Brandsma seems to say to us today, adopting the words of the Apostle to the Gentiles.

"If we have died with him, we shall also live with him" (2 Tim 2:11).

"The word of God is not fettered" (2 Tim 2:9), it has demonstrated its salvific power in the martyr's death.

This martyr is a man of our century. He is your fellow countryman, dear brothers and sisters of the Netherlands.

"The souls of the righteous are in the hand of God," but the death and the glory of his righteous one belong in a particular way to you, to your Church and your nation.

Do not the expressions which we read in the Letter of Paul on the occasion of today's beatification perhaps speak of this?

"I endure everything for the sake of the elect, that they also may obtain the salvation which in Christ Jesus goes with eternal glory" (2 Tim 2:10).

We wish to refer these words in a special way to the Church and to the nation whose son is the Blessed Titus Brandsma.

Benedictus Deus in sanctis suis et Sanctus in omnibus operibus suis. Amen.

+ + +

Homily at the First Mass of Thanksgiving
Johannes Cardinal Willebrands - November 4, 1985
Basilica of St. Mary Major

Titus Brandsma, martyr, that is, one who has witnessed with his blood, in other words with his life, to his faith in Jesus Christ, Son of God and savior of mankind. Thus does Paul speak of the first martyr, Stephen: "While the blood of your witness, Stephen, was being spilt, I stood by" (Acts 22, 20).

The suffering and death of Titus Brandsma have been recognized by the Church as a witness to his faith. He has been given us by the Church as a model of faith, as an intercessor for us, for the people of our time whose faith suffers violence. Thus we honor him in the liturgy, in the worship of the Church, as a witness for Jesus Christ.

The witness of his death was the completion and crown of the witness the whole life of Father Titus lived. He strove to be wholly filled with Jesus Christ. His person was a witness for Christ.

As a boy he chose Carmel, and this choice was in keeping with his attraction for spirituality and mysticism. In his youth and student years he showed a lively spirit with a keen mind and flashing insight, which not only grasped quickly but penetrated in a particular, personal way what was presented to him in his studies. This caused him sometimes to appear wilful and by some even to be suspected of being a danger to the traditional teaching of the Church and the traditional form of Carmelite spirituality. To those who judged him in this manner he was all the more dangerous because he always tried to give practical form to his insights. This applied to both the purpose and orientation of studies in the Order and, later, to the structure and interpretation of philosophy in a Catholic university. He had a passion for study and learning, inspired by his love for God, because he saw God as the origin and final explanation of all things. His learning was directed to the deepening and enrichment of man in society.

That is why his interest and activity was directed to all facets and areas of life. As a man of learning and a professor he could not limit himself to abstract study, to problems for the sake of their own theoretic importance and significance; his insatiable thirst for knowledge and understanding was directed to their practical value and feasibility for life.

He was a mystic in the true sense of the word: to be absorbed in God, to become one with God, but not to shut oneself up in God and seclude oneself from man and his world. God himself shares himself as creator and savior, God is love. Titus was a mystic and a mystagogue, that is, he drew others with him in his ascent to God. Something radiated from him: his quiet happiness, fruit of his union with God. He spoke his opinion freely, but at the same time he was modest and humble. He recognized and appreciated the good in others. He could speak out, but also listen. In prison he suffered a profound crisis, in the sight of suffering and death, in the dark night of abandonment. What was left of all that he had built up? Did not his life collapse, incomplete and useless, under that weight of vulgarity, hate, and godlessness?

Titus was a mystic. In the trial of abandonment his union grew with Christ, the abandoned on the cross, and he felt himself one with God. "O Jesus, when I look on you, My love for you starts up anew. *Vultum Domini requiram.* I will seek your face, O God." He discovered the face of God even in his executioners. They too are human beings, made in the image of God. This image is not yet wholly effaced and can revive. Titus himself had rediscovered his joy, his happiness in God. He calls his cell in Scheveningen "an intimate sanctuary."

"Never was Our Lord so close to me."

"I am willing to remain here always, if he so disposes. I have seldom been so happy and contented."

There he writes his well-known poem, "O Jesus, When I Look On You." In Scheveningen he wrote the life of St. Teresa. In Amersfort he lectured to his fellow prisoners on Gerard Groot and the mysticism of the Low Coumries, on the Christian meaning of suffering. Dachau becomes the high point of the *imitatio Christi*, the scourging of Christ, the thirst of Christ upon the Cross. In this way he experienced and endured his own passion.

At the beginning of this sermon I referred to Stephen, the first martyr. In the account in the Acts of the Apostles of the death of Stephen there are various traits which recall the account of Christ's passion. Stephen's last prayer was, "Lord, do not account this a sin for them." Christ on the cross heard the prayer of the good thief. "This day you will be with me in paradise." Blessed Titus in his suffering and death was the image of reconciliation. To the one who gave him the mortal injection he gave the only thing he had been able to keep: his rosary. The peace and joy of his countenance witnessed to reconciliation and love. This expression of union with God, and of reconciliation and union with men issuing from it, was not lost even on those who killed him. The martyrs, witnesses to faith in and love for Jesus Christ–Titus in particular for our time–are the sign and foundation of reconciliation in the midst of the mystery of evil. *Defunctus adhuc loquitur.* In death he speaks to us yet.

+ + +

Homily at the Second Mass of Thanksgiving
Most Rev. John Malley, O. Carm. - November 5, 1985
Our Lady of Mount Carmel in Traspontina

My dear friends, sisters and brothers in Jesus Christ, it is a great joy and a very special privilege to share this Eucharist with you this evening. During the past three days we have celebrated the beatification of Blessed Titus. There was a procession and rosary at the Court of St. Damasus in the Vatican on Saturday evening. We had the beatification itself in St. Peter's on Sunday. And yesterday we had the wonderful thrill of an audience with his Holiness, Pope John Paul II.

This evening we ask ourselves how do we describe the life and death of Blessed Titus? A Dutch Carmelite, a priest, a professor, a journalist, a martyr. I think of the life and death of an English saint, St. Thomas More, also a scholar, a writer and a martyr for the faith for political reasons. And there is a play written about St. Thomas by Robert Holt which is entitled *A Man for All Seasons*. And I think this phrase, *a man for all seasons*, describes the life and the death of Father Titus.

He was a man for all seasons, because of a deep sense of awareness of God's presence in his life. Perhaps it is the very heart and core of Titus' message: this awareness that God was always with him. As we sang in the Responsorial Psalm: "Jahweh I know you are near, standing always by my side," because this was his commitment as a Carmelite, this awareness that truly God lives in whose presence each of us stand; that truly God is with us every moment.

He made his profession as a Carmelite to live in allegiance to Jesus Christ, to walk in his foot steps, to meditate day and night on his Word, and firm in trust and stout in his convictions, to be unswerving in his service of the Master. This key of God's presence as he walked in the footsteps of Jesus was the reason why Titus could truly be a man for all seasons.

But we must ask ourselves, how did he live out his allegiance to Jesus Christ as priest and Carmelite? There was a story told by Bishop Fausto Vallainc about Pope John XXIII. The Bishop mentioned that when he had given the book (about Titus) to Pope John, the following day the Pope told him, "You are responsible for my not sleeping at all last night." The Bishop of course was a bit concerned. Pope John went on to explain that he had started to read the book as he went to bed in the evening and continued reading the book about Blessed Titus all through the night. I mention this because I truly believe that Blessed Titus, thirty years before, was really a man of the Second Vatican Council.

It was before that Council that Pope John XXIII wrote his encyclical *Peace on Earth* in which he mentioned four particular values which were at the very heart and core of Christian and Catholic life. And those virtues were: truth, love, justice, and freedom. And as we see the life of Blessed Titus, as he lived out his allegiance to Jesus Christ, we see a quest for truth, a commitment to love, a striving for justice, and a defense of freedom.

His quest for truth was something that was so much part of his life. From the first moment of being a Carmelite, he investigated the writings of St. Teresa of Avila and St. John of the Cross. He researched the mystical life especially in his own country. He became truly a scholar, a professor. In his search for truth, in his sharing of truth with his students, with each one that he met, this became the goal of his life. For truly truth was not only a mystery to be discovered, it was something to be lived out. And truly he followed the words of St. Paul: "to live out the truth in love." So often we have read that Titus was truly a mystic, a contemplative. But the definition we have of a contemplative from St. Thomas Aquinas is that contemplation is a simple gaze on truth. But for the Carmelites there was an added dimension. A famous school of theology in Spain said: to be a contemplative was not only to gaze on truth, but always under the influence of love.

So Titus committed himself to live out the truth in love. And he did this in so many different ways. Truly committed to the life of community and fraternity in Carmel, the very basis of our life is that we are brothers and sisters of the Blessed Virgin Mary of Mt. Carmel, united with one another in compassion, respect and care. Titus brought this love from his own Carmelite community to each one whom he encountered. He was well known in the Netherlands for his ability to relate to the little ones, to those who were neglected, to those especially who seemed to have no one else to care for them. He carried this love even into the concentration camp. The Gospel spoke today about the love of enemies, that ability to reach out to those who persecute. Titus had that opportunity and lived it out so well. There's a story told that in one of the concentration camps, after he himself had been struck and beaten, he was encouraging his fellow prisoners that they must love the guards, those who had inflicted punishment on them. One of his fellow prisoners indicated how difficult it was, that it was impossible. You could not love someone who was that brutal and cruel. And Titus with that twinkle in his eye, had the ability to say, "You must love him, but perhaps not all the time, not all day, not at each moment." Love means reaching out to someone, even an enemy.

Titus also had a striving after justice. Many years before the word ecumenism became popular, Titus had the ability to reach out to others in the Netherlands who belonged to other Churches: the Eastern Christians, the Protestants, but especially he reached out to the Jewish people in their persecution. He somehow realized that each man, each woman was made in the image of God, and justice truly meant to seek God's image within that person.

Finally, he defended freedom. It was for his defense of freedom that he was put to death. The Nazis occupied his country. He was able to speak out for the freedom of Catholic schools, for the freedom of the press, and for the freedom of each individual's conscience. God has given us a human dignity, a value and a worth, and it was this value that Titus never forgot: the freedom to be oneself, to develop one's gifts in the service of the Church was a value that he held so precious. Even as he was being persecuted, even as the injustices were being heaped upon his country, he could still pray,

> God bless Holland, God bless Germany; God grant that these two peoples may soon stand side by side in full liberty and peace, in full recognition of his glory for the good of two countries so closely related to one another.

It is for these reasons—his quest for truth, his commitment to love, his striving for justice, and his defense of freedom—that we say that Titus truly is a man for all seasons. I would like to think that as I began with that quote from the play by Robert Holt that Titus is "a man for all seasons," that there is another quote from perhaps our greatest English writer, William Shakespeare, which so beautifully sums up the life of Blessed Titus. In his play *Julius Caesar*, as Mark Anthony praises Brutus after his death, so we too may take the words and say of Bl. Titus: "His life was gentle; and the elements so mixed in him that nature might stand up and say to all the world: This was a man."

And the Church has said this past Sunday of Fr. Titus: This is a Blessed of the Church!

+ + +

Homily at the Final Mass of Thanksgiving
Pietro Cardinal Palazzini - November 6, 1985
San Martino ai Monti Carmelite Church

Cardinal Palazzini was the Prefect of the Congregation for the Causes of the Saints at the time of Titus Brandsma's beatification.

Reviewing once again the stages of the tortuous and heroic life of Blessed Titus Brandsma, we are led to ask ourselves why is it so difficult for men, all of whom are brothers, to live together, to dialogue, to love. Blessed Titus was a Carmelite of the Ancient Observance, born in Bolsward, professor and Rector Magnificius in Nijmegen, arrested on January 19th 1942, transferred from one prison to another, from one concentration camp to another, finally interred in Dachau where he died after numberless physical and moral sufferings. We ask: how can some men take it on themselves to forbid others to believe and to point out to others who wish to listen to them the authentic way to eternal salvation?

Surely these problems cannot be enlightened by the romantic lyricism of poets, nor by the wishful discourses of laicist humanism.

Only the Gospel can tell us something. Only the saint can vaguely outline the unsearchable designs of God. Only the saint inspires us with trust because we find in him at once the suffering and the joy of believing in a God who loves us through the veil of so many twisted phenomena of history. Only a person who accepts Christ can understand why this redeeming suffering is necessary.

However, we remain thoughtful and tormented. Why this knot of human, or rather inhuman acts? What sense of fatality leads people to concentration camps, to the *desparesidos*, to a whole horrible death-dance?

At times ambition, egoism, thirst for power seem to dominate uncontested. History, with these absurd aspects, seems to unfold independently before the face of Christ who does not react, who is willfully powerless. Willfully powerless again before the persecutions against the Church–the persecutions of yesterday and of today. These latter are more subtle and more cunning but none the less cruel. We need only call a few names to mind: Dachau, Mauthausen, Auschwitz. Why this dogged obstinacy against the name of Christian in a society which speaks so much, even to the point of abuse, of freedom? The answer is easy.

After Christ's birth in Bethlehem, he himself, the Incarnate Word, was the object of persecution by a pretentious provincial king, Herod. Later he was hounded by a disorderly mob of scribes, pharisees, leaders of the people as well as a new Herod, while Pilate, the representative of the governing power, thought he was avoiding trouble by nervously washing his hands of the whole affair.

And the Just One *par excellence* suffered the ignominy of the cross, after having spoken to Pilate in vain about truth and about his mission to give witness to the truth.

"If they persecuted me," he warned his disciples, "they will also persecute you." (Jn 15: 20)

And the persecution of Christ was transferred to the Church from its very beginnings. The Church throughout the centuries continues the mission of Christ, to preach the truth, to serve the truth cost what it may. Our Blessed Titus Brandsma also preached, served the truth, teaching in the university, in newspapers, in the pulpit.

He had to face Nazism, which like many other ideologies, claimed and claim now to dominate the world, taking the place of God. He knew well that the Church would remain. Periodically, some people foretell the Church's demise, as they identify as mortal illnesses what really are only passing crises. Blessed Titus knew that even while oppressed by the Nazis, the Church continued to be more alive than ever, and would continue throughout the centuries to proclaim the message of truth and of life. And his preaching instilled fear in them.

There you have the reason for so many persecutions: like Christ, the Church instills fear in the enemies of truth.

That defenseless friar, firm in his ideas and intransigent in putting them into practice, instilled fear in the Nazis who had occupied the Netherlands. He instilled this fear not because he was part of the group involved in the preparation of the atomic bomb in competition with the great physicists of the Reich, but because he protected the persecuted, because even as a journalist he came to their aid, because as prestigious adviser to the Dutch bishops he induced the Catholic bishops to enter the battle to condemn the deportation and the extermination of the Jews, because that unarmed religious instinctively rebelled against abuse of power, against cruelty. He did what he could to protect the victims of violence, camouflaged under legalism and the pretext of war rights.

The truth that had to be preached at that time in answer to Dutch National Socialism was the call to respect for human dignity.

Against the attempt to eliminate the influence of religion and to restrain the profession of one's faith in society, against the ferocious persecution of a race and of a people, Titus Brandsma, using all the means at his disposal, raised a cry that rose from the depths of his soul. It echoed the cry of those whose human dignity was threatened: the cry of the oppressed and of the offended, the cry of victims of systematic terror practiced by totalitarian regimes. It was also the cry of accusation of all those who feel themselves involved in cases where the dignity of man is despised.

To this cry was also added the bitterness of the desperate silence of so many others who seemed to be deaf and blind to so many shameful crimes, to vegetate in a void of senselessness. In self-imposed isolation and in miserable egoism, it was as if they did not live in the midst of so many like themselves, involved as they were in the same problem of the defence of human dignity.

Fr. Titus Brandsma's protest was based not only on the fact that human dignity was particularly threatened (to tell the truth, it always has been), but also on the evidence that it was trampled on for precise ideological principles: racist hatred, religious hatred, ideologies of race superiority. Every totalitarian ideology despises man in favor of some group or people or state (to the extent that it is not the state at the service of man, but man made a servant of the state). This ideology is a substantial attack on the dignity of man because it lowers the individual into an instrument, an insignificant cog in the machinery of the whole state.

Our Blessed Titus knew very well that there is no human law which can guarantee the personal dignity and freedom of man as much as the Gospel of Christ, left to the Church. In fact, this Gospel proclaims and announces the freedom of the sons of God, rejects all slavery, which ultimately derives from sin, honors as a sacred trust the dignity of one's conscience, does not tire in warning all about what corresponds to the basic law of the Christian way of life. Blessed Titus knew this well and put it into practise.

Blessed Titus was well aware how centuries of immanistic rationalism, committed to the denial and destruction of Revelation, had stripped man of his transcendental dignity. They had denied the metaphysical dimension, stripping man of his sacredness and of inviolability as the first value of creation. And he saw its bitter fruits in the Dutch Nazi movement.

He saw that the killing of one or many men, the sacrifice of entire generations in the name of race superiority, was made possible by the denial of man as a creature of God. He saw that it was a result of the fact that man was considered in function of society or of productivity or of the State and not vice versa. Man was "a thing," man was "an instrument" and not the end of society.

The spiritual preparation for what was to be his heroic sacrifice had matured during the period of his novitiate, in his exemplary religious life, in his commitment to study, in his teaching, in his application to journalism and in a whole gamut of activities undertaken in a harmonious fusion between a life of prayer and apostolic activity.

He was arrested for a circular letter which he prepared and addressed to the Catholic press. He insisted on the Gospel *non licet* in order to avoid becoming silly servants of the Nazi crimes. Blessed Titus, in his suffering, seemed to be someone who was not suffering. Perhaps a better way to say this, he took suffering as the normal thing, something that concerned him, something that was he. Segregated from the world, he did not complain of his isolation, of his sufferings, of his wholesale indigence, even of the comfort of a human word.

"Thy kingdom come" was, through all and despite all, the spark of his activity and strength in his suffering. What value do prison and a fiasco in men's eyes have? What does matter is to remain, with the grace of God, on one's feet before the eyes of the Father. Good Carmelite that he was, Blessed Titus retained Our Lady as his light, as his comfort. He constantly called on her when in prison and in the concentration camp. The unbelievers of his time, like the iconoclasts of old, were furious in their denunciation. He loved Our Lady to the bitter end; he was her fearless knight, strenuous, tireless. Surrounded by suffering he found nothing more pleasing than the love of Our Lady.

His greatest secret was the life of prayer. How much his life of prayer can tell us! How eloquently it speaks to us priests, committed to the salvation of the world. Without prayer and the life of grace we can do absolutely nothing, neither for this world nor for the next. Blessed Titus never ceased, even in his internal and external sufferings, to live the life of prayer! A life of prayer! He prayed with his lips, with his physical suffering, without one complaint. In his spiritual suffering he always prayed. If prayer is purity of intention, if it is the willed and accepted will of God, if it is his kingdom even in suffering, if it is the one scope of every battle, then certainly Blessed Titus prayed uninterruptedly.

Against this spiritual background should we see the work and the martyrdom of Blessed Titus Brandsma.

The basic act by which a man shows his dignity is prayer. When he prays he consciously fulfills what he is—and what is fulfilled by him is worthy and right. As a consciencious being, a person does not merely recognize his creatureliness, but he appreciates it with all his heart– *ex toto corde*– with grateful joy he acknowledges that as a creature he is the result of God's love. This is what the person who prays expresses in the depths of his being, in the wholesome adoration of love for his Creator and for his Redeemer. In this prayer of adoration, which begins with reverential fear and includes the fear of offending God by sin, man realizes, so to speak, his very being which is a "gifted" being, given that he possesses being by his very essence. He thanks Him who gave him this being, "which wondrously created was re-created even more wondrously" since he has been called to a new share in the working of the love of God.

St. Augustine writes in *De Trinitate* (XII.11) that the dignity of man consists in his being in the image and likeness of God. It is preserved only if it constantly tends towards Him by whom it was given.

The supernatural dignity of man is actualized in the love of neighbor in the same way as in prayer. Such love is the raising and deepening of natural human solidarity because in it man is affirmes as "a brother of Christ." He is given the answer of a respectful love of service which belongs to him for the love of God.

The accomplishment of Blessed Titus Brandsma, his life of prayer, his Gospel strength which never diminished even in the month after month of his painful Calvary, in the most degrading experiments to which he was subjected, can teach us a great deal about the dignity of man.

Today we are threatened by dangers that may be less visible, but which nevertheless attack human dignity and the life of others (abortion, euthanasia, drugs). These less visible dangers are no less serious. We should take the example of this great Carmelite and of those other martyrs who were his contemporaries– St. Maximilian Kolbe, the Servant of God Edith Stain– who had to pay the price in their very persons in order to keep the faith. From their example we should draw the strength and the pride to be worthy, through prayer, and even at most critical moments, of such a glorious history.

There– I have finished speaking about him, about Blessed Titus. Surely my discourse was quite insipid. It has been the talk of someone who has not lived out the heights of heroism of which he is speaking. But as I bring my words to a conclusion, a prayer rises from my heart:

> Be praised, O my Lord, for Blessed Titus Brandsma, who like our brother fire has brightened the night; and he is pleasing and robust and strong.
>
> Be praised, O my Lord, for the heroism of this heroic life, because yours are the praises, the glory, the honor, O Most High, Omnipotent, O Good Lord!

+ + +

Papal Audience
Pope John Paul II - November 6, 1985
Pope Paul VI Audience Hall

During the regularly scheduled Wednesday audience, the Pope recommended Blessed Titus' example to three particular categories of pilgrims: young people, the sick, newly-weds.

My dear young people!

I'm very happy with your ever welcome presence! I greet you with affection. At this meeting of ours, I wish to bring to your attention the figure of Fr. Titus Brandsma, whom I solemnly declared a Blessed of the Church last Sunday. I urge you to read his biography, which will be of great help to you in your formation. He died on July 26, 1942, in the death camp of Dachau, after terrible suffering. He was a martyr for Truth, which he courageously upheld and defended. Invoke him in your difficulties. Learn from his example to be strong in faith and courageous in your witness! I bless all of you with all my heart.

✝ ✝ ✝

My very dear sick people!

To you too I wish to address myself in a special way—to greet you, to thank you for your participation at this audience, to assure you of my understanding and very good wishes in your suffering, You are constantly present to me in thought and prayer. I wish to encourage you to an ever deeper and patient love for God. I quote what Blessed Titus Brandsma wrote. He was a dynamic journalist, and also a deep mystic. "Consider life as a Way of the Cross, but carry the cross with joy and courage, because with his example and with his grace Jesus has rendered it light." May the heroism of his martyrdom, accepted with love be for you a comfort and a stimulus to holiness. My blessing accompanies you.

✝ ✝ ✝

My very dear newly-weds!

Accept my heartfelt greeting together with my good wishes and blessing for the new life which you have begun with the sacrament of Matrimony. May the Lord remain with you always with his enlightening word and with his grace! Father Titus Brandsma who was completely immersed in the situations and problems of his times, and still cultivated such a deep spirituality, is a teacher and example for you too, immersed as you are in your daily preoccupations. The conviction of the presence of God in the events of history and complete trust in his Love, accompanied him throughout his life and especially in the harsh period of his imprisonment. Learn from him to be persevering in goodness, in patience, in charity, and above all in trust in Him who has united you forever by means of the sacrament. May my affection and my blessing also be a comfort for you.

Appendix IX

Chronology of Titus Brandsma's Life

1881 - February 23: Anno Sjoerd Brandsma is born to Titus and Tjitje (née Postma) at a settlement made up of a handful of farmers known as Oegeklooster, near Bolsward in eastern Frisland. His father is a successful farmer. The Brandsmas will have six children, four daughters and two sons. While one daughter will marry, the other children will become religious.

1892-1898: Anno attends the Franciscan school in Megen, in the province of North Brabant. While studying there, his vocation to religious life matures. It is thought he will enter the Franciscan Order, but his fragile health denies him that possibility.

1898 - September 22: Anno enters the Carmelite novitiate in Boxmeer. He takes the religious name of Titus, the same name as his father.

1899 - October 3: Titus Brandsma professes his first vows as a Carmelite.

1900-1905: Titus continues his studies in philosophy and theology at the Carmelite houses in Boxmeer, Zenderen, and Oss.

1901: Titus publishes his first book: a translation from the French of an anthology of the writings of the Spanish Carmelite mystic, St. Teresa of Jesus. His work is titled *Bloemlezing uit de werken der H. Teresia* (Anthology of the Works of St. Teresa).

1905 - June 17: At 24 years of age, Titus Brandsma is ordained a priest in the cathedral of Den Bosch in Brabant.

1906-1909: Brandsma is sent to the international student house in Rome, Italy. He attends the philosophy program at the Gregorian Pontifical University and takes sociology classes at the *Istituto Leoniano*. He also begins writing for some Dutch newspapers and magazines.

During his summer vacations Titus travels to Mainburg in Bavaria, Germany. During one summer break, he has a reoccurrence of his stomach illness and is sent to the Carmelite house in Albano, near Rome, to recover.

1909 - October 25: Titus passes the doctoral exam in philosophy with the grade of *probatus*. He returns to the Netherlands the next day.

1909-1923: Brandsma begins his teaching career with the Carmelite students in Oss. He is assigned classes in philosophy and Church history. He is also named Regent of Studies.

1912: Brandsma starts a magazine about Carmelite culture called *Karmelrozen* (Rose of Carmel) which later is renamed *Speling*. After two years it has more than 13,000 subscribers.

1918: With a team of collaborators, Brandsma begins the translation (from the Spanish) and publication of a planned seven additional volumes of the works of St. Teresa in the Dutch language.

1919-1923: Titus is named editor-in-chief of the dying newspaper *De Stad Oss* (The City of Oss). It revives.

1923-1942: Brandsma becomes a professor at the newly founded Catholic University of Nijmegen. He teaches philosophy, the history of philosophy, and the history of Dutch mysticism.

1929: Brandsma travels in Spain where he gains a deep appreciation for the country's gentleness and culture and Carmelite heritage.

1932-1933: Brandsma is elected *rector magnificus* of the Catholic University of Nijmegen, a one-year position. To celebrate the opening of the school year, Brandsma gives his celebrated speech on the concept of God (*Godsbegrip*); he completes an official trip to Milan and Rome as *rector magnificus*.

1933: The elections in Germany are won by the National Socialist Party, and Adolf Hitler becomes chancellor.

1935: The Archbishop of Utrecht, Johannes De Jong, names Brandsma as the ecclesiastical assistant to the Association of Catholic Journalist (*R. K. Journalistenvereniging*), a group of approximately 30 publications. He obtains his international journalist card.

Brandsma travels to Ireland and the United States where he gives conferences on Carmelite spirituality and tradition, subsequently collected in the book *The Beauty of Carmel* (La bellezza del Carmelo).

1938-1939: Titus gives lectures on the National Socialist (Nazi) ideology, criticizing its pagan and anti-human approach.

1940 - May 10: The German army invades the Netherlands, Belgium, Luxembourg, and France, gradually imposing its own ideology.

1941 - January 26: The Dutch Church, through their bishops, reacts firmly. Fr. Titus actively collaborates with them. Moreover, he was entrusted with the presidency of the Association of Catholic Schools.

1941 - December 30: Archbishop De Jong summons Fr. Titus for a discussion about the difficult situation of the Catholic press.

1942 - Early January: During the first days of January, Brandsma visits the editorial offices of the Catholic newspapers to deliver the directives of the bishops and to encourage the editors to resist Nazi pressure to publish their propaganda.

1942 - January 19: Upon returning from the university, Fr. Titus is arrested at the Carmelite monastery in Nijmegen. He passes his first night in the Arnhem jail.

1942 - January 20-March 12: Brandsma is taken to Scheveningen prison where he is interrogated. He strongly reaffirms his anti-Nazi positions. The official in charge of the questioning, a secularized priest, did not destroy the notes from the interrogation. They become part of the beatification process.

Titus is allowed to keep two books with him: *The Life of St. Teresa of Jesus* by Thomas Kwakman and *The Life of Jesus* by Cyril Verschaeve. During this time, he decides to write the life of St. Teresa, a project conceived many years before but never brought to fruition. In the absence of paper, he continues writing his manuscript between the lines of the book *The Life of Jesus*.

1942 - March 12-April 28: Brandsma is transferred to the "transit" camp of Amersfoort. He is forced to work and live in very difficult conditions. On Good Friday he delivers a conference on Geert Groote, an important figure in Dutch spirituality.

1942 - April 28-May 16: Fr. Titus returns again to the Scheveningen prison camp for a follow-up interrogation.

1942 - May 16-June 13: Brandsma is relocated to the Kleve "transit" camp. He finds some relief from the suffering endured at

Amersfoort. At Kleve he is allowed to participate in Mass and have spiritual talks with the chaplain of the camp. In the meantime, his religious superiors try, in vain, to change his sentence to house arrest so he is permitted to live in a German religious house.

1942 - June 13-19: Brandsma is transported with other prisoners by train in an animal car via Cologne, Frankfurt, and Nüremberg, to the infamous Dachau concentration camp.

The Dachau internment camp had been constructed at the beginning of the 1930s, initially for political prisoners. During the war, the camp holds at least 110,000 people, of which only 30,000 survived. Inhumane experiments are performed on some prisoners, especially those who are disabled or too weak to be productive in the forced work details.

1942 - June 19-July 18: Brandsma is housed in Block 28, set aside for religious and priests. He meets his fellow Dutch Carmelite Raphael Tijhuis, a brother from the community in Mainz, Germany. Brother Raphael is imprisoned because he complained about the difficulty of finding stamps in a letter to his family. Brother Raphael becomes Brandsma's companion in his final days. He will be a principal witness at Brandsma's beatification process.

1942 - July 18-26: Fr. Titus is kept in the prison hospital. A nurse gives him a lethal injection of carbolic acid at 2 pm on Sunday, July 26. A short time before his death, he gives that nurse a rosary made by a fellow prisoner. The woman later converts to the Catholic faith and testifies in Brandsma's beatification process.

1955: The diocesan process for the beatification and canonization of Brandsma is initiated in the Diocese of Den Bosch, in the Netherlands.

1971: The first examination of the letters by the Congregation of the Causes of the Saints takes place.

1973: The process for beatification is introduced a second time for procedural reasons.

1979: The Acts are presented to the Congregation for the Causes of the Saints.

1983: The cause is readmitted as a case for martyrdom.

1984: The theological consultors and the Congregation of Cardinals give positive opinions for Brandsma's martyrdom. Pope John Paul II signs the decree on martyrdom.

1985 - November 5: Pope John Paul II solemnly proclaims Carmelite Titus Brandsma as a blessed and as a martyr of the faith.

1992: In Brandsma's native Frisland, an Archive of Catholic Frisia is created on the occasion of the 50th anniversary of the death of St Titus. A presentation on this noble son is organized and the idea of creating a permanent museum and archive on the life of Titus Brandsma takes hold. The museum opens its doors in 2003 and is officially inaugurated in January 2004. Over time, the story of Fr. Titus is promoted, and various presentations and temporary exhibits are organized at the museum.

The tapestry from the beatification is temporarily loaned to the church of St. Francis in Bolsward by the Postulator General of the Carmelites, Fr. Giovanni Groso, as a homage to his birth city and to the parish where he received and nourished his faith during the first years of his life.

2005: Titus Brandsma is chosen by the citizens of the town as *Nijmegen's Greatest Citizen of All Time*.

2007: Cardinal Simonis, as president of the Dutch Episcopal Conference, writes a letter on behalf of the other Dutch bishops to Cardinal Saraiva Martins, prefect of the Congregation for the Causes of the Saints, encouraging the canonization of Titus Brandsma. The letter highlights the very positive effect that his canonization would have on the Dutch Church and Dutch society.

2010 - October 1: The Titus Brandsma Memorial is inaugurated in the City of Nijmegen. Participating are many Carmelite communities from around the world and their names appear on the bricks which create the memorial. In the center is a beautiful monument constructed by the Dutch artist Arie Trum. He wished the artwork to reflect the openness of St. Titus, his skill at dialogue, his devotion to St. Teresa, and the strength of his principles.

2012-2013: In recent years, two provinces of the Carmelite Order adopt Titus as protector and take his name. The first is the newly united province of Germany, fruit of the union of the long-established Upper German Province and the Lower German Province which Titus Brandsma played a role in re-establishing after the Secularization. The new province was erected in 2012 and assumed the name "The Province of Blessed Titus Brandsma." The other province is that of the Philippines, erected as province in 2013. The Carmelite foundation in the Philippines had been a mission created 70 years earlier by the Dutch Carmelite province.

2018 - August: While participating in a formation course for Carmelite students from various provinces around the world, the Prior General of the Order, Most Rev. Fernando Millán Romeral, unveils a plaque in the Memorial of Dachau to honor the Carmelites who were interned there, some of whom died in the camp. After the simple ceremony of unveiling the plaque, the group celebrates Eucharist in the chapel of the Heilig Blut Carmelite monastery.

2020 - November 26: The Medical Consultation, appointed by the Vatican Congregation of the Causes of the Saints, recognizes the impossibility of scientific explanation for the cure from cancer of the Carmelite, Fr. Michael Driscoll. The cure is attributed to the intercession of Titus Brandsma.

2021 - May 25: The Congress of Theological Consultors recognized the miracle attributed to the intercession of Titus Brandsma, O. Carm., relating to the scientifically inexplicable healing of Fr. Michael Driscoll, O. Carm., from cancer.

2021 - November 25: During an audience given to Cardinal Marcello Semeraro, prefect of the Congregation for the Causes of the Saints, Pope Francis authorized the Congregation to promulgate the decrees regarding the miracle attributed to the intercession of Titus Brandsma.

2022 - March 4: During the Ordinary Public Consistory, Pope Francis announced the canonization of Blessed Titus Brandsma to take place on Sunday, May 15, 2022, in St Peter's Square in Rome.

2022 - May 25: Pope Francis canonized Carmelite Titus Brandsma as a martyr for the faith during a Eucharistic celebration in St. Peter's Square. Nine other blesseds were also canonized.

+ + +

List of Illustrations

page	description
8	Parents of Titus Brandsma
11	Brandsma Family 1891
13	"Anno" (Titus) Brandsma at age 17
23	Titus Brandsma at age 22
26	Brandsma with Carmelite Humbertus Driessen
31	Brandsma Family 1918
41	Titus Brandsma in Njmegen garden 1935
43	Central Board of the Apostolate of the Union of Eastern Christians
57	Titus Brandsma in robes of Rector Magnificus
73	Titus Brandsma at age 49 in 1930
101	Titus Brandsma enjoying boat to USA and Canada
131	Titus Brandsma and architects of the Nijmegen monastery
147	One view of Cell 577 in Scheveningen Prison
149	Another view of Cell 577 in Scheveningen Prison
165	John Don's portait drawing of Titus Brandsma
203	Arial view of the Dachau Concentration Camp
	Gate at the Dachau Concentration Camp
229	Raphael Tijhuis, O. Carm., drawing of Titus Brandsma at the Dachau Concentration Camp
245	Plaque commemorating Carmelite Dachau victims Hilary Januszewski and Titus Brandsma, both "blesseds" in the Catholic Church
251	Carmelites from around the world visit Dachau in 2018
261	A rosary of Titus Brandsma
262	A second rosary of Titus Brandsma
263	The Chapel of the Agony of Christ in the Dachau Concentration camp

Bibliography

Agasso, Domenico. "Beato Tito Brandsma." *The Voice of the Martyrs* at www.persecution.com.

Alderson, Calvin J., O. Carm. Review of *Un periodista martir* by Miguel Arribas, O. Carm. *The Sword* 45:1 (April, 1985), 63-64.

Alkire, Thomas John, O. Carm. "The Titus Brandsma Commission." *The Sword* 24:1 (February 1964), 26-29.

Alzin, Josse. "Cordero de la Iglesia: ¿Quien es Titus Brandsma?" *Dans le Sillon Missionnaire* No. 224 (1984), 7-26.

Alzin, Josse. "Lamb of the Church." *Dans le Sillon Missionnaire* No. 224 (1984), 7-26.

Alzin, Josse. *Un piccolo frate pericoloso: Tito Brandsma.* 1985, 32 p. Collana Pionieri, 32. Edictrice Elle Di Ci. ISBN: 88-01-00332-3.

Antista, Aurelio, O. Carm. "Spiritual Profile of Father Titus Brandsma." *Carmel in the World* 24 (1985), 163-171.

Arribas, Miguel María, O. Carm. *El precio de la verdad: Tito Brandsma Carmelita.* 2ª edición de Un periodista martir[1984]. 1998, 358 p. Roma: Postulación General de los Carmelitas. ISBN: 88-87275-00-9.

Arribas, Miguel. *The Price of Truth: Titus Brandsma, Carmelite.* 2021. 230 p. Darien, Il: Carmelite Media. And Office of the General Postulator of the Carmelites. Printed Book ISBN: 978-1-936742-26-4 E-Book ISBN: 978-1-936742-27-1.

Arribas, Miguel María, O. Carm. *Un periodista martir.* 1984, 374 p. Madrid: Conferencia de Provinciales de la Región Ibérica Carmelita. ISBN: 84-398-1710-X.

Arribas, Miguel María, O. Carm. "Próxima beatificación del Carmelita P. Tito Brandsma." *Escapulario del Carmen* 80 (1984), 162-169.

Aukes, H. W. F. "A Priest Sabotaged." *The Sword* 45:1 (April 1985), 3-47.

Aukes, H. W. F. *Het leven van Titus Brandsma.* Voorwoord van Bernardus Kardinaal Alfrink. Derde bijgewerkte druk. 1985, 347 p. Het Spectrum. Utrecht. ISBN: 90-274-7159-2.

Beatification of Father Titus Brandsma, Carmelite (1881-1942), The Martyr in Dachau. Edited by Redemptus Maria Valabek, O. Carm. 1986, 160 p.,

18 plates. Rome: Institutum Carmelitanum. ISBN: 88-7288-002-5.

"Beato Tito Brandsma, Carmelita, periodista y mártyr." *Servicio Informativo Provincia Bética* 26:287 (1992), 1-47.

Benevento, Francesco. *Piccolo florilegio mariano.* 1978, 32 p. ill. Frati Franciscani–Grotta delle Tre Fontane.

Berben, Paul. *Dachau: Historia oficial del campo de concentración nazi, 1933-1945.* 1975 Madrid.

Berben, Paul. *Dachau 1933-45: The Official History.* Translated by Bernard R. Hanauer. 1968, 1975, 200 p. Comité International de Dachau, ISBN 0-85211-009.

Besalduch Segarra, Simón María, O. Carm., *Flos Sanctorum del Carmelo.* 1951. N.p. Barcelona.

Bettinger, Eugene Joseph, O. Carm. "Martyr Titus Brandsma." *The Sword* 58:2 (November 1998), 63-65.

Beuker, Klaas. *Titus Brandsma.* 1983, 96 p. N.p.: Uitgeverij Hamedia.

Bianca Maria dello Spirito Sancto, O.C.D. "Un Carmelitano per il vangelo e per l'uomo." *Ministerium Verbi* 67 (1993), 550-554.

Blommestijn, Hein, O. Carm. "Titus Brandsma Prophet of Peace and Martyr of War." *Carmel in the World* 25 (1986), 21-33.

Blommestijn, Hein, O. Carm. "Titus Brandsma (1881-1942): God wordt geboren in de mens." *Tot op de bodem van het niets: Mystiek in een tijd van oorlog en crisis, 1920-1970.* (1991, 118 p. J. H. Kok–Averbode, Altiora), pp. 9-23.

Blommestijn, Hein, O. Carm. "Titus Brandsma–Vredesprofeet en oorlogsmartelaar." *Speling* 36 (1984), 162-169.

Boaga, Emanuele, O. Carm. "Dio grembo della vita: L'esperienza di Tito Brandsma." *Presenza del Carmelo* No. 53 (1991), 71-76.

Boaga, Emanuele, O. Carm. "Dio, silenzio e lager: Titus Brandsma e Edith Stein." *Cercare Dio: L'esperienza carmelitana* (Collana Fiamma Viva, 34). 1993, 267 p. Edizioni del Teresianum. Roma. pp. 163-184. Also in *Rivista di Vita Spirituale* 47 (1993), 520-541.

Boaga, Emanuele, O. Carm. *Tito Brandsma: Testimone di Dio nei luoghi della sua assenza.* 1985, 27 p. Estratto dalla Revista di vita spirituale.

Bonetto, Christianus. "Il giornalismo cattolico secondo Titus Brandsma." *Carmelus* 41 (1994), 126-164.

Bonetto, Christianus. *Il ruolo dello stampa cattolica nella società contemporanea secondo Titus Brandsma (1881-1942)*. Tesi di laurea, Facoltà di Lettere e Filosofia, Università Cattolica del Sacro Cuore, Milano. 1993, xi, 160 p. ill.

Borchert, Bruno, O. Carm. "The Mystical Life of Titus Brandsma." *Carmelus* 32 (1985), 3-13.

Borchert, Bruno, O. Carm. "Titus Brandsma and the Mystical Life." *Carmel in the World* 24 (1985), 172-197.

Brandsma, Titus, O. Carm. *Aandacht voor goden voor mensen*. N.d., 16 p. Bisdom Breda. Veemarktstraat 48, 4811 ZH Breda.

Brandsma, Titus, O. Carm. "A Poem." *The Sword* 57:2 (November, 1997), 24.

Brandsma, Titus, O. Carm. "Before a Picture of Jesus in My Cell." Translated by Gervase Toelle, O. Carm. *The Sword* 45:1 (April 1985), 48.

Brandsma, Titus, O. Carm. *Carmelite Mysticism: Historical Sketches.* 50th Anniversary Edition. 1986, vi 79 p. Darien, Illinois: The Carmelite Press.

Brandsma, Titus, O. Carm. *Een kruisweg voor Dokkum*.1992, 36 p. ill. H. Peters. Dokkum.

Brandsma, Titus, O. Carm. *Ejercicios bíblicos con María para llegar a Jesús*. Presentado con un estudio preliminar por V. Wilderink, O. Carm. 1976. CESCA. Caudete.

Brandsma, Titus, O. Carm. *Engagierte Mystik*. Engeleitet and übersetzt von Elisabeh Hense. 1991, 112 p. Bonifatius Verlag. Paderborn.

Brandsma, Titus, O. Carm. *Geert Groote: Zijn keer naar de Heer*. 1981, 32 p. Titus Brandsma Archief. Karmelietenklooster, Steenstraat 39, 5831 LA Boxmeer.

Brandsma, Titus, O. Carm. "Gemma Galgani: An Introduction to Her Letters and Ecstasies." *Carmel in the World* 33 (1994), 202-209.

Brandsma, Titus, O. Carm. "In the Spirit and Strength of Elijah." *Carmelite Family* N° 14 (2002), 2-3; N° 15 (2002), 2-5.

Brandsma, Titus, O. Carm. *Jardin cercado, pensamientos para ejercicios espirituales*. Datos biográficos por P. Rafael María López Melús, O. Carm. 1978. Caudete: CESCA.

Brandsma, Titus, O. Carm. "Litterae P. Dr. Titi Brandsma, Professoris in Universitate Noviomagensi." *Beati Baptistae Mantuani ex operibus Anthologiam pro studiosa iuventute composuit et commentario adstruxit P. Adelbertus Lokkers, O. Carm.* 1936. Traiecti ad Mosam: Van Aelst Fratres, pp. x-xi.

Brandsma, Titus, O. Carm. "Meditation at Niagara Falls, 1935." *The Sword* 44:2 (October 1984), 33-34.

Brandsma, Titus, O. Carm. "Peace and the Love of Peace." *Carmel in the World* 33 (1994), 4-16.

Brandsma, Titus, O. Carm. "Pointers for a Retreat: The Saints of Carmel." *Carmelite Digest* 8:2 (1993), 39-46.

Brandsma, Titus, O. Carm. "São Joán da Cruz, 'Doctor Mysticus' mariano." In "São Joán da Cruz no IV centenário de sua morte (1591-1991)." *Carmelo Lusitano* No. 8-9 (1990-1991),219-226.

Brandsma, Titus, O. Carm. *Sulla Via della Croce: Pensieri spirituali del Beato Tito Brandsma Carmelitano.* Introduzione di Vincenzo Mosca, O. Carm. Suplemento a Vita Carmelitana. 1985, 48 p.

Centro Comunicazioni Sociali «Tito Brandsma». Corso Benedetto Croce 180, 70125 Bari.

Brandsma, Titus, O. Carm. *The Brothers of Our Lady.* 1936. The Carmelite Press. Faversham, England. pp. 17-20.

Brandsma, Titus, O. Carm. "The Heart of the Mystical Life: St. John of the Cross and Mary's Motherhood of God." *Carmel in the World* 32 (1993), 116-122.

Brandsma, Titus, O. Carm. "The Saints of Carmel: Pointers for a Retreat." Translated by Redemptus Valabek, O. Carm. *Carmel in the World* 20 (1981), 218-224.

Brandsma, Titus, O. Carm. "The True Nature of Devotion to Mary." Translated by Joachim Smet, O. Carm. *Carmel in the World* 32 (1993), 76-82.

Brandsma, Titus, O. Carm. "Titus Brandsma at Niagara." *The Sword* 44:2 (1984), 33-34.

Brandsma, Titus, O. Carm. "Why We Pray to Mary." *Carmel in the World* 30 (1991), 138-145.

Breij, Aemelius, O. Carm. "The Spiritual Life of Titus Brandsma." Translated by Otger Steggink, O. Carm. *The Sword* 22 (1962), 148-158.

Buscoducen. *Beatificationis seu declarationis martyrii servi Dei Titi Brandsma sacerdotis professi Ordinis Fratrum B., Mariae Virginis de Monte Carmelo (1881-1942). Animadversiones promotoris generalis fidei super dubio an constet de martyrio eiusque causa.* 1981, 30 p. Typis Polyglotis Vaticanis. Romae.

Buscoducen. *Beatificationis seu declarationis martyrii servi Dei Titi Brandsma sacerdotis professi Ordinis Fratrum B., Mariae Virginis de Monte Carmelo in odium fidei, uti fertur, interempti; summarium: super dubio an constet de martyrio servi Dei, necnonde eius causa et de signis seu miraculis, in casu et ad effectum de quo agitur.* 1979, liv, 560 p. ill. Typis Polyglotis Vaticanis. Romae.

Buscoducen. *Beatificationis seu declarationis martyrii servi Dei Titi Brandsma sacerdotis professi Ordinis Fratrum B. Mariae Virginis de Monte Carmelo: informatio super dubio an constet demartyrio eiusque causa.* 1981, 114 p. Typis Polyglotis Vaticanis. Romae.

Buscoducen. *Beatificationis seu declarationis martyrii servi Dei Titi Brandsma sacerdotis professi Ordinis Fratrum B. Mariae Virginis de Monte Carmelo: responsorio ad animadversiones promotoris generalis fidei super dubio an constet de martyrio eiusque causa.* 1983, 76 p. Typis Polyglotis Vaticanis. Romae.

Buscoducen. *Beatificationis seu declarationis martyrii servi Dei Titi Brandsma sacerdotis professi Ordinis Fratrum B., Mariae Virginis de Monte Carmelo: sylloges probationum iudicialium de martyrio servi Dei.* 1981, 83 p. Typis Polyglotis Vaticanis. Romae.

Buscoducen. *Beatificationis seu declarationis martyrii servi Dei Titi Brandsma sacerdotis professi Ordinis Fratrum B., Mariae Virginis de Monte Carmelo. Votum promotoris generalis fidei super dubio an eius causa introducenda sit.* 1971, 25 p. Romae.

Buscoducen."Canoniztionis servi Dei Titi Brandsma sacerdotis professi Ordinis Fratrum B., Mariae Virginis de Monte Carmelo in odium fidei anno 1942 interempti. Super dubio: An constet de martyrio eiusque causa et de signi seu miraculis, in casu et ad effectum de quo agitur." *Acta Apostolicae Sedis* 77 (1985), 175-178.

Canal, Antonio Augusto, O.Carm. "Tito Brandsma giornalista martire." *Rosetti del Carmelo* 37:2 (1985), 4-10.

"Carmelitano olandese vittima del furore nazista, Un: Il Servo di Dio Padre Tito Brandsma a quarant'anni dalsuo olocausto." *L'Osservatore Romano*, 27 ottobre 1982, p. 9.

Chalmers, Joseph, O. Carm. "York Minster Homily." *Assumpta* 2003 46:6 (June 2003), 8-11.

Ciravegna, Giovanni. *Martire per la libertà: Padre Tito Bradsma* [sic]. 1986, 124 p. Edizioni Paoline. Via Paolo Uccello 9, 20148 Milano. ISBN: 88-215-1118-9.

Clarke, Hugh, O. Carm. *Titus Brandsma*. 1985, 24 p. Catholic Truth Society. London.

D'Elia, Donald. "The Life & Thought of Titus Brandsma." *New Oxford Review* 53:10 (December 1986) 10-14.

Dölle, Constant. *Encountering God in the Abyss: Titus Brandsma's Spiritual Journey.* Translated by John Vriend. 2002, vi, 188 p. The Fiery Arrow Collection, No. 5. Peeters. Bondgenotenlaan 153, B-3000 Leuven. ISBN: 90-429-1163-8.

Doyo, M. Ceres P. "A Saint for Press Freedom." *Philippines Panorama* 14:44 (1985), 42-48.

Essays on Titus Brandsma: Carmelite, Educator, Journalist, Martyr. Edited by Redemptus Maria Valabek, O. Carm. N° 2 of *Carmel In the World Paperbacks.* 1985, 317 p. Rome: Institutum Carmelitanum. ISBN: 88-7288-000-9.

Explanationes de fama martyrii et martyrio, attentis voto Rvmi. Promotoris Generalis Fidei nec non relatione et votis peculiaris Congressus diei 25 maii a. 1971. Romae, 1973.

Eykelhof, Anne. "Blessed Titus Brandsma: A Modern Martyr." *North American Voice of Fatima* 43:2 (Pentecost, 2004), 13, 25.

Fava, Nuccio. "A Television Newscaster Meets Fr. Titus Brandsma." *Carmel in the World* 24 (1985), 99-113.

Frequin, Louis. *Wie is Titus Brandsma? een mens een heilige van onze tijd.* 1980, 34 p, ill. Stichting Gedachteniskapel Titus Brandsma. Nijmegen.

Geisbauer, Georg, O. Carm. "Auf blutgetränktem Boden: Station in Dachau." *Karmelstimmen* 52 (1985), 356-363.

Geisbauer, Georg, O. Carm. "Titus Brandsma–Friese–Gelehrter–Journalist–Karmeliter–Märtyrer der katholischen Presse–wird seliggesprochen." *Karmelstimmen* 51 (1984), 206-212.

Gemmeke, Emile, O. Carm. "Een vrome van onze tijd, Titus Brandsma." *Studio* 54:8 (1981), 8-19.

Geurts, Math., O. Carm. *Deze man is gevaarlijk: Titus Brandsma.* 1998, 59 p. ill. Karmel Crabbehof. Dordrecht.

Glueckert, Leopold G., O. Carm. *Titus Brandsma: Friar Against Fascism.* N.d., 24 p. Carmelite Press. 1313 Frontage Road, Darien, Illinois 60559-5341.

Gollarte, Paulo, O. Carm. *Novena poderosa de cura interior ao beato Tito Brandsma.* 1993, 19 p. Editora Vozes. Curitiba.

Gollarte, Paulo, O. Carm. *Quando dizer NÃO é preciso: Tito Brandsma.* 1985, 112 p. Cedicarmo. Belo Horizonte.

Groeneveld, Albertus, O. Carm. *Nos passos de Frei Tito.* Traduzido por H. W. Sanders. N.d., 19 p. N.p. Rio de Janeiro.

Hanley, Boniface, O.F.M. *Through a Dark Tunnel.* N.d., 31 p. The Brandsma National Office. 8433 Bailey Road, Darien, Illinois 60559-5341. [Reprint of article in *The Anthonian.*]

Healy, Kilian J., O. Carm. "Carmel: Renewal and Adaptation." *The Sword* 28:1 (February, 1968), 2-11.

Healy, Kilian J., O. Carm. "Elijah, the Spiritual Father of Carmel." *Carmel In the World* 28 (1989), 93-122.

Healy, Kilian J., O. Carm. *Prophet of Fire.* N° 5 of *Carmel In the World Paperbacks.* 1990, 319 p. Rome: Institutum Carmelitanum. ISBN: 88-7288-015-7.

Hemels, Joán. "Titus Brandsma en de pers." National Herdenking Zaligverklaring Titus Brandsma, 10 nov. 1985, pp. 16-21.

Hemels, Joán. "Titus Brandsma: Verteidiger der katholischen Presse, Zu seiner Seligsprechung am 3. November 1985." *Communicatio Socialis* 18 (1985), 333-344.

Hemels, Joán. "Titus Brandsma und die katholische Presse." *Communicatio Socialis* 6 (1973), 1-26.

Hense, Elisabeth. "Gott ist da und offenbart sich in uns: Titus Brandsma." *Karmel-Echo* 29 (1995), 415-422.

Hense, Elisabeth und Leo Groothuis, O. Carm. "Titus Brandsma (1881-1942): Vor Gottes Angesicht." *Geist und Leben* 68 (1995), 47-54.

Het laatste geschrift van Prof. Dr. Titus Brandsma: Geschreven op last van de Gestapo in de strafgevangenis te Scheveningen op 22 janurai 1942. Inleiding van Dr. Brocardus Meijer, O. Carm. 1945, 21 p. W. Bergmans. Tilburg.

Hill, Brennan, O. Carm. and Chester Delaney, O. Carm. "Tributes to Father Titus." *The Sword* 20 (1957), 185-192.

Hogan, Benedict, O. Carm. "Blessed Titus Brandsma: A Modern Martyr." *The Sword* 48:1 (June 1989), 45-48.

Houle, Aquinas, O. Carm. "Father Titus Brandsma, O. Carm." *The Sword* 19 (1956), 3-29.

Il Servo di Dio P. Tito Brandsma, Carmelitano: Profili della sua vita. 1957, 32 p. Tipomeccanica. Napoli.

Informatio super dubio beatificationis seu declarationis martyrii servi Dei Titi Brandsma, Sacerdotis profesi Ordinis beatissimae Virginis Mariae de

Monte Carmelo. Romae, 1968.

Isacsson, Alfred, O. Carm. "Homily on Bl. Titus Brandsma." St. Ignatius Loyola Cathedral, Palm Beach, Florida, June 7, 1986. *The Sword* 46:1 (October, 1986), 55-56.

John Paul II. "121st Annual Supreme Council Meeting: Papal Greetings." *Columbia* 83:10 (October, 2003), 3.

John Paul II. "Allocutio ad peregrinos die 4 Novembris in 'Aula Paolo VI'" *Analecta Ordinis Carmelitarum* 37, 120-123.

John Paul II. "Allocutio ad peregrinos in generali audientia diei 6 Novembris 1985." *Analecta Ordinis Carmelitarum* 37, 124-125.

John Paul II. "Allocutio ad peregrinos neerlandicos meridie diei 3 Novembris 1985." *Analecta Ordinis Carmelitarum* 37 (1985), 120.

John Paul II. "Allocutio in Basilica Vaticana durante Missa in qua Titus Brandsma Beati aureola redimitus est." *Analecta Ordinis Carmelitarum* 37 (1985), 115-119.

John Paul II. "Caelitum beatorum honores conceduntur venerabili Dei servo Tito Brandsma, O. Carm." *Acta Apostolica Sedis* 84 (1992), 490-493.

John Paul II. "L'eroica testimonianza di Padre Tito Brandsma: verso un mondo di giustizia e di pace." *L'Osservatore Romano,* 2-3 novembre 1992, p. 5.

John Paul II. "What Does It Mean to Be a Professional Journalist Who Is Catholic?" Address of the Holy Father to the International Catholic Union of the Press (UCIP), December 6, 2002. *L'Osservatore Romano: Weekly Edition in English.* December 11, 2002, p. 5.

Jong, L. de. "Titus Brandsma." *Het Koninkrijk der Nederlanden in de Tweede Wereldoorlog: Deel 5, Maart '41 -Juli '42.* Tweede helft. Amsterdam. Rijksinstituut voor Oorlogsdocumentatie -'s-Gravenhage. Staatsuitgeverij. pp. 712-724.

Kolathara, Mary Anie, O. Carm. *Tito Brandsma, voce di un testimone della verità.* Dissertazione di Lecenza, Facoltà di Missiologia, Pontificia Università Gregoriana. 1994, 131 p. Roma.

Kosasih, Fransiscus, O. Carm. *The Prophetic Dimension of the Carmelite Charism: New Developments since the Second Vatican Council in the Light of Biblical, Theological and Historical Foundations.* 2001, 259 p. *Vacare Deo* #15. Edizioni Carmelitane. Via Sforza Pallavicini 10, 00193 Roma. ISBN: 88-7288-062-9.

López Melús, Rafael María, O. Carm. *El periodista santo.* Onda (Castellón): Amacar. N.d., 157 p. ISBN: 84-398-4783-1.

López Melús, Rafael María, O. Carm. "Padre Tito: El nuevo beato Carmelita y María." *Miriam* 37 (1985), 193-196.

López Melús, Rafael María, O. Carm. "P. Tito Brandsma (1881-1942)." *La Vida Sobrenatura*l 66 (1986), 53-60.

Lurvink, Bertoldo, O. Carm. "O servo de Deus P. Tito Brandsma O. Carm." *Carmelo Lusitano* 2 (1984), 173-178.

Lüthold, Ida. *Pater Titus Brandsma: Märtyrer in Dachau: Lebensbild.*1963, 35 p. Ars Sacra. Verlag Ars sacra, München.

Lytle-Vieira, Jane E. "Meditations on Blessed Titus Brandsma." *The Sword* 60 (2000), 155-164.

Maccise, Camilo, O.C.D. "Un testigo y defensor de los valores humanos: Tito Brandsma." *Grandes testigos do los valores.* Coordinador: Rafael Checa. 1987, 248 p. Editorial Progreso. pp. 219-229.

Malley, John, O. Carm. "Letter on the 50th Anniversary of Titus Brandsma's Death." *Carmel in the World* 32 (1993), 60-64.

Martínez Carretero, Ismael, O. Carm. "Beato Tito Brandesma, Carmelita: Contemplación y compromiso." *Escapulario del Carmen* 88 (1992), 200-204, 244-251, 253-255, 329-332, 352-356.

Martínez Carretero, Ismael, O. Carm. *Figuras del Carmelo*. Vol VI de *Los Carmelitas: Historia de la Orden del Carmen*. 1996, lii, 549 p. Madrid: Biblioteca de Autores Cristianos. ISBN: 84-7914-174-3.

Martínez Carretero, Ismael, O. Carm. *Y tras la noche, la libertad: Breve semblanza del beato Tito Brandsma, Carmelita.* 1993, 34 p. Confer. Madrid.

Martino, Alberto, O. Carm. "Padre Tito Brandsma carmelitano martire della verità e della carità in Dachau." *La Madonna del Carmine* 36:9 (1982, 18-25.

Mary Angela, S.M. "Dachau–That Holy Place." Reprint from the Annals of Saint Anthony's Shrine 9:2 (1946), in *The Sword* 11 (1947), 31-34.

Meijer, Brocardus, O. Carm.. *Titus Brandsma.* 1951, 480 p. Uitgeverij Paul Brand N. V. Bussum.

Melsen, Jacobus, O. Carm. "Mysticism: The Aim in Life of Fr. Titus Brandsma." *Carmel in the World* 20 (1981), 85-102.

Millán Romeral, Fernando, O. Carm., "Campo de concentración de Dachau." *Escapulario del Carmen* 93 (June 1996), 212.

Millán Romeral, Fernando, O. Carm. "Carmelitas in Dachau: La apasionante historia de los carmelitas polacos qui vivieron el drama de los campos de concentración, *Escapulario del Carmen* 91 (1994), 120-129.

Millán Romeral, Fernando, O. Carm. "Carmelitas en Dachau: Las Cartas del P. Albert Urbanski desde el lager en el 50 aniversario de la liberación." *Carmelus* 42 (1985), 22-43.

Millán Romeral, Fernando, O. Carm. "El apostolado de la mística carmelitana (Conferencia del P. Tito Brandsma sobre Teresa de Lisieux)." *Revista de Espiritualidad* 57 (1998), 669-689.

Millán Romeral, Fernando, O. Carm. "El Padre Tito Brandsma: La santidad de la humanidad." *Carmelo Lusitano* N 10 (1992), 33-51.

Millán Romeral, Fernando, O. Carm. "El Padre Tito e la paz." *Carmelo Lusitano* No 11 (1993), 47-63.

Millán Romeral, Fernando, O. Carm. "El Padre Tito: Modelo de tolerancia para lost Carmelitas de hoy." *Escapulario del Carmen* 91 (1995), 120-129.

Millán Romeral, Fernando, O. Carm. "El P. Tito Brandsma y Teresa de Lisieux: Algunos aspectos comunes de suespiritualidad." *Escapulario del Carmen* 94 (1997), 94-98, 132-134, 167-172.

Millán Romeral, Fernando, O. Carm. "La Mariologia del P. Tito Brandsma." *Escapulario del Carmen* 84 (1988), 154-162.

Millán Romeral, Fernando, O. Carm., "Un testimonio de primera mano sobre la muerte del P. Tito," *Analecta Ordinis Carmelitarum* 44:1 (1993), 34-39.

Monari, Elia, O. Carm. "Tito Brandsma uomo di pace." *Presenza del Carmelo* N 36 (1988), 38-43.

Mosca, Vincenzo, O. Carm. "P. Tito Brandsma: Un modello di vita." *Presenza del Carmelo* N. 35 (1985), 29-52.

"Necrologia: Titus Brandsma." *Analecta Ordinis Carmelitarum* 11 (1942), 253-255.

Neglia, Alberto, O. Carm. "Nell'inferno dell'olocausto: La testimonianza del P. Tito Brandsma." *La Revista del Clero Italiano* 67 (1986), 455-464.

Nijenhuis, John, O. Carm. "Bl. Titus Brandsma, O. Carm., On the Presence of God." *The Sword* 48:2 (October 1988), 3-26.

O'Connor, John, Cardinal. "Blessed Titus Brandsma: The Importance of Life." Homily in St. Patrick's Cathedral, New York City, December 14, 1985. *The Sword* 46"1 (April 1986), 49-52.

Orrù, Giuseppe, O. Carm. "Dal Carmelo a Dachau: Padre Tito Brandsma martire per la fede." *L'Osservatore Romano*, 19 febbraio 1982, p. 8.

Orrù, Giuseppe, O. Carm. "Dal Carmelo al 'inferno' di Dachau: l'eroico calvario di un giornalista cattolico olandese prigioniero delle SS." *La Vice* 30:4 (1982), 2.

Os, Henk van. *Titus Brandsma: De man Gods uit Bolsward: Over heiligenverering vroeger en nu.* 1998, 61 p. Titus Brandsma Instituut -Valkhof Pers.

Overduin, Hendrik. "Titus Brandsma, 1881-1942: An Enduring Symbol for Freedom of the Press." *Carmelus* 37 (1990), 146-169.

Pawlak, Leszek, O. Carm. E-mail letter to translator. January 22, 2003.

Peréa, Romeu. *Tito Brandsma, reitor de universidade e restaurador da mística em pleno século XX.* 1977, 143 p. Editora Universitária. Universidade federal de Pernambuco.

Pettinati, Guido, S.S.P. "B. Tito Brandsma (1881-1942." *I santi canonizati del giorno*, Volume 7 (1991), Edizioni Segno. Udine. pp. 271-280.

Proper of the Liturgy of the Hours of the Order of the Brothers of the Blessed Virgin Mary of Mount Carmel and of the Order of Discalced Carmelites. 1993, 492 p. Rome: Institutum Carmelitanum. ISBN: 88-7288-028-9.

Rainer, Hans. *Los horrores nazis.* 1977. Barcelona: n.p.

Rees, Joseph. *Titus Brandsma: A Modern Martyr.* 1971, 192 p. London: Sidgwick Jackson. ISBN:0-283-97817-1.

Rhodes, Elinor D. *Carmel to Calvary: The Story of Father Titus Brandsma, Mystic and Martyr.* 1957, 18 p. Carmelite Publications. 60 Aungier Street, Dublin.

Rogge, Louis P., O. Carm. "Created for Joy." *Carmel in the World* 25 (1986), 6-20.

Rogge, Louis P., O. Carm. "Obedient unto Death." *New Covenant* 14:10 (May 1985), 20-23.

Russell, John F., O. Carm. "Titus and Thérèse: Witnesses to Integrity of Life." *The Sword* 62 (2002), 19-27.

Sacra Congregatio pro Causis Sanctorum. *Buscoducen. Beatificationis seu declarationis martyrii servi Dei Titi Brandsma sacerdotis professi Ordinis Fratrum B. M. V. de Monte Carmelo. Relatio et vota alterius congressus peculiaris super introductione causae die 9 octobris anni 1973 habiti.* 1973, 39 p. Tipografia Guerra e Belli. Roma.

Sacra Congregatio pro Causis Sanctorum. *Buscoducen. Canonizationis servi Dei Titi Brandsma sacerdotis professi Ordinis Fratrum B. M. V. de Monte Carmelo in odium fidei, uti fertur, interfecti (1881-1942). Relatio et vota congressus peculiaris super martyrio de 22 maii an. 1984 habiti.* 1984, 111

p. Tipografia Guerra. Roma.

Sacra Congregatio pro Causis Sanctorum. *Buscoducen. Canonizationis servi Dei Titi Brandsma sacerdotis professi Ordinis Fratrum B. M. V. de Monte Carmelo in odium fidei anno 1942 interempti. Super dubio an constet de martyrio eiusque causa et de signis seu miraculis in casu et ad effectum de quo agitur. Analecta Ordinis Carmelitarum* 37 (1984), 34-36.

Sacra Congregatio Rituum. *Buscoducen. Beatificationis seu declarationis martyrii servi Dei Titi Brandsma sacerdotis professi Ordinis Fratrum B. Mariae Virginis de Monte Carmelo. Positio super scriptis.* 1962, 87 p. Roma.

Scapin, Santino, O. Carm.. *Nella notte la libertà: Tito Brandsma giornalista martire a Dachau, con una antologia dei suoi scritti.* 1985, 212 p. Editrice Rogate. Via del Rogazionisti 8, 00182 Roma.

Scapin, Santino, O. Carm. "Titus Brandsma and the World of Ideas." Translated by Dennis Graviss, O. Carm. *The Sword* 45:1 (April 1985), 49-50.

Scapin, Santino, O. Carm. and Bruno Secondin, O. Carm. *Tito Brandsma: Maestro di umanità, martire della libertà.* 1990, 181 p. ill. Edizioni Paoline. Milano.

Schweizer, Paul, O. Carm. "Bl. Titus Brandsma: Mystic and Prophet in the Press." *The Sword* 62 (2002), 28-35.

Scurani, Alessandro, S.J. "Per lui il cielo si schiuse su Dachau: Padre Tito Brandsma carmelitano." *La Civiltà Cattolica* 137:1 (1986), 15-29.

Secondin, Bruno, O. Carm. "Tito Brandsma y su espiritualidad." *Paradigmas de santidad en el Carmelo, leídos desde América Latina y el Caribe.* 1997, 196 p. PP. O.C.D. Quito. pp. 143-154.

Shortis, F.C., O. Carm. *Father Brandsma: Carmelite, Educator, Journalist, Nazi Victim.* 1956, 30 p. The Advocate Press. Melbourne, Australia.

Sicari, Antonio M., O.C.D. "B. Tito Brandsma." *Il grande libro dei riratti di santi.* 1997, 925 p. Editoriale Jaca Book. Milano. pp. 757-774.

Sicari, Antonio M., O.C.D. "Der selige Titus Brandsma." *Das geistliche Leben des Christen: Glaubenserfahrung und Wege zur Heiligkeit.* Lehrbücher zur kathiolischen Theologie, 17. 1998, 440 p. Bonifatius Verlag. Paderborn. pp. 107-122.

Slattery, Peter. "Blessed Titus Brandsma, Martyr." Chapter 7 of *The Springs of Carmel: An Introduction to Carmelite Spirituality.* 1992, xviii, 152 p. Alba House. 2187 Victory Boulevard, Staten Island, New York 10314. ISBN: 0-8189-0604-9.

Smet, Joachim, O. Carm. Review of *Het laatste geschrift van Prof. Dr. Titus Brandsma: Geschreven ap last van de Gestapo in de strafgevangenis te*

Schevingen op 22 Januari 1942 and Mijn cel, en dagorde van een gevangene van Prof. Dr. Titus Brandsma. The Sword 11 (1947), 61-63.

Smet, Joachim, O. Carm. *The Carmelites: A History of the Brothers of Our Lady of Mount Carmel.* 1976-1988, 4 volumes. Darien, Illinois: Carmelite Spiritual Center.

Smet, Joachim, O. Carm. *The Mirror: A Brief History of the Carmelites.* 2011, 812 p., Darien, IL: Carmelite Media. ISBN: 1936742012.

Staring, Adrianus, O. Carm. "Bibliografia di Tito Brandsma (1881-1942)." *Carmelus* 31 (1984), 209-233.

Staring, Adrianus, O. Carm. *Boletín del "Comitato Italiano Tito Brandsma,"* 1984-1985.

Staring, Adrianus, O. Carm. "Chronicon Provinciae Neerlandicae (durante bello)." *Vinculum Ordinis Carmelitarum* I (1948), 61-68.

Staring, Adrianus, O. Carm. "Fr. Titus Brandsma and St. Teresa of Avila." *Carmel in the World* 20 (1981), 40-50.

Staring, Adrianus, O. Carm. "Joy in the Life of Fr. Titus Brandsma (1881-1942)." *Carmel in the World* 21 (1982), 56-67.

Staring, Adrianus, O. Carm. "Love of Neighbor in Fr. Titus Brandsma." Carmel in the World 23 (1984), 190-200.

Staring, Adrianus, O. Carm. The Beatification Process of Titus Brandsma. Translated by Joachim Smet, O. Carm. 1964, 12 p. General Curia of the Carmelites. Via Sforza Pallavicini 10, 00193 Roma.

Staring, Adrianus, O. Carm. "The Brandsma Dossiers: A Providential Sign." *Carmel in the World* 24 (1985), 92-98.

Staring, Adrianus, O. Carm. "The History of the Process of Beatification of Titus Brandsma." *The Sword* 45 (1985), 51-55.

Staring, Adrianus, O. Carm. "The History of the Process of Beatification of Titus Brandsma." Translated by Dennis Graviss, O. Carm. *The Sword* 45:1 (April 1985), 51-55.

Staring, Adrianus, O. Carm. "The Simplicity of Fr. Titus Brandsma (1881-1942)." *Carmel in the World* 22 (1983), 129-136.

Staring, Adrianus, O. Carm. "Titus Brandsma (1881-1942) and the Mysticism of the Passion." *Carmelus* 28 (1981), 213-225.

Staring, Adrianus, O. Carm. "Titus Brandsma's Trust in God." *Carmel in the World* 22 (1983), 229-241.

Steggink, Otger, O. Carm. *La reforma del carmelo español: La visita canónica del general Rubeo y su encuentro con Santa Teresa, 1566-1567.* Textus et studia historica carmelitana, 7. 1965, lv, 518 p. Institutum Carmelitanum. Via Sforza Pallavicini 10, 00193 Roma

Steneker, Johan, O.Carm. "Gott ist ganz nah: Das Lebenszeugnis des Titus Brandsma." *Karmelstimmen* 53 (1986), 224-229.

Stolinski, David C. "The Dogs Aren't Barking." *New Oxford Review* 69:11 (December 2002), 35-37.

Struyker Boudier, Kees."De vele gezichen van God: De Godsidee van Titus Brandsma O. Carm." *Ons Geestelijk Leven* 63 (1986), 234-245.

Summarium super dubio beatificationis seu declarationis martyrii servi Dei Titi Brandsma, sacerdotis profesi Ordinis beatissimae Virginis Mariae de Monte Carmelo, Romae, 1965.

Summarium super dubio beatificationis seu declarationis martyrii servi Dei Titi Brandsma, sacerdotis profesi Ordinis beatissimae Virginis Mariae de Monte Carmelo, Romae, 1979.

Tamura, Kaoru. "Bl. Titus Brandsma, O. Carm.: A Reflection on the 50th Anniversary of his Martyrdom." *Carmel in the World* 33 (1994), 31-41.

Teresa de Jesús, O. Carm. *Obras completas.* Edición manual: Transcripción, introducción y notas de Efren de la Madre de Dios, O.C.D., y Otger Steggink, O. Carm. Quarta edición revisada. 1974, xlix, 1179 p. Biblioteca de Autores Cristianos. Madrid.

Teresa of Avila, O. Carm. *The Collected Works.* Translated by Kieran Kavanaugh, O.C.D., and Otilio Rodriguez, O.C.D. 3 volumes. ICS Publications. 2131 Lincoln Road N.E., Washington, D.C., 20002-1199.

Theunissen, W. "In Piam Memoriam: Dr. Titus Brandsma, O. Carm." Translated by Linus Kemps, O. Carm. *The Sword* 10 (1946), 317-321.

Tijhuis, Raphael, O. Carm. "Dachau Eye-Witness." *Essays on Titus Brandsma: Carmelite, Educator, Journalist, Martyr.* Nº 2 of *Carmel in the World Paperbacks.* (Rome: Institutum Carmelitanum, 1985), pp. 58-67.

Tijhuis, Raphael, O. Carm. "Martyr for the Catholic Press." *The Sword* 34:2 (June 1974), 53-63.

Tijhuis, Raphael, O. Carm. *Nothing Can Stop God from Reaching Us.* 203 p. Rome: Edizioni Carmelitane. 2007. ISBN: 9788872880.

"Titus Brandsma ... Carmelite." *Mary* 42:3 (May-June 1981), 2-4.

"Tito Brandsma: 50 anni dal martirio." *La Madonna del Carmine* 46 (1992), 2-21.

Titus Brandsma: die is gaaf. Samenstelling: Aalt van de Glind. 1991, 64 p. ill. Uitgeverij Auctor. Apeldoorn.

Titus Brandsma 1881-1942: Carmelite and Martyr. N.d., 24 p. *The Carmelites.* 1313 Frontage Road, Darien, Illinois 60559.

"Titus Brandsma: A Heart on Fire I." Prepared by Robert Murphy, O. Carm. Carmelite Provincial Chapter Workbook, June 10-14, 2002, Province of the Most Pure Heart of Mary. Section IV: Titus Brandsma -Four Essays. pp. 20-28.

"Titus Brandsma: A Prophetic Message for Carmelites in Every Season: Wisdom on the Spiritual Life from His Writings and Lectures." *Carmelite Provincial Chapter Workbook*, June 10-14, 2002, Province of the Most Pure Heart of Mary. Section IV: Titus Brandsma -Four Essays. pp. 34-37.

Titus Brandsma, Mystiker des Karmel, Märtyrer in Dachau. Herausgegeben von Georg Geisbauer, O.Carm. 1987, 127 p. ill. Weinand Verlag. Köln.

"Titus Brandsma Will Have a Museum in His Native Town." *CITOC*, May-June, 2000, pp. 53-54.

Troy, Leander, O. Carm. "Blessed Titus Brandsma's Trip to the United States and Canada in 1935." *The Sword* 52 (1992), 25-35.

Valabek, Redemptus Maria, O. Carm. "Blessed Titus Brandsma." Homily in St. Matthew Cathedral, Washington, D.C., February 23, 1986. *The Sword* 46:2 (October 1986), 3-9.

Valabek, Redemptus Maria, O. Carm. "I Santi: la giovenezza e freschezza della Chiesa: P. Tito Brandmsa, O. Carm." *Presenza del Carmelo* No. 22 suppl. (1980), 67-77.

Valabek, Redemptus Maria, O. Carm. "Mary and Ourselves: God-Bearers." *Essays on Titus Brandsma: Carmelite, Educator, Journalist, Martyr* (Rome: Institutum Carmelitanum, 1985), pp.183-204.

Valabek, Redemptus Maria, O. Carm. "Mary and Ourselves: God-Bearers: Our Lady of Mt. Carmel in the Life of Fr. Titus Brandsma, O. Carm." *Carmel in the World* 18 (1979) 148-171.

Valabek, Redemptus Maria, O. Carm. "Prayer Is Life, Not an Oasis in the Desert of Life." *The Beatification of Father Titus Brandsma, Carmelite (1881-1942): Martyr in Dachau.* pp. 114-123.

Vallainc, Fausto. *Un giornalista martire: Padre Tito Brandsma.* Prefazione di Raimondo Manzini. 2ª Edizione. 1963, 239 p. Milano: Editrice Àncora.

Vandenheuvel, Anthony. *Titus Brandsma: A Modern Martyr for the Truth.* 1989, 128 p. ill. The Friends of Titus Brandsma. Welland, Ontario.

Walters, Leo J., O. Carm. "Father Titus Brandsma, O. Carm., R. I. P." *The Sword* 6 (1942), 422-423.

Weber, John-Benedict, O. Carm. "Titus Brandsma: A Heart on Fire II." *Carmelite Provincial Chapter Workbook,* June 10-14, 2002, Province of the Most Pure Heart of Mary. Section IV: Titus Brandsma -Four Essays. pp. 29-33.

Weber, John-Benedict, O. Carm. "Titus Brandsma: A Life Spent for Christ." *Carmelite Provincial Chapter Workbook,* June 10-14, 2002, Province of the Most Pure Heart of Mary. Section IV: Titus Brandsma -Four Essays. pp. 15-19.

Weiterink, Alphons. "More about Titus Brandsma's Rosaries." Translated by Frans Bruning. *The Lighted Candle N° 24* (May, 2002), 4-5.

Welch, Rory [John], O. Carm. "A Time for Our Prophet." *The Sword* 27:1 (February, 1967), 19-29, 64-66.

Werling, Norman G., O. Carm. *Journey to Dachau: Blessed Titus Brandsma, O. Carm., 1881-1942.* Unpublished notes. Carmelite Provincial Archives, Province of the Most Pure Heart of Mary, Darien, Illinois.

Wermers, Manuel María, O. Carm. *Prof. Dr. Tito Brandsma, Carmelita: O primeiro mártir da Nova Era.* 1959, 39 p. Edicões Carmelitanas. Fatima.

Wysbek, Leopold. Letter to Prior General Hilary Doswald. *The Sword* 9 (1945), 296.

Recommended Carmelite Websites

FOR MORE INFORMATION ABOUT THE CARMELITES TODAY, OUR SPIRITUALITY AND OUR MINISTRIES WORLDWIDE, VISIT:

The Carmelite Order
ocarm.org

The Most Pure Heart of Mary Province
carmelites.net

Center for Carmelite Studies at Catholic University of America
carmelites.info/CenterForCarmeliteStudies

Carmelite Institute of North America
carmeliteinstitute.net

Instituto de las Americas
institutocarmelitano.carmelitas.org

FOR A LISTING OF CARMELITE PROVINCES WORLDWIDE, VISIT:
carmelites.info/provinces

FOR A LISTING OF MONASTERIES OF CARMELITE NUNS, VISIT:
carmelites.info/nuns

FOR A LISTING OF CARMELITE HERMITAGES, PLEASE VISIT:
carmelites.info/hermits

FOR A LISTING OF SITES ABOUT LAY CARMELITES:
carmelites.info/lay carmel

FOR A LISTING OF AFFILIATED CONGREGATIONS AND INSTITUTES:
carmelites.info/congregations

FOR OUR WORK WITH THE UNITED NATIONS, VISIT:
carmelitengo.org

FOR MORE INFORMATION ABOUT PUBLICATIONS, VISIT:
carmelites.info/publications

www.ingramcontent.com/pod-product-compliance
Lightning Source LLC
Chambersburg PA
CBHW050125170426
43197CB00011B/1722